Won't Quit!

An Escalante Desert Love Story

by Dick Johnston

First published in 2014
Juniper is an imprint of Southern Utah University Press
Cedar City, Utah

ISBN: 9780935615456
Library of Congress Control Number: 2014941810

Edited by Janet Seegmiller
Layout and design by Sheri Butler
Cover design by April McPherson

Printed in the United States by Lightning Source

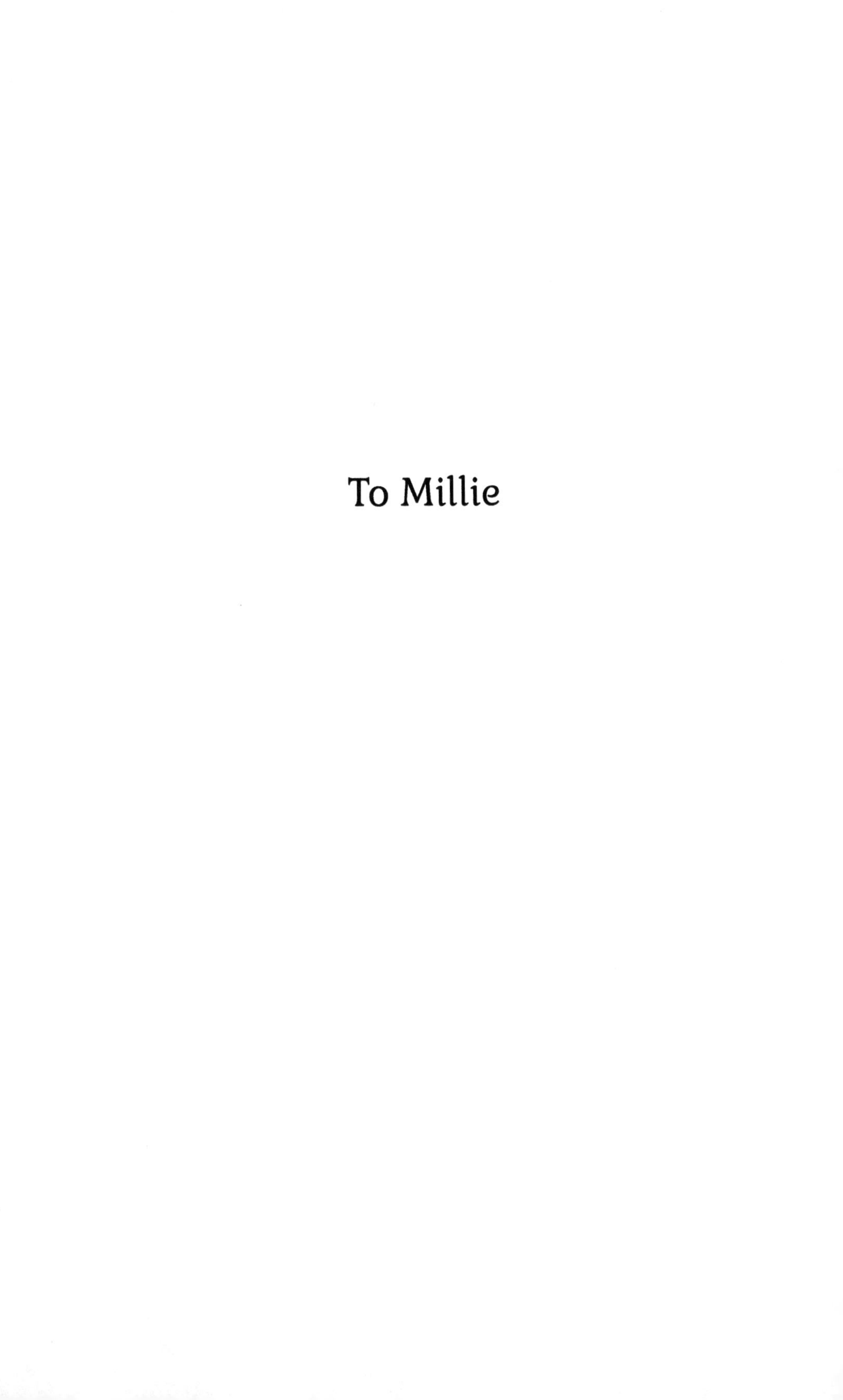

To Millie

John Harlan (Harley) Johnston   Mary Dora King Johnston
circa 1914

Photo Credits

Unless noted, all photos are from Dick Johnston's family photo collection. Grateful acknowledgement is made for permission to reproduce the following images:

Southern Utah University, Special Collections, 37, 118, 120, 124 (middle, bottom), 128, 129, 141, 142, 147, 167, 179, 243
Campbell's 1907, 52
http://www.dogonews.com/2007/11/29/the-tumbleweed-queen, 97
Ruby Seegmiller, 124 (top)
https://www.flickr.com/photos/dok1/3254313822/, 152: cropped and gray-scaled
First Wind Company, 288
Milgro Newcastle, Inc., 290

Table of Contents

Preface and Acknowledgements

Theoretically, it would seem, a book-length memoir should be comparatively easy to produce—a person needs merely to put down memories and hope that they are sufficiently unique or interesting to attract a publisher, impress friends and relatives, and maybe even find some readers willing to pay a few bucks. I enjoyed writing *Won't Quit!* but discovered, as might be expected in today's media turmoil, that catching the attention of a "regular" publisher was difficult. The alternative was to join the thousands of self-published authors annually who pay companies for book design and printing.

In original drafts of *Won't Quit!*, I thought the hopefully unique angle of a pretty, vivacious, and well-educated young woman giving up a comfortable and fun-filled life in lovely Santa Barbara, California, to spend the rest of her life with a farm-obsessed husband in a desolate desert in Utah would catch the attention of one of the thousands of literary agents who screen book proposals for big-time publishers. But after sixty submissions to carefully selected agents yielded no requests for the manuscript, I began researching what the book industry calls "small presses" especially those in the West's mountain states where this book's Utah setting and farming/ranching descriptions might catch attention. The Southern Utah University Press was an obvious target so, on a visit to Cedar City in 2012, I got an appointment there to submit my manuscript. I had expanded the book to include more of the history of the Escalante Valley desert and hopefully make it more appealing to a university press. It worked!

I cannot give enough thanks to the Southern Utah University and the handful of members of the staff of the Gerald R. Sherratt Library there who work part time on publication of a few books per year. My appreciation starts with the SUU Press reviewer, Janet Seegmiller, Special Collections Librarian, who recommended publication of my family saga, and my gratitude extends to Matthew Nickerson, Chair of the SUU Press, who agreed with the Janet so that work on publication could begin early in 2013. I am also deeply indebted to Janet and Sheri

Butler for their skill in editing the manuscript, selecting photographs, and formatting the book. Their patience in dealing with my corrections, additions, and changes was a blessing. Janet was the author of an impressively researched book, *A History of Iron County—Community Above Self*, on which I constantly relied for facts and history. Sheri, bless her heart, wrapped up the final complex process for submission to the printing company where copies of the book become available on a print-on-demand basis.

My thanks go also to April McPherson for the cover design and to Susan Nelson Christopher, of the library staff, whose sheep owner father reviewed part of my text.

Won't Quit! probably would not have been possible without the boxes full of handwritten letters, faded documents, and old photographs that my mother had saved for fifty years and left in an antique trunk in an attic. Those materials gave me enough framework for the first twelve chapters so that I could imagine the rest of the narrative. As is usually the case for collections of old photos, the ones from 1900 to 1915 in Santa Barbara had no dates or names on them but I remembered enough faces to identify more than enough pictures for the book. Also, the totally charming old photos enhanced the description of life then and there.

The Special Collections section in the Sherratt Library at SUU was a constant and in-depth source of materials about the Escalante Valley region. A visit to the Frontier Homestead State Park Museum in Cedar City confirmed my descriptions of what was essentially pioneer life in southwestern Utah. Michael Redmon, director of research at the Santa Barbara Historical Museum, was very helpful in providing me with information and materials about "old time" Santa Barbara. The staff at College Hill Library in Westminster, Colorado, with whom I have had a wonderful working relationship for many years, found a bunch of books for my research. Donna Glidewell's book about Wasatch Academy, Mt. Pleasant, Utah, where she and I graduated, was a pleasure for me to read and use. Maps of the region were obtained from the U.S. Bureau of Land Management and U.S. Geological Survey.

Fay Frahske Burns, whom I knew all her life as the last member of a homestead family to live in Lund, shared with me her extensive collection of memoirs, documents, and photographs which refreshed my recollections of life in the Escalante desert. Jim Holyoak, of Salt Lake City, a lifetime friend, and his uncle, Paul Holyoak of Cedar City, shared timely memories with me. In 2013, Charles Reeve of Hurricane, Utah, took me on an enjoyable pickup truck tour of the area south of Lund where he now owns part of my father's homestead land.

My journalist daughter, Kit Johnston, provided useful comments on early drafts of *Won't Quit!*, and my son, Kirk Johnston, was my computer technology advisor. A longtime friend Joe Marisco of Arvada, Colorado, an oil company land man, drew the book's customized map of the Lund area.

My beloved wife, Loretta, cheerfully tolerated my immersion in book writing for two decades, constantly proof-read drafts, and gave me strong support at every step along the way. My son-in-law, Dave Debus, arranged a delightful visit to Santa Barbara where we visited my mother's now drastically-changed neighborhoods.

Richard (Dick) Johnston

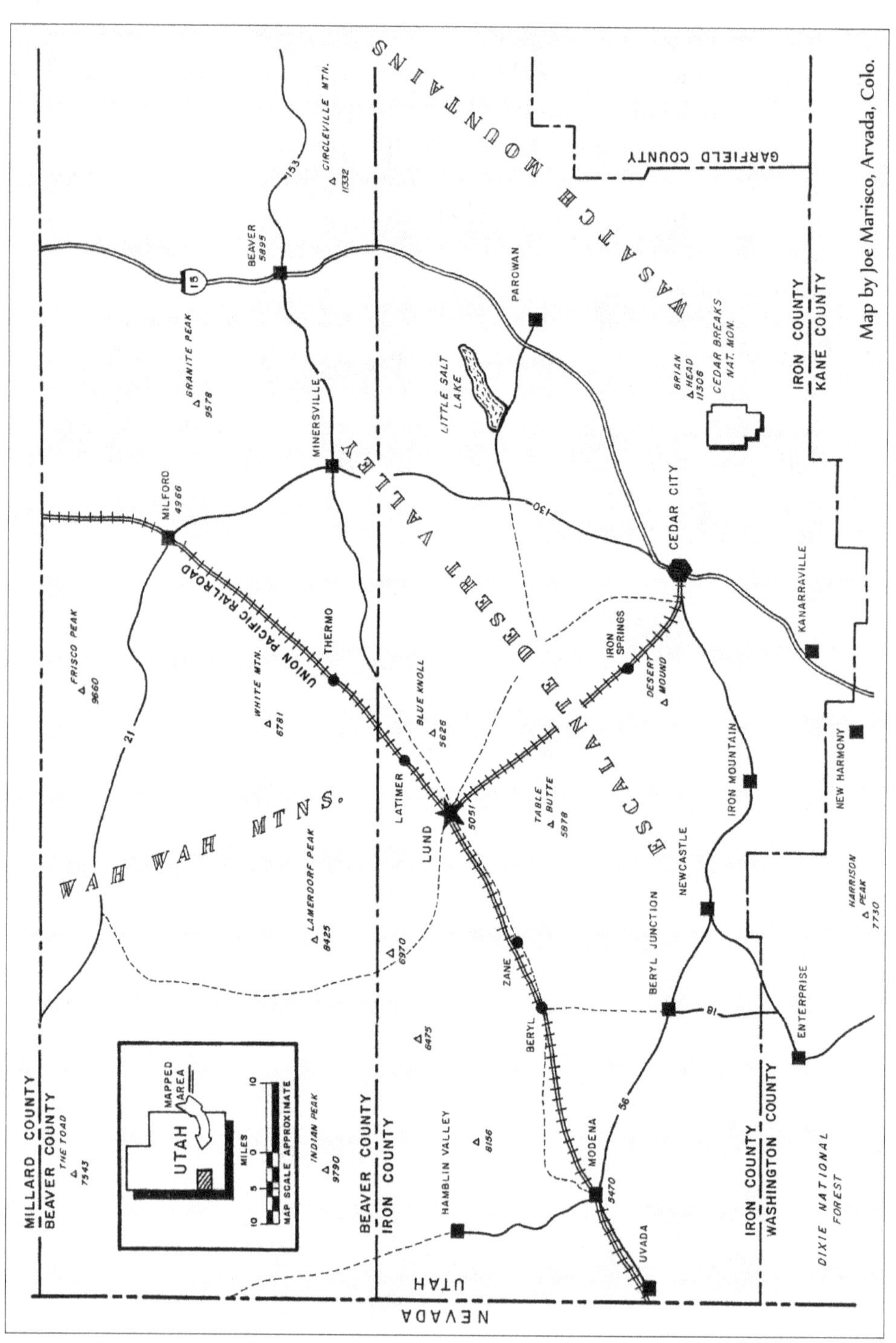

Map of Escalante Desert Valley

Chapter 1

Harley Meets Mary

"What are you looking at, Harley? From the expression on your face, it must be a naked woman."

Bill Thompson circled the scarred wooden counter in Wacona's General Merchandise Store and joined Harley Johnston, the store's other clerk, who was holding up a newspaper advertisement.

"No, it's not a naked woman but for me, believe it or not, this advertisement about getting a homestead farm is exciting."

The ad said:

OWN YOUR OWN FARM!
For ONLY $18!
320-Acre Homesteads Now Available
In Southern Utah's Escalante Valley

"Oh, boy!" Bill snorted. "You've got a big problem if that turns you on! Why would anyone want to leave Los Angeles to go farm in Utah, of all places? From what little I've heard about Utah, it is mostly barren desert."

Harley, a wiry little guy with ice blue eyes and blond hair parted in the middle and slicked down on one side in the fashion of 1914, replied, "I know it sounds dumb, but I'm going to look into it. I've been working for years trying to save enough money for my own place. I've been reading about homesteading but from what I can tell all the good land the government made available has been taken up and what's left is in hills or too far from any markets. If land in this valley in Utah is bad desert, why is it being offered for farms?"

"Good question!" Bill declared, "And anyway, from what I've heard about homesteading, like up in Montana, you work your butt off to get any kind of a crop, you freeze your butt in winter, and you get hungry and go broke in a few years. I like it here in southern California where you don't have to wear a coat. This city is growing so fast you can always find a job, and you don't have to work sunup to sundown and on Sunday."

Harley smiled. "You'd sure never be a farmer! You're too lazy. As you know, I was a farm hand in the Midwest before I came out here to look around. I like farming. I'm going to find a pretty young wife and go to Utah."

Bill laughed. "You better get humping then. I got the idea that you've been kicking around the country for so long you haven't lit anywhere long enough to get a wife, let alone a pretty young one. And you admitted the other day that you are 37 years old. I'd say your time to find a pretty young wife is running out. You may have to settle for an ugly old one."

"Okay! Okay!" Harley shot back. "You wait and see. When I've got a bunch of kids and a farm covered with crops, I'll come back, and you'll still be here picking your nose."

Harley was using his pocket knife to cut out the homestead advertisement in the newspaper when another ad caught his eye:

TREE TRIMMERS NEEDED.
No experience necessary.
Some travel around southern California.
$4 per day plus expenses.
Contact the Dependable Landscaping Company.

Harley was making $3 a day at the Wacona store, and the higher wage would boost his savings for a farm. He cut out the second ad, waited impatiently for the store to close, and caught a streetcar to Pasadena where he got room and board for $30 a month from his sister, Lu Strahan, and her husband, Ray.

That evening, he penciled a letter to the "Escalante Locators, P. O. Box 10, Lund, Utah" asking for details about the homestead program there. He reread the ad's small print reference to "Excellent Opportunities for Application of the New Technique of Dry Land Farming" and made a mental note to find out how that kind of farming would be different from agriculture in the moist land of river valleys in the Midwest.

Lu entered the room and said, "Brother dear, you were talking at dinner about going to a homestead farm in Utah. Don't you think you should have a wife to go with you?"

Wacona Store in Los Angeles, circa 1914—Harley on right

"Well, now that I've gotten a pretty clear idea of what I want to do, yes, I better get serious about finding a wife. You got any suggestions?"

"Well, no, not right now, but I'll work on it. Why don't you just settle down here? When Ray and I got married and came out here from Valentine, Nebraska, he found a job right away, and our sisters, Jennie and Ruby, followed me and soon found work and husbands. If I find you a pretty young wife like they found husbands, will you stay?"

"Nope. I want a farm of my own. I was very happy as a farm hand plowing a straight furrow in bottomland black soil on a beautiful spring day in Missouri, but it was clear I'd never be able to buy land like that. So, as you know, I came to visit you girls and found out I can't afford the land prices here either. I can get 320 acres for almost nothing in Utah, and I'm getting close to having enough money to buy the equipment and livestock I would need to make the move."

"I can't understand why you are so stuck on being a farmer. You remember when we were kids, the family moved every few years because Dad was always looking for a better farm or ranch job. I've forgotten how many times we moved from Knoxville, Iowa, where you were born until we ended up in the sand hills of northern Nebraska.

You want your kids to be like us, walking two miles to a one room grade school?"

"We didn't have to walk all the time! In the winter we got to ride horses. Anyway, it wasn't so bad. We always had enough to eat and a warm house to sleep in. And we all got to finish the eighth grade before we had to go to work. I kind of liked working on different kinds of farms before I came out here."

"And in all those years you never found anyone to marry?"

"Well, I did have a few freckle-faced farm gals try to get me into haylofts but I didn't want to get caught until I was ready to settle down on my own farm. I kind of kept thinking I'd fall in love somewhere along the line. So far it hasn't happened. On Saturday nights at the country barn dances, a lot of the guys I worked with would get likkered up and find out later there were girls' fathers with shotguns looking for them. I never liked drinking, especially not that white lightning stuff in jugs the guys passed around outside the dances. So, I was sober on buggy rides home."

"Well, if you are so keen about getting a homestead farm, how come you're going to try for that job with the landscape company?"

"Mainly because it pays a lot more than working at Wacona's store. But another reason is that I like hard physical work, and I'm starting to get soft being a clerk. I'll have to be ready to work hard to start a new farm. Doing tree trimming and planting stuff will be good for me."

"Okay, have it your way but I think you're being stubborn." Lu shook her finger at him and left the room.

The next day Harley got permission from the store owner to take a long lunch hour. He rode a street car to the Dependable Landscaping Company and filled out a job application, stressing his physical fitness and experience on farms.

Hank Ibsen, the company owner, was in the office and interviewed Harley, emphasizing that the job involved climbing up and down ladders or scaffolding, cutting down trees, and digging up shrubs. He said, "You're the kind of wiry guy that does best in this kind of work."

"Good. I'm sure I can handle it," Harley replied.

"When can you start?"

"Well, I'd like to give a week's notice at my present job, so how about a week from tomorrow? I'll be here at eight o'clock."

"That will be fine. Be sure to bring a hat and you might want to have some gloves."

A few days later Harley got a reply letter from the Escalante Locators in Utah briefly describing the homestead application process. The letter said the land bordered a new railroad line, and the railroad company wanted homesteaders to help develop the area. The information strengthened Harley's resolve to go to Utah although he was totally naive about deserts and dry land farming.

At the Dependable Landscaping Company, Harley got strenuous on-the-job training in the use of ropes and tools. He learned how to clear brush off land, how to make a tree fall in a certain direction, and how to pull up stumps with a team of horses. The crews normally worked ten hours a day six days a week. On Sundays, Harley usually visited his two other sisters in Pasadena.

The company got contracts as far south as San Diego and as far north as Santa Barbara, sometimes using trains to ship horses, equipment and the crew to large commercial jobs.

Early in March 1914 the company landed a prized contract to clear some land on the Hope Ranch that sprawled for 10,000 acres up the coastal mountain range behind the ocean-front town of Santa Barbara. The horses and equipment were left each night on the Hope Ranch work site, and the men stayed in a rooming house in town where they got breakfast, dinner, and a sack lunch. After the long workweek, most of the guys spent Saturday nights in saloons and spent Sundays nursing hangovers, sleeping, or just loafing.

Harley had tried a few saloon evenings with his buddies, but he disliked the smoky atmosphere and what he regarded as a waste of time and money.

His parents were nominal Methodists, but in pioneer Nebraska there were no regular church services and Harley had little interest in religion. However, on the first Sunday morning in Santa Barbara he was bored and was strolling around town when he saw a group of young men and women all dressed up and chatting merrily as they entered the Grace Methodist Church.

Harley followed the group and sat down in a corner pew. Although he bowed his head during prayers, he continued to watch a group of young ladies across the aisle. One of them had brown hair with a Marcel wave, a dazzling smile, a hint of dimples, and an air of quiet confidence. When she caught him staring at her, she lifted her chin slightly, looked straight at him, then averted her eyes. Harley was hooked.

He waited outside the church until she came out, laughing and talking with several friends. She caught sight of him, looked boldly at him, and then turned away. He went back into the church and picked up a program for the Sunday events including a vespers service at 7 p.m.

Harley hurried back to the rooming house and dug into his suitcase for his cap, a clean shirt, a skinny blue tie, and a white celluloid collar that was the fashion of the day. He bummed some black shoe polish from the landlady, brushed the Hope Ranch dust from his boots, and shined them. He laid out his black suit pants between the bed's springs and mattress and lay down on the bed for a couple of hours so that the pants would be "pressed" and almost have a crease in them.

Back at the church a few minutes before vespers, Harley spotted the young woman in a circle of friends. With cap in hand, he approached her and stammered, "Hello, I'm Harlan Johnston from Pasadena. Most people call me Harley. I hope you don't think I'm rude but I've been waiting all day to meet you. May I sit with you?" She looked him up and down for a second, noting the intense blue eyes, straight pointed nose, and breeze-ruffled blond hair. She glanced at her friends who were edging into a pew, whispering behind their hands and watching her with obvious curiosity.

With a defiant toss of her head, she turned to Harley, and said, "I'm pleased to meet you. I saw you in church this morning, and I'm glad you came tonight. I'm Mary Dora King. If you don't mind, we can sit with my friends."

She introduced him very briefly to several young women and went to the far end of a pew where they sat down. Before they had a chance to talk, the service began, and they sat stiffly in silence through the program, stealing sidelong glances at each other. Mary was dressed in a full length gray plaid skirt, a white blouse, and a large blue kerchief tied loosely in front. Her brown ankle-high shoes had buttons up the sides.

Harley mumbled his way through two hymns and "The Lord's Prayer," but religion was obviously not the main thing on the minds of both of them. When the service was over, they paused in the aisle, and Harley, twisting his cap with both hands, said, "I sure want to get to know you. Can I walk you home?"

"Yes, that would be nice. I live about five blocks from here, and we can talk as we walk," Mary replied and waved to her friends as a signal that they should not wait for her.

The couple walked out of the church into a balmy early spring evening with a thin band of sunset pink in the western sky and shimmering pink reflections on the languid ocean that could be glimpsed down some palm-tree-lined streets. They strolled through a residential neighborhood with rows of brick bungalows, each with a white-painted front porch and a patch of tan-tinged lawn. A pale saffron glow from a street light at each corner competed with darkening shadows.

Harley, eager to assure Mary that he was a "regular" guy, summarized his farm background, saying "I was born in Iowa, and when I was six years old, my family moved to Nebraska where my father worked on farms and then on a small cattle ranch. I have five brothers and sisters. When I was fourteen, I started working as a farm hand in Nebraska and then spent about ten years on farms in Missouri."

"How come you ended up out here in California?" Mary interrupted.

"My three sisters moved out here, and all of them live in Pasadena," Harley replied. "I get room and board with my oldest sister. She wrote me a long Christmas card two years ago about how fast the Los Angeles area was growing, so I thought I would come and see what it's like. I rode Union Pacific trains to get here. The farm work here is different from what I'm used to so I ended up working in a store for a while. Now I work for a landscaping company that got a big contract here on the Hope Ranch."

"I know the Hope Ranch very well," Mary commented. "My father was a foreman there for about fiteen years. My family lived in a ranch house a few miles from Santa Barbara and I was raised there until I was in grade school. My father, who was about twenty years older than my mother, died in 1903, and we moved to town where my mother could find work."

"That's too bad about your father. How is your mother?"

"She is well, thank you. She has had to work very hard at cleaning houses to get me and my three brothers through school and old enough to get jobs and help pay the bills."

"Where do you work?"

"I'm the secretary for the director of administration at the California State Normal School downtown. The school is a two-year college."

"If you're a secretary in that place, you must be pretty well educated. I barely got through the eighth grade before I had to go to work farming, but I do fairly well with reading and numbers, and I helped keep the books at the store in L.A."

Mary showed no adverse reaction to his eighth grade education since she knew quite a few people who had not gotten very far beyond grade school. "I graduated from Santa Barbara High School two years ago. I got pretty good grades and won a scholarship to the Normal School for a year while I worked part time. I studied bookkeeping, typing, English and grammar—stuff like that so I could get a job as a secretary. I couldn't afford to keep going to college so I started working full time there."

"Sounds like you're a hard worker. I am too."

They walked in awkward silence for half a minute. Harley, desperate to keep the conversation going, asked, "Where were your parents from?"

"They met at a gold mining camp called Nevada City at the edge of the mountains near Sacramento. I think that was about 1880. It's a ghost town now. Mom's name is Nancy. Her maiden name was Cooper. She grew up in the gold mining region and was about eightreen when she met my dad. He was Walter Riley King, a tall, good-looking Irishman with red hair. He came west from Maine hoping to get rich in

King family, circa 1902
Sitting: Walter (father), unidentified, Nancy (mother). Standing: Alfred, Eugene (Quil), Walter, Mary

gold mining. I'm not sure about just how they met but when the gold mining faded away they got married in Sacramento and headed south. He hoped to find permanent work on a ranch. They ended up here on the Hope Ranch. I was born there January 24, 1893."

Mary stopped walking, turned to Harley with a giggle, and said, "My goodness, how I prattle on, telling you my life story all at once."

Harley was almost paralyzed by the giggle and stammered, "I want to know more. I want to know all about you."

Harley was aware that they were approaching her home and was panic-stricken at the thought he might not see her again. He blurted out, "How often do you go to church? I mean, when are you going to be there again? I mean, when can I see you again?"

Mary stopped and gestured toward a modest house with a low wire fence and iron scrollwork gate. "This is my home. And, yes, you can see me again. I have to work all week but I'll be at the church next Sunday. I hope you will come."

Harley took off his cap and began twisting it. "I'm not sure how long the job on the Hope Ranch will last. If it goes on for another week, I will for sure be at the church Sunday. But even if we return to Los Angeles, I'll try to catch a train up here Saturday night 'cause I sure do want to see you again."

Mary laughed. "That would be sweet of you to make a special trip on the train to see me. We still have a lot to talk about, don't we? Maybe one of these days, you can meet my mother and my brothers. But for now, goodbye, and thanks for walking me home."

Harley resisted the urge to grab her hand and stuttered, "Thank you for letting me come with you. And I would like very much to meet your family. Anyway, I will see you at church next Sunday morning."

Mary opened the gate, stepped onto the porch, turned and waved, and disappeared into the house.

Harley began walking back to the rooming house, almost skipping, and thinking, "She's young and pretty, and I'm going to marry her."

As he entered the four-bunk bedroom he shared with other Dependable workers, one of them was reading a pulp magazine about cowboys, and two were getting ready for bed, showing signs of a heavy-drinking weekend. "So, lover boy," one of them wisecracked, "What did you find at that church deal you said you were going to? It was pretty clear that you weren't going there just to pray."

Harley smiled as he snapped off the celluloid collar and rubbed his neck where it had pinched him. "I'll let you know later. But for now, I'll just say I found something I want to keep."

The week of hard hot work on the Hope Ranch passed very slowly for Harley, and he was glad for the physical labor that kept his mind off Mary for hours at a time and put him into deep sleep at night. However, in the dream time just before waking up, he had visions of Mary's face floating in sun-flecked clouds.

He had hired the boarding house matron to clean and press his fraying suit so that he felt as presentable as possible when he hurried off to the church Sunday morning. He arrived a half hour early and stood near the front door, anxiously scanning the ebb and flow of parishioners. It was a warm cloudless morning in Santa Barbara with a breeze whispering in from the Channel Islands, and the parishioners were in a cheerful mood.

Finally, he saw her. She was wearing a full-length gauzy pink dress with a collar that covered her neck and was fastened with a cameo brooch. Wavy brown hair framed her lightly powdered face, blue eyes, and rounded nose that was a bit large but not enough to detract from her attractive face. She found him near the door and, with a faintly mocking curtsey, she said, "Good morning, Harlan Johnston. I heard through the grapevine that your job continued all week so you didn't have to hurry back here from Los Angeles. You would hurry back, wouldn't you?" Her appearance, mischievous smile, and teasing comment left Harley almost speechless. "Yes, yes, I mean I did work here all week, and, yes, I will sure hurry back here to see you, no matter what."

They entered the church, and Mary went to a side row of empty pews, motioning Harley to sit beside her. A few faces in the congregation turned with quizzical expressions to watch the couple. He was a stranger, and Mary was well known in the church from many years of attendance starting when she was in grade school.

When they emerged from the service at noon, Harley asked, "May I take you to have some ice cream or maybe lunch?"

"Yes, that would be swell. My favorite place is Romero's cafe just a few blocks away. You can get a good sandwich and a glass of sarsaparilla for a quarter."

"That sounds good to me. I'd rather take you to the Sunday buffet at the Arlington Hotel, but, as you might guess, I can't afford that."

They strolled as if on clouds to the restaurant, talking a bit self-consciously about the church service and the pastor's sermon titled "Turn the Other Cheek."

"If everybody in the world turned the other cheek, maybe we wouldn't have wars," Mary mused.

Harley shrugged and said, "I don't know much about what happens around the world, but I have to think that if all the good people turned the other cheek when they got hit, the bad people would simply make them obey orders or get hit again."

Mary gave him a sharp look. "You sound like a pessimist!"

"No. I'm not as skeptical as I may have just sounded, but I think you have to watch out for yourself, work hard, and mind your own business, then you won't have to worry about what other people might do to you."

"Well, I guess that's true but I think the better you treat other people the better they will treat you."

"Okay, you're an optimist, and I'm a pessimist. Maybe we would be good for each other."

Mary gave him a sidelong glance, and Harley thought to himself, *"You dumb head! You're going way too fast."* Mary caught the look of consternation on his face and smiled, "Maybe, just maybe."

At the restaurant, they had tuna sandwiches, and Harley got root beer rather than sarsaparilla. Mary, devout Methodist that she was, began to carefully probe Harley's personal habits. "I notice you don't smoke or it appears that you don't. I haven't smelled smoke on you or is that just because it's Sunday?"

Harley threw his shoulders back and his chest out. "I don't smoke—never have and never will. I tried a cigar once that a guy gave me when his wife had a baby. I thought it tasted terrible and smelled even worse. Stogie is the best name for a cigar. I've been around quite a few guys who are heavy smokers, and I don't like the way some of them cough. It's none of my business if they want to smoke but I have a hunch it's bad for your health. I've been healthy all my life, and I want to stay that way. But probably another good reason I don't smoke is because I don't want to spend money on tobacco. My father was part Scotch, and I'm afraid I inherited his stinginess."

The oration was longer than Harley usually talked, and he glanced at Mary to see if she was bored. She was looking at him with a pleased expression on her face. She fingered her glass of sarsaparilla and said, "What about drinking? I'll bet you don't do that either—at least I hope you don't."

Harley chuckled, "No, I don't drink. Of course, I've seen a lot of people get happy with booze, and I've seen what can happen when it becomes a habit and the trouble it can cause. Like the case of the cigar, I've tried whiskey several times when the guys I work with dragged me to a bar. But, again, I simply don't like the taste of it, and I don't like the feeling that I might lose control. Basically, I guess I just want to be sure I can always take care of myself. And, besides, I hate to waste money."

Mary reached across the table and touched his hand. "I'm glad. My father was mostly Irish, and there were times when he drank too much."

They finished their first lunch together, and Harley, with a feeling of gallantry he had not felt for many years, paid the bill, declining her offer to "go Dutch."

Mary said, "It's such a lovely day. Let's go down to the beach."

In 1914, Santa Barbara was a comparatively minor seaport in California. A valley named after the town is nestled at the base of the Santa Ynez Mountains. They rise to 4,000 feet altitude on the east and curve westward around the north side of the opalescent sea that became known as the Santa Barbara Channel.

The first Europeans to see the site were Franciscan monks traveling north to Monterey in 1769. Spaniards built an adobe fort in 1782, and on December 4, 1786, Father Lasuén consecrated the start of a Catholic mission church which became one of the most notable and best-preserved of a string of mission buildings along the southern California coast. Until the Yankees arrived six decades later, Santa Barbara was a classic colorful Spanish colony with vaqueros and dons rich in land and cattle.

From 1900–1910, during Mary's youth, the town was primarily residential with some business supported by travel up and down the coast and by farming in the valley. The waterfront had a wooden wharf stretching far out into the bay where the water was deep enough to allow ships to use dock facilities. The wharf was flanked by broad sandy beaches where gentle waves were barely knee-high except during storms. Fishing from the wharf and in the surf was popular.

High temperatures hovered between 70 and 80 degrees Fahrenheit in summer with constant sea breezes, and low temperatures ranged in the 30s and 40s in wintertime. Rainfall was about 22 inches per year with most of it occurring in the winter months.

Santa Barbara was a very pleasant and healthy place in which to live.

Harley and Mary strolled down State Street between rows of palm trees, walked out onto the wharf, and sat down on a splintery old bench. Seagulls soared on motionless wings overhead. Sandpipers skittered on twiggy legs along the beach below, dodging the edge of waves and the forays of children of sunbathing parents. A thin layer of stratus clouds rested on the ocean horizon, and the Channel Islands were vague humps 30 to 40 miles out in the haze.

Waving toward the four-story bell tower of the Methodist Church that loomed over the edge of downtown, Harley turned to Mary and said, "I like your church. I feel comfortable there. So often when I've gone to churches in other places, I felt like a stranger in the congregation. That doesn't happen here, but probably that's because of you."

"Well, I have kind of taken you under my wing. But the young adults group I'm a member of likes to welcome newcomers," Mary responded. "I've been busy in the church ever since I was in high school and started singing in the choir for early services. That led me into wanting to learn to play the piano. My oldest brother, Walt, paid for some lessons for me, using one of the pianos at the church. Now I play well enough to accompany the singing at some church socials and vespers."

"I notice you seem to be pretty popular with that bunch of people I see you coming to church with. Are you all part of some kind of a club?"

"Yes, sort of, but it's pretty informal. There's about ten of us, guys and gals, and we do a lot of things together—picnics, parties, some dances, hikes in the canyons."

"Well, I can whistle but I can barely carry a tune so I won't sing very loud. I've done some country dancing, and I like to go walking, and I like to eat at picnics so hopefully, with your help, I can fit in."

"You'll fit in. I'll make sure of that."

As the afternoon shadows began to lengthen, Mary said, "I better be heading home. Mom has not been feeling very well, and I need to go fix dinner. I'd like to invite you to come to dinner but that might be rushing things, don't you think? My family may need a little more time to get used to the idea of you being around."

Harley thought to himself, *"We're not rushing things fast enough,"* but said, "That's probably true. When the time comes, I look forward to meeting your mother and your brothers."

The couple walked slowly back up the slight slope of the town. "It's too bad we don't have time to visit the old mission church," Mary exclaimed, "It's the biggest attraction in Santa Barbara. It's almost 150 years old."

The church was rebuilt several times in Spanish colonial days. The main structure, with its domed bell towers and tile roof, was 170 feet long and forty feet wide with a ceiling 28 feet high. The surrounding acreage was landscaped with many of the trees and other plants native to California plus gardens where flowers bloomed nearly year around. Emphasis was on golden poppies, adopted as California's state flower in 1903. Old wooden carts used by Spanish pioneers were scattered around the grounds.

As they neared Mary's home, Harley stammered. "My crew will return to Los Angeles Tuesday, and, of course, I have to go to keep my job. I don't know when I'll be able to come back. Can I write to you?"

"Certainly. I'd like that," Mary replied. She dug into her small purse and took out a pencil and a slip of paper. "Here's the address."

Harley took the note and held her hand for just a moment. "I will be back just as soon as I can."

He turned and started walking to the rooming house. Mary watched him for a few seconds, clasped her hands in a gesture of prayer, and entered the house.

Chapter 2

The Courtship

Four days after their second date, Mary got her first letter from Harley, addressed to "Miss Mary King, 519 W. Haley, Santa Barbara, California." It was written in pencil on notebook paper and had sporadic punctuation.

> Dear Mary,
>
> I am not much good at writing I would rather talk to you. The last two Sundays with you were really swell. If it is OK with you I will come up a week from this Saturday and will stay at the rooming house Saturday night and catch the train back to LA Sunday night. The train as you probably know gets to the Santa Barbara station about 5 in the afternoon so maybe we can have dinner. Please write to me if this is OK. The address on the envelope is for my sister Lu where I get my mail.
>
> Hopefully,
> Harley

Mary read the letter several times, tucked it inside her blouse, and hugged herself.

Her bedroom was the smallest of three in the bungalow. Her brothers, Walter, the oldest, Alfred, and Eugene, best known as Quil from his middle name of Aquila, a year younger than Mary, shared a bedroom. Mother King had the "master" bedroom with a brass frame double bed topped by a thick goose down quilt. Everybody shared the tile-floored single bathroom which had a washstand, flush toilet, and a bathtub on lion-claw legs.

After dinner, Mary tried to seclude herself in her bedroom to compose a reply to Harley, writing on top of a chest of drawers which had to double as a desk. The bedroom door opened, and Quil came in. He was six feet tall, slim and handsome with a shock of unruly reddish hair that he had inherited from his Irish father, twinkling blue eyes, and the quick-to-laugh face of an extrovert. He and Mary, being the youngest, were the closest members of the family. He stood near the doorway with his hands on his hips and nodded his head toward the pieces of paper on the chest of drawers. "So, little sister, what is going on? You've been acting a little strange lately. You want to tell your dear brother something? I'll bet it's that blond guy who was with you in church and who walked you home last week."

Mary blushed and replied, "Well, if it's any of your business, smarty pants, it is a man. His name is Harlan Johnston, and he works for a landscaping and tree trimming company in Los Angeles. The company had a job at the Hope Ranch, and we met at church, and now he wants to keep coming to see me."

"Well, well, well! The way you are acting, he must be quite a guy. I thought you were waiting for someone tall, dark and handsome."

"Oh, aren't you a smart alec! Harley's not very tall, he is blond, and he is good-looking. He is very nice, and I think he likes me a lot."

"So, Miss Prim, when do we get to meet this Prince Charming?"

"I'll let you know. But til then, Quil, please don't make a big to-do around the family. I need more time to think about the whole thing and about what I should do."

"All right, I'll keep my mouth shut for a little while. But I get to be the first to know if it gets serious, okay?"

"Yes, that's a deal. Now get out of here and leave me alone."

Mary checked the address on Harley's letter, decided she liked the name of Harlan better than his nickname, and started writing:

> Mr. Harlan Johnston
> C/O Lu Strahan
> 1191 N. Los Robles Ave.
> Pasadena, California
>
> Dear Harlan,
>
> I was very glad to hear from you so soon. Yes, please do come up here a week from Saturday. I will meet you at the station and, yes, we can go to dinner. Then maybe we can go to an organ recital at the church. On Sunday, after church, I want to take you home to meet my family and have dinner. My favorite brother, Quil, is getting very nosey and will start spreading rumors if he doesn't meet you soon.

Mary leaned back, looked at the ceiling and pondered how to end the letter. "Yours truly" and "Sincerely" sounded much too distant and formal. "Fondly" seemed a bit presumptuous. She looked at Harley's letter and decided to set the same tone that he did with "Hopefully."

P.S. I know you said most people call you Harley but I like Harlan better.

A week from Saturday, Harley stepped off the train at the Santa Barbara station a few minutes after 5 p.m. After an anxious moment of scanning the platform, he saw her hurrying toward him, waving both hands. He was wearing a fashionable new straw hat with a black band. He doffed the hat, bowed, and kissed her hand. Wide-eyed, she whispered, "Oh, my goodness! Such chivalry!"

Harlan

She left her hand in his for a moment after his quick kiss. "Am I glad to see you! Have you been working hard? It looks like you got sunburned."

Mary

Harley's blond complexion was a bit more ruddy than usual, but the color was due to blushing as well as sunburn. "Yes, we were out where the desert starts east of L.A. for a few days, and it was pretty hot. But look at you! What a pretty dress!" Mary was wearing her best green chiffon dress with long ribbed sleeves fitted snugly on her arms. The dress color complimented her brown hair.

"It's a little bit early for dinner," Mary said. "The recital at the church isn't until eight o'clock, so we have plenty of time. How about a walk through one of my favorite parks near here?"

"Whatever you want to do is fine with me," Harley replied.

They walked past the Haley Street playground to Oak Park which surrounded a Spanish-style fountain. There were tall ferns, some clusters of bamboo, colorful patches of hibiscus, poinsettias, myrtle, acacias, and jacarandas, with live oaks, some cypress trees, and California laurel as backdrops. The late afternoon sun was starting to cast deep shadows that accentuated splashes of golden sunlight on the flowers.

"I love this place," Mary murmured. "It's so peaceful. I sometimes come here on Saturday afternoons and read. It's especially lovely at this time of year, which reminds me—Easter is just two weeks away. I hope you can come again then. It's one of my favorite times of the year."

"I will come for Easter. My company lets its workers off for Good Friday and a three-day weekend. I should spend Good Friday with my sisters in Pasadena, but I could come up again on the train the Saturday before Easter like I did today."

"That will be absolutely wonderful for us to spend Easter together. We can double-check by mail next week."

After a Mexican dinner and the organ recital, they walked to Mary's home. "I'll meet you at the church a little before 11 o'clock tomorrow morning," Mary told Harley. "After church, we'll go home and you can meet my family. We usually have dinner around four o'clock on Sundays so you can catch the evening train to L.A. Okay?"

"Yes, that will work out good. I guess I have to meet your family sooner or later but, of course, I'm pretty nervous about it. These are my best clothes, and they are pretty well worn. I hope they understand that I'm a working man and trying to save money."

"Pshaw! All my brothers are working men and can't dress any better than you do. Now good night, sleep tight, and don't worry. I'll see you in the morning."

Mary extended her hand to Harley who took it gingerly and, for a panicky second, wondered what he should do—shake her hand vigorously like a man, kiss it, or just touch it and drop it. Mary sensed his concern, smiled, placed her other hand on top of his, and let her finger tips slide off his hand. Harley shivered and stuttered, "Well, good night, then, and you sleep tight too." Mary turned at the door and waved. He blew her a kiss and skip-walked away down the street.

The next day as they left the church service, which ended at 12:30, Mary and Harley paused on the steps. "Well, Sir Lancelot, are you ready for the jousting match?" Mary asked, tugging at his sleeve.

Harley was not sure who Sir Lancelot was or what jousting meant, but he knew she was referring to the challenge he faced in meeting her family. "I guess I'm as ready as I'll ever be. Tell me what we are having for dinner, and I'll think about that 'til we get to the house."

At the Haley Street bungalow, the King family was waiting in the living room. Mother King stood at the front window, peeking around the yellow flower print curtain toward the street. "Here they come," she whispered, and hurried to her rocking chair.

Mary and Harley entered the room to find the family arrayed in a semi-circle facing a sofa where the couple was to sit. Mary took Harley's hand, glanced saucily around the room, and said, "This is Harlan Johnston from Pasadena. He's my new boyfriend!" She pointed a finger at each of the men, turned to Harley, and said, "These are the brothers I told you about. They are really nice guys, and I'm lucky to be their only sister."

She led Harley slowly around the room, introducing him to each member of the family. The couple sat down on the sofa, and Harley, clutching his straw hat and feeling like he was in a police station, braced himself for the interrogation.

Seated directly across the room from him was Mother King, wearing metal-rim eyeglasses, dressed in a gray striped dress with a prim white lace collar, her gray-streaked black hair in a tight bun, her hands clasped sternly in her lap. Next to her was Walter—Walt for short—the oldest and biggest son at six feet, two inches, wearing a large mustache, white shirt with black pants and black string tie, his black hair parted in the middle. On the other side of the mother was Alfred—Alf, for short—wearing a short black beard on his gaunt face, dressed in a dark brown suit and open neck shirt, and appearing to be as nervous as Harley. Quil was standing to one side, leaning nonchalantly on a bookcase and surveying the scene with a faint smile. He was dressed in the latest fashion, a plaid suit in a light mustard color.

Mary patted Harley's arm and said, "As I told you all yesterday, Harlan works for a tree-trimming and landscape company out of Los Angeles and likes to come to Santa Barbara. His nickname is Harley. We met at church vespers a few weeks ago, and I think we kind of like each other, and I decided he should meet my family, so here we are. He's staying for dinner and then he has to go back to L.A. this evening."

Mother King was the first to speak. "Welcome, Mr. Johnston. Any friend of Mary's is, of course, a friend of ours. Most of us usually go to church but the boys have been working extra hard this spring and have been resting on Sundays. Walter is thinking about getting married and moving out this summer. He works in the city public utilities department. Alfred works at the city's stables and is a bit of an expert on work horses. And Quil, over there, works part time at the docks on the end of the pier. Mary hasn't told us much about you, Mr. Johnston. She did say you've been a farmer most of your life."

"That's true. But, please, call me Harley. I was born in Iowa and worked as a farm hand in Nebraska and in Missouri. I like farming, and I hope to have a place of my own. But, as you might guess, I couldn't save much money as a hired hand so I came to California two years ago hoping to find work that pays better so I can save enough to buy some land."

"Have you looked around here in the Santa Barbara Valley?" Walt asked.

"Yes, a little bit but the main crops here are lemons, walnuts and olives, and I don't know much about them. And, besides that, any land around here worth trying to farm costs $50 to $100 an acre. It would be a long time before I could buy anything near here. The federal government has a homestead program that offers free land."

Harley, realizing that he had not given Mary even a hint about his interest in a farm in Utah, hastened to add, "However, that program is just a possibility that I might look into. And, anyway, right now I'm just trying to save as much money as I can."

"Mary mentioned that you and your company cleared some land at the Hope Ranch," Alf said. "That must have been pretty hard work."

Harley, grateful for the change in subject, replied, "That's true but I'm used to hard work." He paused for a moment, wondering what he should say about his wages and working conditions. "I make four dollars a day, and when my crew is on the road we get rooms and meals at a rooming house. We usually work six days a week and have Sunday off. I just happened to go to church here last month and was very lucky to meet Mary there."

Mary gave a thumbs up sign and set out to lighten up the conversation. "Maybe Quil can get a job with your company but, then again, he doesn't like hard work."

Quil waggled a finger at her, then turned to Harley. "I'm very glad you came to visit. We were becoming aware that Mary had met someone at church that seemed to catch her fancy. But, I must warn you, she's been known to flirt with a lot of guys."

"Quil, stop it!" Mary giggled and shook her fist at him. Harley shuffled his feet and thought desperately for something clever to say. "Yes, I'll bet she's very popular. She's so lively and pretty."

The King family nodded approval in unison. Then Mother King returned to the interrogation. "Where do you live in L.A.?"

"I rent a room at the home of my oldest sister, Lu, in Pasadena, and I ride a streetcar to work in the middle of Los Angeles," Harley answered.

Mother King reached for her crochet needles on a table and asked, "What about the future? Do you think you'll be working for the landscaping company for a long time?"

Harley sensed that his position with the mother and perhaps the whole family depended on his answer but he did not hesitate. "No, to be honest, I don't expect to be with the landscaping company or with any business for that matter for a long time. I want to be my own boss, and, since the only thing I know much about is farming, I am determined to save enough money to get my own place as soon as possible and to raise a family in the country rather than a city. Compared with most of the guys I know, I save quite a bit of money by not smoking or drinking. As I have told Mary, I don't like tobacco or booze, and I don't want to waste money on them."

Mary looked at Mother King and her brothers for their reaction to Harley's almost vehement declaration. Everyone was silent for a half minute. Mother King was having a mixed reaction as she considered the possibility of her beloved daughter's future with this man. Her concern about Mary going off to a farm somewhere was partially offset by her approval of Harley's opinion about smoking and drinking. The brothers worried about losing their only sister, but they did not share his views about liquor and tobacco.

Harley squirmed on the sofa, hoping the questions would end soon but from the look on Mother King's face, he knew another tough inquiry was coming. "How old are you? It seems like you spent a lot of years as a farm hand."

"I'm thirty-seven, and I know you're probably thinking I should be married and settled down by now. But about all I can say is that, so far anyway, I haven't met someone I've fallen in love with." He thought it best not to tell the whole truth—that he was hoping to find a woman much younger than he so she could take care of him in his old age.

Mary, sensing that Mother King was getting uncomfortable with some of Harley's answers, interrupted, "Mom, we have to look at the roast in the oven, and we better go start fixing dinner." Mrs. King agreed and followed her daughter to the kitchen.

Harley, relieved that the inquisition was over, at least for the time being, turned to Alf, "So, you work at the city's stables. What kind of horses do you have, and how do you use them?"

Alf, pleased to hear that Harley was interested in his work, described the kind of horses and some mules at the stables, and how they were used for deliveries, pulling city maintenance equipment, and digging ditches, for example. "Of course, the time is coming when the animals will be phased out and replaced by what everybody is starting to call motor vehicles. I'll probably have to start learning about internal combustion engines."

Walt interrupted, "Yeah, I got a look yesterday at the new Metz 25 touring car with an electrical system for start-up and lights, a speedometer, and plate glass that replaces isinglass. But I doubt I'll be getting one soon. It costs over $1,000—a lot more than the Model T Fords that everybody is buying."

"Yes, but horses and mules are still going to be around for quite a few more years, especially outside of cities where the roads aren't paved, and a car can get stuck in mud more than a buggy," Harley commented. "Even here, there's only one paved highway."

Quil changed the subject to Harley's declaration about smoking and drinking. "I have a year to go before I'm old enough to drink, but I kind of look forward to finding out what it's like to have a couple of beers. And, Harley, you should know that my brothers are not teetotalers. Alf smokes little cigars, and Walt has been known to belt down a shot and a beer in his favorite bar. But they have a problem here at home. Mom won't allow tobacco or booze in the house. So, you're safe here, Harley." Everyone laughed.

Mary bounced into the living room and announced, "Dinner's ready! Come and get it!"

The smell of roasted beef and potatoes filled the kitchen, and Harley wolfed down the home cooking, showing the bigger men that he had an appetite as big as theirs.

After dinner, Mary told Harley, "We often play cards after dinner Sunday evenings, but we don't have time to get a game going before you have to catch the train."

"That's all right. I don't know much about cards. But I'd be glad to have you teach me."

"And I'll be very glad to be your teacher. But now I'd better teach you the way to the train station."

As the couple went out the front door, Walt tugged at his mustache. "Mary's almost as tall as he is. I hope she knows what she's doing."

At the station, Mary turned to Harley, took both his hands and said, "Thank you for being so honest with my family. They mean the world to me, and I want them to know what I'm doing. If my mother seemed tough on you, it's mainly because I'm her only daughter, and she wants to protect me."

"That's okay. I understand. I only hope I didn't disappoint them because I'm not going to let you go," Harley replied.

"You're sweet! Write to me soon." Mary gave him a quick kiss on the cheek and walked away. Harley watched until she turned a corner and was out of sight.

He returned to Santa Barbara for the Easter weekend and joined the King family at Sunday events at the church and Sunday dinner at home. There was a young adults picnic Saturday, and Harley had to make small talk with Mary's many friends who obviously were very curious about this "older man" and about what Mary saw in him. She

The young adults of Mary's church on a picnic, circa 1913.
Mary is seated in the center right.

was busy with activities at the church, and Harley wished they could spend more time alone together but he began to understand her quiet faith in her religion and the inner strength and energy it seemed to give her.

May and June were very busy months for the Dependable Landscaping Company, and Harley was barely able to squeeze in a few Saturday nights and Sundays in Santa Barbara.

On one Saturday, the young adults group had an outing on the Hope Ranch. Mary showed Harley where she had spent her early childhood, and he showed her the area where he had worked on trees and bushes in March.

That evening, on the way to her house, Harley suggested they sit for a while in Oak Park so that he could start to explore her reaction to his plans for the future.

"You know, Mary, how often I've mentioned wanting to have my own farm somehow. Well, I've started looking into a federal government program called homesteading. Under the 1909 law, a guy like me can get a big piece of land in some western states for only a few dollars. I got some information about what looks like a good deal in a valley in Utah. There's a new railroad there, and it offers cut rate shipping for people who want to move there."

Mary, basking in the afterglow of a very pleasant afternoon, murmured, "I don't know very much about Utah. How far away is this place you're talking about?"

"It's in a corner of Utah closest to California and is easy to reach on a new railroad line."

"If the land is almost free, why would you need a lot of money to have a farm there?"

"I'd have to build a house there and buy some livestock and a lot of farm equipment."

"Would I like it there?"

"I don't know because I haven't been there, and it will be quite a while before I can check it out and have enough money."

Harley's comments were vague enough that Mary stopped asking questions and started reviewing the social events of the day.

For the Fourth of July holiday, Harley had a four-day weekend, and he was torn between the urge to see Mary whenever possible and the expense of staying in a hotel or rooming house for four days and paying for meals. His internal debate did not last long however as passion easily won out over penury. He wrote Mary about his train schedule, his desire to see her, and what they might do together. He sensed that during this visit some kind of crisis was eminent. There would probably be a dance, and he would hold her in his arms.

The evening of Independence Day, following a parade and a party hosted by one of Mary's girlfriends, Harley and Mary arrived at her gate on an exquisitely beautiful evening. A polished brass moon was flirting with wisps of clouds above the palm trees.

Mary had been walking with an arm in the crook of his elbow, and she prattled on about the fun of the day's events, laced with gossip about her friends and their latest love affairs. "Some of them are wondering about us," she whispered as they stopped at the gate. "They are asking me if we are in love."

Harley had sense enough to know she had pushed open a door and dared him to enter. He had kissed a few farm maidens on moonlight buggy rides, but never had he felt so overwhelmed and tongue-tied as he did at this moment.

He took a deep breath and blurted out, "Mary, I love you! I'm crazy about you!"

She spun halfway around, threw her arms around his neck, and whispered, "Oh, Harlan, I'm so glad! I love you so much." She leaned her head against his chest for a moment, and then lifted her face for a kiss—their first. Their lips touched tentatively at first, then pressed hard together. Harley hugged her tight with one arm, and with the other hand in her hair he held her face against his. Then, alarmed by his impulsiveness, he released her and leaned back, searching her face for her reaction. She smiled, touched his face with her fingers, and murmured, "That was nice. Let's do it again." They did and then she whispered, "I'd better go in before somebody sees us."

Harley stammered, "When I come back, I'm going to bring a ring because I want to start making sure that I can keep you away from all those guys you see when I'm not here."

"Don't worry, darling. I'll be here, waiting just for you, and I can't wait to wear your ring," Mary murmured. They kissed again and Mary went into the house.

Chapter 3

Engaged

A week after the July 4th holiday and Harley's and Mary's first kiss, he hurried back to Santa Barbara with a ring in his pocket. It was a painfully thin gold band with a diamond chip but it was all Harley felt he could afford.

That Saturday evening after dinner, they strolled down State Street to the moonlight-drenched beach where a few hardy fishermen were casting lines in silhouette against the glistening wine-dark waves. Mary and Harley sat on the sand a few feet above the rising tide.

Harley cleared his throat. "Mary, my love, the past few months have been the happiest and most exciting time of my life. I know I'm a lot older than you, but will you marry me? I know I can make you happy." She threw her arms around his neck, kissed him, and almost shouted, "Yes! Yes! I've been waiting, hoping, wondering if you would ever propose. I was almost ready to ask you myself."

With fumbling fingers, Harley slipped the ring on her finger. "Now we are engaged, and you belong to me. When can we tell your family and all your friends?"

"Tomorrow! We'll tell the whole world tomorrow after church!"

"I don't know when we can get married. I need to keep working at Dependable Landscaping to save a little more money before we can set a date."

"We'll work it out. For now nothing matters except that we love each other."

Harley was suddenly aware of all the implications of their engagement for the future. "I don't know a darn thing about getting married. I hope you know what we have to do."

Mary leaned her head on his shoulder, took a deep breath, and said, "Don't worry. It will be fun, lots of fun, and we'll have lots of parties to celebrate."

A few days later, Mary received the first of a torrent of letters and postcards from Pasadena, and nearly every one ended with a string of "XOXOXOXOXO" meaning hugs and kisses. She replied in kind.

On the last weekend in July, Harley returned to Santa Barbara, and reluctantly agreed to join Mary and her "club" on a over-night junket to the little town of Goleta on the coast a few miles northwest of Santa Barbara. It was much less strait-laced than the bigger and older town and offered a popular escape for the younger set. It had a campground for tenting and a large picnic platform near a small lake. Mary's group pitched a tent for the men and one for the women and installed Army-style cots.

Impromptu skits were all the rage for outings, and Mary and Harley, being newly-engaged, were singled out for the main show. It involved a family with two babies so Harley and Mary had to wear diapers created out of bed sheets. While Harley was allowed to wear only the sheet, Mary, in the interest of modesty, wore a baggy black bathing suit that covered her from knees to shoulders under the big diaper.

Harley was an embarrassed actor but he had no choice about proceeding if he were to keep Mary happy. Being the oldest guy in the group was tough enough without trying to act like a baby.

Harley's main competitor for Mary's hand had been Alvin Lloyd, a handsome young man a year older than Mary. His trademark was wearing his gray fedora at a rakish angle.

Ebullient, gregarious, energetic, a bit mischievous, Mary wore her heart on her sleeve, scribbling joyously in letters to Harley about life in the good old summertime in good old Santa Barbara. Naively, she wrote about Alvin in an August 10 letter to Harley:

> Alvin heard you were out of town so he said he would visit me at 7:30. I told him he would have to bring me a box of candy and take me to a show. He came but I got cold feet and wouldn't go with him. He said he would come again, but I told him he would not be expected. What are you going to do with me, Harlan? You better come back quickly, don't you think? But, darling, never mind. You are more to me than anyone else on earth! Thanks for the XXXXXs and OOOOOs. They are not half so nice as some I have had from you.
>
> P.S. I miss you dreadfully. When will you come back to Santa Barbara?
>
> XOXOXOXO

Harley replied swiftly with a briefly worded postcard reminding her that they were engaged and that she must tell Alvin to stay away. There were only a few Xs and Os.

Mary's continuing lack of guile resulted in even more of a lovers' spat, detailed in several letters that revealed Harley's straight-arrow view of life and the problems of living 90 miles from his betrothed.

On August 16, Mary wrote:

> Had the time of my life last night in Goleta. I haven't made such a fool of myself since the last time we were in Goleta. Do you remember that time, kiddo? I stayed all night with my good friend, Maude, after two fellows tried to take us home. One of them rang me up the next morning and wanted to take Maude and me to church. I said I would go, but then I remembered what you told me the last time you were here so I rang up Maude and told her 'nothing doing!' Maude said to tell you she wished I was not engaged so that we could go out with those fellows. But I'm glad I'm engaged because I love you!
>
> XOXOXOXOXOXO

(She did not say how one of the "fellows" had gotten her telephone number.)

In a rambling reply August 18, Harley wrote:

> Was glad to hear from you but do not know whether I am very much pleased with the way you seem to be cutting up when I have not been away two weeks. I thank you very much for telling me all about it and it was all right for one of your friends to bring you home and if you will not have that other fellow that is very much stuck on himself [an apparent reference to Alvin Lloyd] around, then everything will be alright. Maybe I better stay away another week or I may come up some night in my dreams and you better be true or I may see you then. My darling girl, I may be somewhat cranky but I do not want to be mean so do not get angry at what I write. I love you.
>
> XOXOXOXOXO.

On August 20, Mary wrote:

> My dear Harlan,
>
> When I came home tonight, I had the blues. Consequently, when I read your letter it made me cry. I never dreamed that you would not trust me or else I would not have been so frank. I think you must be a little bit sensitive so I'll forgive you and, believe me, I'm going to stay home every night until you come back.

In another letter two days later, Mary told Harley about being "awfully lonesome" and about going to a church social.

> You will laugh when I tell you who walked home with me—old man Burchett. Ha! Ha! But I couldn't stop him without being rude. Now I suppose you will scold me again. I don't believe you care whether you come back or not, the way you talk. I don't want you to come in a dream, I want you to really come. It's been awful since you left. I'm glad to hear from you soon after my letters but please, please, don't scold me. XOXO

On Aug. 22, Harley wrote:

> Well Dear I'm very sorry I made you cry over what I said in my letter. I know you did not think about what you were doing but I could not help getting a little peeved. Yes Dear I am coming back to Santa Barbara and it can't be any too soon to please me because I do want to see you something awful . . . I have a bad cold but I would love to take you in my arms and hug you and kiss you just like before. Do not think I do not trust you for I do and if Burchett wants to walk home with you I will not scold you.
>
> With lots of love to my intended wife.
>
> XOXOXOXOXOXO

Harley was no smarter than Mary in saying the wrong thing at the wrong time. In his next letter he wrote, "I may go up to Utah before I come up to Santa Barbara again."

Mary promptly replied:

> It seems you have been gone for more than three weeks. Mother says that if you went to Utah, I would never see you again. I told her that you would not go without me. I don't want you to go to Utah!! If you do, I'll be mad at you . . . Gee, if you are to be away many more Sundays, I'll go crazy. Guess I am foolish but I can't help it. I never realized what it would mean to have you away so long and I never thought I would miss you so much but it means now I know that I really love you, Sweetheart. Take care of your cold.
>
> XOXOXOXO

Harley decided he had better wait a while before going to Utah to see about homesteading. He visited Santa Barbara for another Saturday night and Sunday, and he and Mary kissed often and made up and pretended to forget about the letters. After church, they joined several of her friends for an afternoon swimming party and picnic at the beach, using dressing rooms in the bath house at the Plaza del Mar. The sun was hot but the waves were a cool 65 degrees. Nearly everyone wore black swimming clothes—the men in shorts and tank tops, the women in baggy blouses and bloomers.

A week later, at a retreat at the Painted Cave Resort, the guys rode some donkeys, and the gals staged a fashion show of hats that included

Swimming party at Santa Barbara beach, 1914.

Retreat at Painted Cave Resort, 1914.

many with wide brims and piles of flowers, one with the front brim turned up like a Pony Express rider, and several tams.

Throughout late August and into the fall, Mary and Harley continued their barrage of letters and postcards:

> Harlan Johnston, I have a bone to pick with you. Please return those Xs and Os you borrowed from me. I need them now! . . . Write more often.
>
> Dear Mary,
>
> I miss you as much as you miss me. I long to be with you . . . So you will be mad if I go to Utah will you! Well if I go you need not think I will stay without you. You do not need to worry about me coming back . . . You are invited to come to visit in Pasadena. My brother-in-law said for you to come and stay with me. I do not know what for — do you? My dear girl, I am sending you a box of chocolates and a box of Xs and Os.
>
> ***
>
> My Dear Harlan,
>
> You had better come home before you go to Utah because if you stay away too long I will get another fellow, see! I meet lots of new nice-looking fellows at Normal [college] so you had better look out, old man. But I do love you best of all. I hope you come home next week. P.S. My brothers ate most of the chocolates.
>
> ***
>
> Dear Harlan,
>
> I need your advice on whether I should buy a Mason and Hammond piano from a friend for $175. It is a bargain and I am crazy to have it. I also have enough money to pay cash for it. If you think we will stay in Santa Barbara, I'll take it. Otherwise, we would not want to haul it around over the country. I want it awfully bad.
>
> ***
>
> Mary Dear,
>
> Well I am coming up to Santa Barbara after finishing the job I was on yesterday. I wanted to come sooner but some of the other workers had problems so I had to stay . . . Well Sweetheart I hardly think we will make our home in Santa Barbara for a while anyway. I think a change would be better and after we get settled we could buy a piano then . . . With buckets of love to you and how anxious I am for a real kiss.
>
> XOXOXOXOX
>
> ***
>
> Dearest Harlan,
>
> You are so good to me but, Sweetheart, you must not be too good to me because then I may not appreciate it. I am awfully glad you are coming home. I wish you could have come tomorrow night so you

> could be here for the picnic at Oak Park. If it were within the laws of etiquette, I would go to the station and meet you and kiss you then but you see how it is. When you are my husband, I won't care what people say, will I? I'm keeping my promise not to go anyplace. I love you. Good night.
>
> XOXOXOXOX

That Saturday night, they attended a dance at the pavilion in Goleta. One of the church group brought a new Victrola record player (made by the Victor Talking Machine Company with patents in 1901–1909) and a dozen thick black records. Among the "hits" of the day were the international award-winner *Macushla* by tenor John McCormack, *I've Got the Time and the Place But It's Hard to Find a Girl* by tenor Henry Burr, and a waltz *After the Ball.*

Instead of another visit to Santa Barbara, Harley arranged for Mary to visit Pasadena for a few days. She was ecstatic about a friend of Harley's taking them on a long tour of Los Angeles in his new Ford auto.

By mid-autumn, despite Mary's notes about loneliness and her objections to him visiting Utah, Harley began firming up a plan for the rest of his life—a marriage that would last for many generations on a homestead farm of his own in a place called the Escalante Valley. There, life would be as simple as the cycle of growing crops, and their children would smell new-mown hay.

He waited to disclose any specifics of the plan to Mary and her family until he could be fairly sure of getting a 320-acre homestead for a few dollars. A pamphlet he had received from the Escalante land office in Milford, Utah, rhapsodized about the "wonderful and exciting potential" for farms in the region and about the "amazing new science of dry land farming." It stressed the railroad access to thousands of acres of flat virgin land.

At the Dependable Company, Harley had been promoted to tree surgeon specializing in saving old and valuable trees on many of the large estates of wealthy owners in southern California. He got a pay raise so that he could squeeze out almost $2 a day into a bank account for the move to Utah. He began calculating and re-calculating a budget for the biggest gamble in his life, and he figured he could finance a marriage by the end of the year and the homestead deal by early 1915.

When he outlined the basics of the plan to Mary on a visit early in November, she realized fully for the first time that she would have to leave her cherished home and family, her church, her circle of friends, and the places of many memories in Santa Barbara. She had passed up the opportunity to buy a piano, and she now sensed there would be no piano in Utah.

However, she could not comprehend what life would be like on a pioneer farm. Her early childhood on the Hope Ranch, while it involved daily chores and no money for candy, was mostly a pleasant memory, spiced with frequent visits to the "city." She had never been outside of southern California, and now she had a sense of adventure about moving to a strange land populated by people called Mormons with a strange religion. Anyway, she was not prepared nor inclined to ask tough questions.

The evening after Harley returned to L.A., Mary summoned her family to a meeting in the living room and repeated what Harley had told her about his plan. The family's reaction was a mixture of dismay, anger and curiosity.

Her mother was furious. "I don't think this is a good idea at all. I don't mind you getting engaged to Mr. Johnston, but I am upset that he is 15 years older than you and now he wants to take you off to what is probably a desert. He seems like a hard worker and can take care of you but why can't he stay in California and you could live here happily ever after, close to your family and home? I think it's pretty selfish of him to want to drag you off to Utah just because he wants a farm of his own, regardless of any consequences."

Mary was prepared for her mother's onslaught and refrained from an immediate argument, waiting to hear from her brothers.

Walt asked, "Where is he getting the money for this escapade? Is he going to want money from you?"

Alf asked "Why does he want to go up there next winter? He can't start farming until spring."

Quil asked, "Are you sure you love him enough to leave here and go work your butt off on a new farm and maybe go hungry for a while?"

Mary began to realize the scary scope of the venture but quietly and firmly replied to the bombardment. "Harley has been saving every penny he can, especially since he got promoted, and he is sure he has enough to pay the cost of getting a homestead, buying a team and some farm equipment here, shipping it to Utah, and building a house for us and a barn to start out. He wants to get that done in time to maybe plant a first crop in the spring. He says he has enough money for that but the savings account I have can be a backup in case of emergencies. I love him very much, and I am sure he loves me. He has warned me that life on a homestead can be very hard but we feel that as long as we are together it will work out okay."

Mother King interrupted, "Why do you have to have him for a husband? There are a lot of nice young men here that you know and that would be glad to marry you if you gave them a chance."

Mary sighed, "Yes, Mother, there are several guys that say I should give them a chance. But, let's face it—I'm twenty-one years old and I probably should be married by now or I might become a spinster. I just can't see spending the rest of my life with any of the men you are probably referring to. For example, Alvin Lloyd has had a cough that makes me nervous, and now he's being treated for tuberculosis. Dave Delaney has a big belly and a big ego. Bill Hastings likes liquor and usually has a flask with him at our parties. Don Waring is simply lazy; he hasn't been able to keep a job more than a few months. Bob Billings pays more attention to baseball than to girls. And so on. You should know by now exactly what Harley is like and that we can all depend on him. He is strong and healthy and would make a good father. I want to have children by him."

"All that may be true but why can't he just stay here and be a good husband?" Mother King fired back.

"Because he wants to be a farmer and have his own farm and he can't do that here. As he told Walt a while ago he can't afford to buy land here and he is not familiar with California farming which is different from what he did for many years," Mary replied.

Quil, the most vocal and liberal-minded of the brothers, interrupted. "Well, it appears to me that the two of them are very much in love and it's hard to stop the results of that and maybe we should not try to change Mother Nature. Let's look at the bright side. Mary is convinced she will be happy and we can hope for sure that she will be. It's her life, and I think she can handle whatever happens. Finally, Mom, you don't have any grandkids yet. Walt and Alf and I aren't doing much about that."

Mother King smiled, "Well, I guess you may be right but I still don't like it. And now that you mention it, when am I going to get some grandchildren?" She looked with arched eyebrows toward Walt and Alf who were studying a crack in the ceiling.

The next weekend, Mary told Harley about the family conference. He was happy. "Well, that's maybe better than I thought would happen. Thank you, my Dear, for straightening things out and having faith in me. Which reminds me, when can we start having children? You know what we have to do first, don't you?"

Mary laughed and fired back, "I can hardly wait!"

Harley turned serious. "Now I know for certain that you want to go along with me and the family won't try to stop you, I need to get going on the homestead deal. So I must tell you now that I'll be going to Utah in a few days. I'll take a Union Pacific train from L.A. to a town called Milford where I will find out all the details about getting some land and then I'll probably go to a new town called Lund where most of the homesteading is going on. I'm not sure when I'll be back, but my boss at Dependable said I could have a week off. Most of the guys at the company think I'm crazy but they know how determined I am to have my own farm."

Mary's panic-stricken look left Harley frozen for a moment. He hugged her, kissed her cheek, and whispered, "Don't worry, my darling, I'll be back before you know it. I love you, and everything will be all right."

Mary brushed away a tear, kissed him and replied, "I know, I know. I'll wait and pray day by day until you come back." Harley hugged her tightly but his mind was already shifting to the next step in the "plan."

Two days later, Harley took a train to Utah, and wrote a letter postmarked November 8 at Milford:

> My Dearest Mary,
>
> Everything is going okay on the homestead deal. I am sure not the only one looking for free farm land. Nearly every day, the trains from Salt Lake City and Los Angeles bring a few people here to sign up. I talked with two men from L.A. who are about in the same boat that I am, and I have heard that quite a few of the land lookers are new in America, from countries in Europe.
>
> I had to wait a day to get my turn to go out in the country with a man who has maps showing homestead land. The land is pretty much desert but it should be alright for what they call dry land farming. I'll tell you all about it when I get back and return to work at Dependable and then visit you as soon as possible. Then we can

talk about getting married and how we can get started on our farm early next year.

I miss you very much.
Your loving husband-to-be,

Harley
XOXOXOXOXOX

Mary read the letter several times. She was a bit taken back by the speed at which the Utah homestead program was progressing. She had secretly hoped that the deal would fall through and Harley would stay in California. However the cloud of concern began to be partly replaced by the excitement of getting married and thoughts about what the wedding night would be like. And in the background of her mind was the yin and yang anticipation of an adventure, leaving California for the first time in her life and speeding off to a kind of life she could only vaguely imagine.

Chapter 4

The Homestead Deal

Milford train station, circa 1914

Harley had barely stepped off the train in Milford when the station master took one look at him and pointed to a building that was the headquarters for the Escalante Valley homestead program. This office housed the agents who processed and verified claims. They referred homesteaders to land locators who for a few dollars would take visitors out into the desert and show them exactly what land had been surveyed and staked out for homesteads.

Harley spent a day examining maps at the office and quizzing the agents and land locators about roads, wells, and soils in the valley. He should have been discouraged but he wasn't.

An agent told Harley, "When the railroad came south from Salt Lake, Milford was its terminal for many years. Then a guy named Lund wanted to start selling lots in a new town where steam locomotives would stop for water when the railroad line was extended southward. He and the railroad are promoting homesteads. Sections and half sections of land, mostly on the east side of the railroad line, have been staked out for about 10 to 20 miles south of here past the new town."

The homestead program officials had heard about the so-called new theory of dry land farming, but carefully declined to advise Harley about whether the technique would work in the Escalante desert.

On the advice of the officials, Harley took a train to the new town of Lund to work with a land locator there. He stayed overnight in

Lund's Root Hotel which consisted of a half dozen small bare rooms, a common bathroom, and a lobby with one fraying sofa.

The next day he met a locator named Stan Brown and helped him start a dusty Model T Ford by working the magneto lever on the steering column while the locator wrestled with the crank at the front of the car. As they set out into the desert on a dirt road parallel to the railroad track, Brown said, "The flattest land available is a few miles northeast of Lund so that is where we'll go first, and then if you don't like the looks of the ground there, we can go a few miles southeast of the town. There are some pretty good sites there near the railroad. There are too many sand dunes directly east."

The car turned away from the railroad track onto a faint trail through thick brush. After about a mile, the locator stopped, pulled a cardboard-mounted map from behind the seat, pointed to a spot on the map and then to a patch of land. "This is Section 5, Township 32 South, Range 13 West, Salt Lake Meridian. This area has been getting a lot of lookers because it's only about a mile from the railroad and a few miles from the main road to Cedar City which is over there at the foot of that blue mountain range called the Wasatch Mountains. People who look for a homestead around here key in on the little butte over there to the north that's being call the Blue Knoll. About a year ago, I brought a German guy out here named Oscar Frahske—can barely pronounce his name let alone spell it—and he filed on a half section over there in an area called Latimer after the name of a siding on the railroad."

Even though Harley went in a Model T Ford, most homesteaders rode the Knell Stage Coach (above) to tour the land.

Harley walked around in the middle of Section 5 for about 15 minutes, examined a handful of the soil, and returned to the car. "The soil is pretty heavy like it's mostly clay. I'll bet it's a bit hard to plow and is pretty sticky when it's wet." Brown, leaning against the car, replied, "I don't know much about farm land but you're probably right about the plowing. Let's go see if there is something you like south of Lund."

After lunch at the all-purpose Lund Store, they headed south on a comparatively well-traveled road that continuously paralleled the rail tracks toward the next tiny town of Sahara, ten miles away, and fast-growing Beryl, five miles farther. (The railroad soon changed the name of Sahara to Zane after the then-famous western novelist Zane Gray because the original name was discouraging visitors.)

After a few minutes of driving, Harley noticed the cross-arms of a sign that marked a railroad siding named Ford. The locator stopped, took out the map, and pointed eastward to a gently sloping patch of low brush. "This is the corner of the north half of Section 6, Township 33 South, Range 14 West. I think it's one of the better sections of land around here close to the road to Lund. A guy named Bentley has filed on the south half of the section. He has started hauling stuff for his house and barn along the section line where you can see some wheel tracks."

Harley walked out into the brush and examined the soil in several spots. He gazed at the snow-rimmed top of the Wasatch mountain range to the east beyond the hazy tan flat land of the Escalante desert. To the south a brown butte loomed up in lonely splendor with a rocky cliff crown above the valley floor. Behind it, in faded blue, were mountains that Harley learned later were called the Pine Valley Mountains. They separated the Escalante valley from the region known as Utah's Dixie. To the west, across the railroad tracks, the land sloped slowly up to a horizon of brown foothills. To the north, beyond a water well drilling tower visible in Lund, the desert floor flowed around the Blue Knoll now blurry in the distance.

"I kind of like this place," Harley told Brown. "The soil is lighter than the first place we went to and is likely to absorb and hold moisture better. And from what I've read, dry land farming depends on soil that holds moisture. And there's a patch of sage brush. That's supposed to indicate fairly good land. I'm going to walk around some more and see what other kind of brush is here. You can take a nap in the car." Brown climbed into the back seat and pulled his cap down over his eyes.

When Harley returned, he asked the locator, "Do you know anything about well water here—how deep do you have to go to get water?"

"No," Brown replied, "but I understand that well depths vary considerably. So do you think you want to follow up on this half section?"

"Yeah, I think so. Do you have the paper work in Lund?"

"Yes, we can fill out the papers with the legal description, your name and address and citizenship and so on, but you'll have to take the forms to the Milford office to actually file the claim and pay the filing fee. I need to collect $5 here, and I have to have cash because, as you can guess, I can't depend on personal checks in this business."

They returned to Lund, and Harley took the papers to Milford on a train the next morning. To his dismay, he had to wait most of the day for the "bureaucrats" to process other claims before they got to him.

Harley listened to the conversation of a half dozen men lounging in the office of the homestead agents. One man complained loudly about the fee the locators charged "for just a few hours of driving around." Another man, who like Harley had worked on farms in eastern Nebraska, was excitedly describing how he planned to grow tall corn on his homestead, feed it to cattle to fatten them, and make big money selling thousand-pound steers. Harley started to argue with him that dry land farming in the Escalante desert would not produce even half as much corn as land in Nebraska but then thought to himself, "I'll bet that guy loses his enthusiasm fast enough within a year." The group was joined by a weather-beaten man in oft-patched overalls who announced he would farm his homestead as long as possible then sell it and retire in comfort. Of all the dreams in the room, his would turn out to be the most bitter.

There were fragments of conversation about a kind of dry land farming called the Campbell Method, but Harley remembered the look of the flinty homestead sites and he wondered about separating fact from fantasy. However, adding to the general optimism in the group was the probability that grain prices would rise because of the war that had started in Europe six months earlier.

Harley went back to the Lund Store for a sandwich and joined two men there when he overheard them talking with the store owner and discussing how to obtain building materials and farm equipment for their homesteads. After half an hour of exchanging notes, the visitors, who it turned out were all from the Los Angeles area, had a better idea of what would be required on a homestead, what the costs would be, and whether they should try to buy everything from businesses in Lund and Milford or buy the "stuff" in California and freight it to Utah. Throughout the discussions, there was a feeling of excitement and anticipation.

After he completed filing his homestead claim in Milford, Harley caught the evening train to Los Angeles. Before drifting off to an uneasy sleep in his train coach chair, he debated with himself for several hours about pursuing his dream of a farm in a desert valley where Christ would have lost his sandals.

Harley loved Mary deeply and worried that she might decide at any time to give him up if he insisted she leave her beloved family and beloved Santa Barbara for a life of hardship and extreme loneliness. Realistically, he would never find another woman to marry as young, pretty, and vivacious as Mary. Dry land farming in the desert he had just seen up close would be a massive gamble and would most probably use up all the money he had scrimped to save for two decades. Purchasing all the materials, equipment, and animals he would need for the new farm, shipping them to Lund, building even a small house and barn, and clearing land for the first planting would be a tremendous effort squeezed into a few months that would test even his stamina for hard work. If he stayed in California, he would undoubtedly spend the rest of his life working for wages and never plow another furrow. If he didn't return to Lund and didn't do something on the homestead, he would lose the land and the money he had paid for the claim and other expenses. If he proceeded with the homestead farm and couldn't make a living there by the end of a three-year test, would he be able to find a job in or around Lund or would he have to sneak back in embarrassment to Santa Barbara or Pasadena? At his age and with the way the last remaining land for homesteads was being gobbled up, this could be his last chance to have a farm of his own.

The uneasiness stayed with him all the next day as he got back to sister Lu's home in Pasadena and prepared to return to work at the Dependable Landscaping Company. However, after a good night's sleep in a comfortable bed, his resolve to have a farm returned as strong as ever.

Chapter 5

Getting Married

While Mary was waiting to get married and was corresponding every few days with Harley, she was also exchanging letters with a longtime friend, Flo Nelson, who had gotten married several years earlier and had moved to Phoenix, Arizona.

In a July 6 letter, Flo said she had heard that Mary had a "new beau in a whirlwind devotion" and wanted to know all about him:

> Is he a Sweed? Is he a Christian? Mary dear, do you love him better than anyone on earth? Is he the best man on earth (except my husband)? What are his good points?
>
> I do not think you can see too much of him before you are married. It is best to know him in every mood and under every condition. How old is he really? In the thirties is rather vague . . . You will have to jump from girlhood up to womanhood for he can't go back in age. There is nothing wrong with that if you are happy all the rest of your life . . . With him, there would be no uncertainty as there would be with a boy your own age.
> With much love,
>
> Flo

She also said Mary should visit her in Phoenix to "learn how to cook and keep house."

Mary replied and confided her feelings to Flo about being "blue, lonely, under nervous strain" and frustrated with "Mr. Johnston" after getting engaged. From then on, Flo, based on her few years of experience in marriage, set out to be mother confessor, marriage counselor, philosopher, and psychologist, assuming that Harley would be some kind of businessman in a town, probably Santa Barbara.

On July 16, she wrote Mary a six-page letter:

> Mary Dear,
>
> Marriage is either the most blissful or the most terrible life anyone can live . . .You cannot always have your way; he cannot always have

his. I'm afraid a man his age has much to overcome; he will be set in his ways. Suppose for a while that you are married, the honeymoon is over, and you are settled down to homemaking. You have all the necessities and luxuries you can afford. He is to discuss his business with you. You are to plan your housekeeping with him. You are business partners as well as companions and lovers. I know this is absolutely necessary . . .

You have been working hard all day and are very tired but have a well-cooked dinner for him and yourself and be prettily dressed yourself when he comes home. Next time, don't do so much for it is as much your duty to be a companion as it is to clean house. Most men prefer a companion to a housekeeper. I never wash my dishes in the evening. . .

Perhaps he comes home tired in the evening and inclined to be cross. KEEP SILENT!

It is one of those times when silence is golden. Don't ever both get cross at once . . .

Then he must take you out in the evening even if he does prefer to stay at home (and a man Harley's age probably will!) for house work is monotonous, and you must have some diversions. No matter how pretty your home is it will be prettier when you get home. Dress yourself neatly in the mornings and prettily in the evenings. These may sound like foolish little things but married life is not all honeymoon and dreams . . .

All these things I've written you must be talked about between you and thoroughly discussed before marriage. Other things too must be discussed but I can't write about them!

It's too bad your mother takes the stand she does but I guess she thinks your ages are too far apart, and it's not unusual that she is afraid. I'm sure your mother doesn't want you to sacrifice your life's happiness for her . . . Come down (to Phoenix) if you can.

Your loving sister,

Flo

On August 12, Flo wrote a five-page letter to Mary:

Dear Little Sister,

Your letter came last night with the pictures. Was glad to hear from you again and to see that wonderful man's photograph. He is better looking than I expected! He looks as if he were good natured and kind and that is best of all . . .

But why do you say you must write nonsense to keep your mind off things (what things?) and to keep you from getting nervous. I'm

> afraid something is troubling you. Your letters read like you are in a terrible nervous strain. Aren't you happy? You can't go on so or you will give 'The Man' a nervous wreck instead of a cheerful loving wife and once your nerves give way you are never as strong. . .
>
> You must keep yourself in the best of health now. You wonder why? Well, if I were there I could tell you but since I'm not, take my word for it that it is most important. When I see you I will tell you why . . .
>
> With love,
>
> Your big sister,
>
> Flo

Mary was unable to visit Phoenix that fall, and by the time Flo got to visit Santa Barbara the next year Mary was married and was in Utah. So they never got together with a chance for Flo to tell Mary about birds, bees, and the sex life of married couples. As a child, Mary had seen what bulls did to cows on the Hope Ranch, but she could not quite translate that into the basic purpose of marriage. Her mother was no help, and Mary had to pry a few pointers from another married friend who was a little more specific than Flo.

Mary had written a letter to Harley at his Pasadena address so he would get it within a day or two of his return from Utah in November.

> Harlan, my long lost love,
>
> Come to Santa Barbara immediately. I can't wait another day to see you and I get hot flashes when I think about us getting married. Of course, you better be prepared to report to the family pretty soon. Maybe you can come up for Thanksgiving.
>
> I'm not sure I understand very much from your letter about homesteading in Utah but I'm sure I will learn pretty fast from now on. XOXOXOXOXOX
>
> Your loving wife-to-be,
>
> Mary

Upon Harley's return to Pasadena, he spent part of an afternoon telling sister Lu and her husband, Ray, about the Utah visit and the homestead proceedings. Ray had worked most of his adult life in a variety of jobs in towns including the past ten years in the L.A. area. He and Lu were politely skeptical about Harley's plans, especially about the very isolated location in southwestern Utah.

"What about the Mormons?" Ray asked. "From what I've read about them they don't like outsiders and call them Gentiles. As I recall, they had a lot of trouble with the federal government for a long time."

Harley replied, "The people I dealt with in Milford didn't say anything about the Mormon religion. Many of them working on the program to provide homesteads on federal land must have been Mormons, but you wouldn't know it in dealing with them. On the one Sunday I was there some of them had gone to the towns of Parowan and Cedar City to attend their church, but I got the impression that the people in those towns are not particularly interested in farming in the Escalante Valley because it is basically a desert, and they have already got the best land near the mountains on the east side of the valley. The Union Pacific railroad line that will help businesses and ranching is their main interest in a place like Lund."

Harley was unable to get away from his job for a week, but finally got to Santa Barbara for a weekend and spent most of that Sunday on an outing with Mary and her friends with a picnic and hikes in Cold Creek Canyon. He got Mary alone for an hour to tell her about the homestead arrangement and promised her he would come back for Thanksgiving Day dinner with her family. He emphasized that he had to keep working hard to keep saving money for the marriage and the move to Utah.

On Thanksgiving Day, Harley joined Mary and her family at church in the morning and went home with them. He sat down in the living room once again and spent a very uncomfortable hour telling them what he had done in Utah and, more vaguely, what he had in mind for the marriage and the move. The mother and the brothers remained skeptical but resigned to the loss of daughter and sister. However, everyone relaxed over the roasted turkey dinner. Walt had popped for a bottle of cheap red wine. Mary and Harley dutifully took a sip and enjoyed the good cheer the wine brought to the table.

Since Mary and Harley were properly engaged, and it was clear that Harley was determined to save every penny he could, it seemed logical that he would stay at the King home on his visits to Santa Barbara. However, the house was small, the brothers' bedroom was already crowded, and certainly there could be no implication that Harley and Mary might get together alone in her own home. So he continued to stay at a boarding house where his room was not conducive to a clandestine meeting even if Mary were so inclined.

During the Thanksgiving holiday, Harley and Mary began planning their wedding. He was not willing to spend money on a church wedding and reception requiring extensive invitations regardless of how Mary may have wanted something like that to show off to her friends. However, she was not surprised at the poverty, knowing him as she did by now and especially remembering the good buy on a piano that he skillfully squelched.

Several of her friends kept demanding to know where and when the big event would take place. They could almost understand skipping a church wedding but they insisted on seeing a lacy wedding dress and at least getting invited to a coffee-and-cake reception. "He's a nice guy and pretty good-looking, and he's healthy and obviously a hard worker but don't you think he's pretty cheap about not even having a reception?" one of them asked as the girls chatted after church when Harley was absent.

Mary could only shrug and reply, "That's the way he is, and I'm afraid I won't be able to change him very much. Besides, we'll need every penny for the move to Utah."

Harley chose Friday of the weekend before Christmas day for the wedding date, noting that he should continue to work every possible day at Dependable Landscaping, and he and Mary would have the holidays and two months together before he would leave for Utah. He did not say so but another reason for the timing was that, in the future, they would save money by combining Christmas and wedding anniversary celebrations and gift exchanges.

Mary made a careful calculation that her menstrual period would, hopefully, not occur during the ten days to two weeks of the honeymoon time. She was aware that she could get pregnant but decided to be risky and not mess with birth control measures. She had learned a few essentials about birth control from one of her married friends so, when the wedding date was near, she went to a drug store and, putting on her most worldly air, purchased contraceptive powder and equipment for using the powder in solution in douches. However, she couldn't ask the druggist how to use them.

Harley also "suggested" that they get married by a justice of the peace in a very simple ceremony at the courthouse in Los Angeles and stay in a hotel in L.A. for a few days. After that, they could stay with Harley's sister, Lu, in Pasadena until time for each of them to move to the Escalante homestead. A quick and simple wedding at the courthouse in Los Angeles would definitely preclude any reception and proceedings with family and friends.

Mother King and the brothers were furious when Mary told them about the tentative plans after Harley had returned to Pasadena at the end of the Thanksgiving holiday. However, they could tell that Mary was upset and struggling to accept what was happening. Although she did not say so, it was evident that she faced an extreme dilemma—go through with the arrangements or call the whole thing off. Her family loved her enough not to suggest an end to the engagement, knowing she did love Harley and wanted to get married. They could only hug her and hope for the best.

However, at one point, Mother King told Mary, "I still don't know why he can't stay here. He's taking my only daughter away."

Mary sighed, "We won't be as far away as it might seem. Remember, there's a main line railroad between L.A. and Utah, and the trip takes only about a day. So I think we'll see each other once in a while."

Her mother retorted, "Maybe, but from what I'm seeing about Harley's attitude toward money, I'll bet he won't pay your train fare for you to come home very often, if at all."

Mary and Harley were married the afternoon of Dec. 23, 1914, in Superior Court in Los Angeles where they had obtained the marriage license. A minister named James Myers who was "on call" at the court for fast weddings performed the five-minute ceremony with a court employee as the required witness. The marriage certificate listed her as age 21, a Caucasian, born in Santa Barbara. The certificate listed him as age 38, a Caucasian, born in Knoxville, Iowa. She wore the pale green chiffon dress that was her best dress. He wore a black suit with a string tie.

After the wedding ceremony, the newlyweds registered at a modest-priced L.A. hotel as Mr. and Mrs. Harlan Johnston of Santa Barbara. Following a leisurely dinner at the hotel, they went to their room and began a self-conscious mating ritual. They were both virgins. She knew only the little she had gleaned from one married friend. He knew more from his many years of dealing with farm animals and from the constant talk by all the men he had known about the physical (but not mental) details of "making love."

Once inside the room, they kissed long and deeply. "You go first," he whispered, pointing to the bathroom. She opened her suitcase, took out a frilly pink nightgown, and waved it at him as she entered the bathroom. In a few minutes she emerged, hung her street clothes in the closet, and slid into bed.

Harley went into the bathroom, undressed, and emerged wearing only his pajama bottoms. She was propped up on two pillows with her cleavage showing like dawn on drifts of new fallen snow. He threw the bedding aside, and took only a minute to consummate the marriage. As he lay still, breathing deeply, Mary thought, *"Is that all there is? What do we do now?"*

They lay in bed silently for a few minutes, then she got up and went into the bathroom. When she came out, Harley was half dressed. "Making love makes me hungry. How about something to eat and drink?"

"I guess so," she replied. "But you'll have to wait until I get dolled up and put on lipstick if we are going out."

When she was dressed, they went down to the hotel coffee shop and shared a piece of pie and a pot of tea. Not sure of what she should be doing, Mary wandered around the gift shop for a few minutes and then found Harley in the lobby, scanning a newspaper. He looked up. "Find anything interesting?"

"Nope. The stuff in shops like this is too expensive."

Harley motioned to a grandfather clock in the lobby and smirked, "Bed time."

She giggled, "So soon?"

They went back to the room and made love. This time it took a lot longer, and Mary felt a lot better about the marriage. To the amazement of both of them, it happened again after they had slept in each other's arms until the pink light of dawn crept through the window.

Mary was a bit more confident now that she could follow Harley to Utah and face whatever hardships might await her there.

When Harley emerged from his turn in the bathroom, he declared, "I'm hungry again. See what you do to me!" Hand in hand they traipsed down to the coffee shop. From the looks on their faces and their determination to keep touching each other, several couples in the coffee shop could tell, with some envy, that Harley and Mary were newlyweds.

They spent their first day of married life wandering around downtown Los Angeles. They purchased modest Christmas gifts for their relatives, had lunch at a Mexican restaurant on old Olivera Street, sat in the gazebo in the plaza where the city was born, and fed popcorn to the pigeons. That evening they made love again but in a much more leisurely way than the first night.

The "official" honeymoon of two days ended as they caught a train to spend the rest of Christmas Day with Mary's family. At the King home, they were greeted with hugs and kisses and exclamations of "Merry Christmas" and "Congratulations!" Mother King's coolness was still evident but she was accepting reality, and she was determined to be a gracious hostess.

Quil hugged Mary and smirked, "So how do you like married life, little sister?"

"It's marvelous," she shot back. "You ought to try it sometime."

During the evening, the family and newlyweds exchanged gifts, lingered over a roast chicken dinner, and heard Mary describe the wedding ceremony. The brothers teased her about being a blushing bride and accused her of getting ready to run away to Utah.

The conversation turned serious for a while when Walt said to Harley, "You've mentioned several times that Lund is in what's called the Escalante desert. If it's that dry, where will you get water for farming?"

Harley replied, "Well, there is a somewhat new theory about dry land farming that's being tested in desert areas. It's called the Campbell Method, and I'm just starting to study up on it."

Now that Harley and Mary were married, they were entitled to stay in the house and use Mary's tiny bedroom. They were well aware that any sounds they might make could be heard in the other bedrooms so they abstained that night from lovemaking for which the 38-year-old Harley was grateful.

They stayed in Santa Barbara for five days, allowing Mary to show off her new husband to her friends and allowing them to throw several holiday parties for the newlyweds. Harley had taken the week off from work and didn't mind the days in Santa Barbara this time because he didn't have the expense of staying at the rooming house.

The day before New Year's Eve they took the train back to L.A. and caught a trolley to Lu Strahan's home in Pasadena. She had fixed up a room for them to stay in for a few months until they could both get moved to the Utah homestead, and she arranged to share meals and cooking. Mary quickly became well acquainted with Harley's three sisters and their husbands as they all celebrated New Year's Eve and New Year's Day together.

Harley went back to work at Dependable for two months to wait for the worst of winter weather to end in Utah and allow him to start work on the homestead when they were there. With Ray Strahan's help, Mary found temporary work as a secretary in offices of the Los Angeles School District, saving money for the "adventure" while helping her sister-in-law with housework and the cost of groceries. She spent a few dollars on two weekend visits to her family.

After a few days, Mary felt comfortable enough with Lu to seek more knowledge about postponing pregnancy but was uncertain about how to bring up the question. One morning after breakfast Mary was fidgeting at the kitchen table, and Lu said, "Honey, what's wrong? Is something bothering you?"

Mary blurted out, "Yes, I don't want to get pregnant just at the time we make the big move to Utah. Obviously, I can't talk to your brother about what to do, so I need to ask your advice. One of my friends told me a little bit about using douches for birth control. Can you tell me exactly how that works?"

Lu, as Harley's older sister and frequent confidante, was more than willing to lend her "expertise" to help assure the happiness of the younger couple. She took Mary's hand, and said, "My dear, you seem to know already what a lot of young women don't find out or are afraid to find out before they are pregnant and a baby is coming whether any one wants it or not. Yes, I know about douches but we will get you an appointment with my doctor who can give you better advice than I can. However, the usual procedure is this. You mix a powder in a warm water solution, put it in a rubber bag like everyone uses as a hot water bottle, and use a curved nozzle to inject the solution inside you. My doctor said the chemicals in the solution kill a man's sperm before it can fertilize the egg in a woman's womb. But, my dear, you should know that it doesn't guarantee you won't get pregnant. The only sure way not to get pregnant is not to make love. And I'll bet that is not an option for you and Harley!"

Mary, who had learned more about birth control in a few minutes than she had learned so far in her lifetime, hugged her sister-in-law. "Thank you! Thank you! You're so good to me. Can we make an appointment with the doctor soon? I don't want to try to make Harley wait."

When she began staying in the bathroom longer than usual after love-making, Harley asked what she was doing. She explained very briefly and emphasized, "I'm trying to not get pregnant."

"Well, Dearie," he commented, "that's a good idea because we don't want to have a baby while we are trying to get a farm started. When we get settled, we can think about having all the kids you want."

Harley showed no further interest in the details of the procedure, and Mary thought to herself, *"Well, it is certainly all up to me. If it works the way it is supposed to, I can decide when I want to have a baby."*

With one of her most urgent worries alleviated, Mary settled down to a comfortable routine of working three days a week, helping Lu with the cooking and housework, and loving Harley. He spent all his free time studying about dry land farming and planning the permanent move to Lund, Utah.

Chapter 6

The Lure of Homesteading and Railroads

In November 1914, Harley had uncharacteristically splurged one dollar on a clothbound book, *Campbell's Soil Culture Manual.* The dark green cover had a camel stamped in gilt with a headline, "The Camel for the Sahara Desert—the Campbell Method for the American Desert."

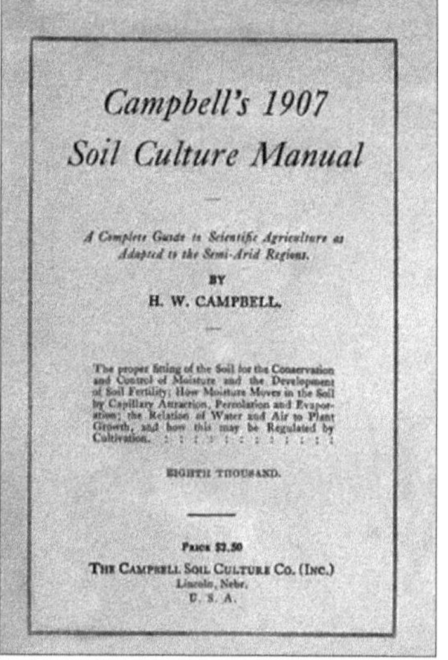

Campbell's 1907
Soil Culture Manual

A Complete Guide to Scientific Agriculture as Adapted to the Semi-Arid Regions.

BY
H. W. CAMPBELL.

The proper fitting of the Soil for the Conservation and Control of Moisture and the Development of Soil Fertility; How Moisture Moves in the Soil by Capillary Attraction, Percolation and Evaporation; the Relation of Water and Air to Plant Growth, and how this may be Regulated by Cultivation.

EIGHTH THOUSAND.

PRICE $2.50
THE CAMPBELL SOIL CULTURE CO. (INC.)
Lincoln, Nebr.
U. S. A.

Campbell's Soil Culture Manual
published in 1902, 1905, 1907

The book, written by Hardy W. Campbell, a University of Nebraska professor, had become famous since the first edition in 1902 for its description of "the highly successful science of dry land farming." It was hailed as the Bible of thousands of gullible homesteaders and would-be homesteaders in the arid and semi-arid parts of the Upper Midwest, the Southwest, and Rocky Mountain states where precipitation was 9 to 20 inches per year. Campbell emphasized dry land farming for high prairie regions east of the Rocky Mountains/Continental Divide, but many readers blindly stretched his theory to cover actual deserts such as the Escalante Valley which often had only eight inches of precipitation per year.

The theory was that farm land soil, with proper preparation, would act as a reservoir of moisture for growing crops in a dry climate. After plowing, the soil surface would need tilling—harrowing and disking—to produce a layer of fine particles of dirt instead of clods. That layer (which unfortunately had a tendency to blow away in the wind in many places) would keep a proper amount of moisture and air in the zone of roots. Through capillary action, moisture would also be drawn upward to the root zone from deeper in the ground.

Campbell claimed his methods could triple the production of many kinds of crops in semi-arid regions He mentioned, but downplayed, the concept that dry land farming often works best when a crop is grown only every two years on a piece of land. For most cash-strapped homesteaders, a crop every other year would not keep starvation away.

Unlike the history of irrigation back to the earliest civilizations, dry land farming in the late 1800s and early 1900s had very little history, few guidelines, no research, no government aid, and no help from weather forecasts. Dry land farmers were edging into western Kansas by 1870, but their first decades of trial-and-error experiences were not documented. Failures and periods of drought flew in the face of perpetual hope.

An International Dry Land Farming Congress was held in Denver, Colorado, in 1907 with representatives from state and county governments around the United States. Speakers included Campbell who touted his theory while the government farm experts derided his "method" as "scientifically unsound."

Under the Treaty of Guadalupe-Hidalgo in 1848 ending the Mexican-American War, Mexico ceded to the United States government all the land in what became known as the Southwest including Utah, Nevada and California that had been part of Spain's colonial empire. In an effort to encourage settlement of the vast public lands in the western half of the expanded nation, Congress passed the Homestead Act of 1862. It allowed a head of household to apply for a homestead farm of up to 160 acres on vacant federal land. An applicant/claimant had to reside on the land for at least three years, cultivate the land to some extent, and make "improvements" such as a tar paper-covered "house" in order to obtain a patent as a form of title. Claimants were initially charged $1.25 per acre.

The concept turned out to be highly popular among millions of would-be homesteaders including many immigrants from Europe. So, in February 1909, Congress passed the Enlarged Homestead Act to allow claims on 320 acres (half of a one-square-mile section of land) in 14 western states. However, filings were limited to lands that the U.S. Secretary of the Interior declared were non-mineral, non-timbered, and non-irrigable. A claimant had to be a U.S. citizen or become a citizen in five years, pay a basic fee of $16 to $18 and "cultivate" at least one-eighth of the land within three years.

Over a period of 120 years, the U.S. homestead program included more than four million applicants, but only 1.6 million completed the process, claiming some 270 million acres.[1] And even for many of those, the dream of a farm on arid land turned into a nightmare.

By 1909, the Western frontier, as defined by demographers and historians, had closed, and most of the "good" land for farming had been bought, homesteaded, or acquired by railroads (between 1850 and 1880 railroads received 175 million acres in federal land grants). Although the Enlarged Homestead Act was in effect a remnant sale of undesirable federal land, many would-be homesteaders from the eastern United States and from poverty-racked parts of Europe accustomed to farms of 100 acres or less, the offer of 320 acres seemed like a bonanza akin to gold discoveries in the West. Filings peaked at 59,000 in 1913. Thereafter, the brutal realities of dry land farming became clear, and filings had almost stopped by 1920. Harley Johnston and his new bride learned those realities starting in 1915.

Land speculation was a characteristic of the American frontier ever since the first colonists began moving westward from the Atlantic Coast settlements. The driving determination to own land, preferably farm land, often overcame common sense. Waves of settlers did not stop at the high plains edge of what was once called the Great American Desert and swept on to the real deserts such as those in Utah. But within a few years most of those migrants and immigrants fled from windowless shanties and wind-scoured lands, leaving a few stubborn survivors to scavenge vacated buildings and acquire the deserters' tracts for a few dollars in back taxes.

In the eastern half of the nation, water for the benefit of human beings, whether in the form of precipitation for farms and forests or in creeks and rivers, was largely taken for granted. But, in the western half, water in whatever form was the pivot point and the subject of conflicts at every level of activity from neighborhood feuds to national politics. A standard comment in the West is, "Whiskey's for drinking, water's for fighting." Homesteaders who didn't get rain could turn to irrigation and discover that a government permit was needed for a well or learn that a filing was needed to take water from a river. Of all the frustrations that homesteaders endured, one of the most painful was watching huge frothy thunderhead clouds gather over a desert and then roll away without leaving a single drop of rain.

Railroads initially opposed the 1862 Homestead Act as competition for railroads selling pieces of their land grants, but later realized that homesteads would help create towns and business along new railroad lines. Those lines were the main means of transportation across the nation for homesteaders from 1870 to 1920 when the auto age was well underway. Even before the 1909 homestead expansion law, the railroads were offering tracts for sale in arid and semi-arid regions, issuing pamphlets filled with lies and statements that, if a piece of land is plowed, rain will automatically fall on it.[2]

The arrival of the Union Pacific Railroad was the key to the initiation of homesteading in Utah's Escalante Valley. For many decades, the railroad was a fickle economic lifeline through the valley. It was the reason the town of Lund was born and was the reason the town died 70 years later.

The UP began in 1848 as a small railroad line in northern Illinois, merged in 1851 with the Missouri Pacific, and in 1862 was chartered by Congress along with the Central Pacific to build a transcontinental railroad line. The UP stampeded westward from Omaha, Nebraska, to join up in 1869 at Promontory Point in northern Utah with the Central Pacific that built eastward out of San Francisco. Ogden, Utah, became a major location serving the transcontinental line.

Thereafter, the Salt Lake City-based Church of Jesus Christ of Latter-day Saints, better known as the Mormon church, badgered the Union Pacific for three decades to help build a line southward through desolate western Utah and hopefully across southern Nevada and into southern California.[3]

The Church, with UP financing, built the Utah Central Railroad from Odgen to Salt Lake City. In 1871, the coalition created the Utah Southern Railroad to proceed south from Salt Lake City to reach mining districts that were popping like dandelions, watered by reports of gold and silver. The railroad would haul supplies to the mines and haul ore to metal-producing mills. After bogging down several times, the Utah Southern in 1880 reached Milford, Utah, in the north end of the Escalante Valley, with a spur line to a big silver mine at Frisco. Work proceeded in 1898–1899 on a line westward through the level Escalante Valley to Uvada, but stalled just west of the Utah state line in rocky canyons and at Crestline, elevation 5,962 feet. Financial backing by the Union Pacific for extensions of rail service was held up while the UP was in bankruptcy in the 1890s.

Sulphur Spring, named after the odor of its meager flow of water a mile west of Lund, was a freighting and stagecoach stop on a route between Milford and mining districts to the southwest as far as Pioche, Nevada.

In 1900, William Andrews Clark, a scandal-plagued U.S. senator from Montana and millionaire mining magnate who wanted to get into the railroad business, emerged as a roadblock to the Union Pacific's monopoly over the planned rail line between Salt Lake City and Los Angeles. Clark took over a 27-mile-long Los Angeles Terminal Railway, set up the San Pedro, Los Angeles and Salt Lake Railroad Company (SPLA&SL), and started building toward Nevada. He and the UP faced off in the canyon area near Caliente, Nevada, after a UP subsidiary had installed rails across the Escalante desert into Nevada.

After a series of bitter legal and political battles over the Nevada route, all parties agreed in June 1903 to a complicated settlement. Clark and E. H. Harriman, Union Pacific president, emerged as co-owners of the SPLA&SL which owned the eventually completed rail link between the two major cities. San Pedro was dropped from the name in 1916 and it was called the LA&SL. The Union Pacific operated the line and used the UP name from then on. Clark sold his half interest in LA&SL to the UP in 1921 for $5 million, but the company remained as a legal entity until it was dissolved by the UP in 1988.

After the 1903 settlement, construction resumed on 300 miles of tracks past what would become Las Vegas. The 800-mile railroad project, then 35 years old, was finished on January 30, 1905, at Sloan, Nevada. It replaced the Old Spanish Trail and the Mormon Trail for wagons through southwestern Utah. The railroad also replaced a ten-passenger Concord stagecoach service between Cedar City and Salt Lake City transporting passengers at a cost of $25 each and baggage limit of 25 pounds per person.

On the railroad line, mile-long sidings to allow trains to pass each other were built every five to ten miles. A traffic control system evolved to include red and green lights on signal poles to govern which trains had the right-of-way on a main line and which trains had to get off on sidings. The steel tracks at the sidings had low voltage electrical current in them supplied by batteries. A train approaching or leaving a signal acted like a light switch to open or close the circuit in the rails

In the golden age of steam locomotives, towns sprang up along new railroad lines to provide coal and water for the engines. Lund, at elevation 5,018 feet in the middle of the Escalante Valley, became a train stop in 1905 for replenishing water from a deep well and storage tanks maintained by the UP. With the railroad, telegraph service came to Lund followed later by party-line telephone service. Other water stops were Beryl and Modena, southwest of Lund.

Although the need for water stops was the railroad's main reason for the birth of Lund and of a string of similar tiny towns, the UP heavy handedly promoted the homestead boom there as a way to increase local business. At one point, a Union Pacific advertisement declared, "Perhaps no portion of the great West today presents to the actual farmer, looking for a place in which to establish a home, so great an inducement as does that portion of the Escalante Valley in Utah known as the Beryl District . . . There is no better farming country in Western America." Beryl was fifteen miles south of Lund. *The Arrowhead*, a free magazine distributed by the railroad, touted "rich soils and abundant water" in southwestern Utah. Photographs purporting to show "oceans of alfalfa in Utah's New Agricultural Empire" were actually taken in other states. The UP also offered cut rate transportation for homestead seekers and their freight shipments.

By 1860, all the good irrigable land along the western side of the Wasatch Mountains range through the middle of Utah had been taken up by Mormon settlers so their church promoted the potential for homesteading to populate the barren deserts stretching west from the mountains to Nevada. Utah's U.S. senator, Reed Smoot, was instrumental in getting the 1909 law passed that allowed enlarged homesteads of 320 acres in western states and started the West's last great land rush. A Utah state government pamphlet called Iron County around Lund "an undeveloped agricultural empire of wonderful opportunities." A "wet cycle" with far above average precipitation in 1912–1913 helped the homestead promotions. An Iron County Fair booklet described Lund, after the turn of the century, as an "exciting place to be, a remote community set down in the vast desert wastelands."

A leading promoter of dry land farming in the early 1900s, especially in the Escalante Valley, was John A. Widtsoe, president of what was then Utah State Agricultural College at Logan, but later a Mormon apostle.

The town of Lund was named after Robert C. Lund, a St. George, Utah, businessman, state legislator, and mine owner who lobbied for extension of railroad service from Milford through Lund. Although

St. George was seventy-five miles away, the businessman recognized the economic impact that a railroad freight connection to the rest of the nation would have on the entire southwest corner of Utah.

Records of the Department of Interior Land Office in Salt Lake City include affidavits dated July 22 and August 13, 1913, by Lund residents H. J. (Harry) Doolittle, J. A. (John) Root, and J. David Leigh about a new town called Lund, platted in Iron County in Section 21, Township 32S, Range 14W, Salt Lake Meridian. They said the town began in the year 1900 (in anticipation of eventual railroad service) and by 1913 had "fifty-two inhabitants, three hotels, one garage, one blacksmith shop, two general stores, one post office, two warehouses, four barns with corrals, one 'camp house,' one windmill, bunkhouses, tents, sheds, chicken coops, fences, and numerous outbuildings." Sam W. Johnson became owner of the Lund Store as it was known for eighty years.

Harry J. Doolittle who had a wholesale business in St. George opened a freight forwarding warehouse on a Union Pacific siding in Lund in 1911 and became a leading businessman and community leader in Lund and Cedar City for two decades.

South of Lund, past Beryl, the Escalante Valley's last locomotive water stop was Modena near the Nevada state line, the start of canyon country, and the location of several mining districts. When railroad service arrived there, Brigham J. Lund, E. M. Brown, and Jose Price started a freighting business to St. George. In 1930, Modena had a population of about 300, larger than Lund, but died as the Great Depression set in. A two-story structure labeled "B. J. Lund & Co. General Merchandise & Hotel" stood boarded up and paintless for 70 years at the State Highway 56 crossing of the railroad tracks. Modena had a weather bureau station for many decades.

B.J. Lund's second general store in Modena, circa 1930

The promotions for homesteading in the Escalante Valley applied to land up to fifteen miles south of Lund and 15 miles to the north at the railroad siding called Nada. Efforts in 1912–1920 to create a town there rivaled similar efforts at Lund.

The Nada experience, woven into the history of homesteading, was detailed in a rambling article titled the "Last Free Land Rush," by Carlton Culmsee, a dean and professor at Utah State University, Logan, Utah[4]. The author was the son of Ludwig A. Culmsee, a native of Denmark, who became a medical doctor in Iowa in 1897 and moved his family in 1912 to California where he became enthusiastically aware of the homestead activity in the Escalante Valley (land rush promoters never referred to the valley as a desert!).

Dr. Culmsee and his wife caught a train to Nada, stayed in a makeshift hotel, chose 320 acres nearby and filed a homestead claim in the Milford land office. Dr. Culmsee, the epitome of an optimist, set up a store and post office at Nada, became an official weather observer/reporter, and had his well-educated wife provide schooling for children of settlers. He persuaded agricultural college officials to create a dry land farm experiment nearby and used them to promote homesteading in the region. Some college visitors tactfully suggested the need for wells and irrigation in addition to dry land farming.

By 1917, as the harsh realities of desert life set in, more homesteaders were leaving than were coming, and Nada, Dr. Culmsee's "community," began to fade although he hung on there until his death in 1936 at age 76.

---

1. "How the Homestead Act Transformed America," *Smithsonian Magazine*, May 2012.
2. A good example, as detailed in Jonathan Raban's 1996 book, *Bad Land: An American Romance*, was the program of the Chicago, Milwaukee, and St. Paul Railway Company as it extended its line through western North Dakota and eastern Montana where annual rain fall averaged only 10 to 15 inches.
3. Hemphill, Mark W. *Union Pacific Salt Lake Route*. Boston Mills Press, 1995, .
4. Culmsee, Carlton. "Last Great Land Rush," *Utah Historical Quarterly*, Winter 1981, 26-41.

Chapter 7

Homestead Start

In Pasadena and Los Angeles, January and February 1915 melted away with Mary working part time for the school district and Harley working at the landscaping company while they prepared in their free time for the greatest challenge in their lives.

Harley's farm-hand background helped him make the critical decisions about what would be necessary for start-up of the homestead farm. He scouted all over the Los Angeles region to arrange purchases of a team of three-year-old mules and harnesses, a well-used wood-sided wagon, an old single blade plow, a small rusty four-blade disk, old and new tools including an axe, shovel, pitchfork, pick, scythe, wrenches, and oil cans. He bought a small canvas tent, lumber, two small carefully-packaged windows, a door and hinges, rolls of tarpaper, concrete blocks for a foundation, fifteen feet of galvanized stove pipe, saws and hammers and nails, some rope, a ton of bales of hay, buckets, metal drums for water, two galvanized tubs, a cast iron frying pan and kitchen pot, a kerosene lamp, a pot-bellied wood-burning stove, a lever-handled cast iron pump for an outside well, a bedstead and straw-filled mattress, two used chairs, sacks of corn seed and alfalfa seed, and a basic supply of non-perishable food. He scheduled the purchases to be completed at the end of February when he would haul the stuff to a Union Pacific warehouse to await loading onto a freight car bound for Lund.

During some evenings, with an increasingly-worried Mary participating, Harley carefully added up the cost of the purchases versus his bank account. He calculated how long it would take to get the shipment to Lund and out to the homestead, how long it would take him, with his limited carpentry skills, to build a house while he lived in a tent, and how to haul cans of water from Lund until he could dig a well.

Then, finally, he and Mary agreed on a tentative schedule for her to join him at their "new home" in springtime. When she came, she would accompany a shipment of more of the basic household items they would need such as pots, pans, dishes, towels, and bedclothes. After she arrived, they would buy more food and kitchen items in Lund.

When the time approached for Harley to leave, he quit his job at Dependable Landscaping, Mary got time off at the school district, and they took a few days together for a mini-vacation and a tension-filled visit to her family in Santa Barbara.

On March 1, Harley rented a Union Pacific freight car to hold five tons for the haul to Lund. With the help of his brothers-in-law and the owner of one lumber yard, he got the freight car loaded and then tied the mules in one corner with some hay and a bucket of water. He got to ride free in the freight car, saving the cost of a passenger ticket.

The next morning, Harley and Mary, accompanied by Ray and Lu, went to the UP freight yard where they watched the "Johnston" car being switched to the end of a freight train. The conductor signaled "All aboard!"

Harley kissed sister Lu on the check, shook Ray's hand, and turned to Mary. As they hugged and kissed, she whispered, "Be careful, my darling. I love you so much I don't want to lose you, and I keep thinking of all the bad things that might happen to you up there working all alone. Write to me as soon as possible and every day if you can. I'll miss you dreadfully."

"Don't worry, dear wife," he replied. "Everything will be just fine, and I will be careful, and I'll write whenever I can get to the post office at Lund. Lu and Ray will take good care of you, and when we see each other again it will be on our own farm! Goodbye now and remember I love you very, very much."

Harley climbed into the freight car and waved, and one of the mules brayed a farewell.

As the train chugged out of the yard and into the desert of southeastern California, the warm afternoon sun gave way to a chilly night. Harley tried to make himself comfortable among the bales of hay after a supper of canned meat, crackers, and water. At dawn, the train pulled into Lund, and Harley's car was switched off onto a spur track leading to the small stockyards at the west edge of town.

A bleary-eyed and raggedly dirty railroad employee emerged from under one of the stock chutes where he had huddled against the morning chill. He confirmed Harley's identification and freight contract, then he and Harley unloaded the mules and the wagon first, hitched up the mules, and piled the first load of farm equipment onto the wagon.

The mules showed no inclination to start pulling the wagon until Harley found a board and pounded their butts. The two animals finally quit jerking around and fell into step.

Harley paid his helper two quarters, stopped at the Lund Store for a cup of coffee and some donuts, bought some bacon and potatoes, and headed out south on the dirt road, parallel to the railroad track, three miles to his "farm" with its crop of scruffy brush. He spent the first day hurriedly hauling loads because he had to empty the freight car within 48 hours.

As the pale sunlight of the winter afternoon faded, Harley set up the small tent, put on a heavy coat, started a camp fire with stalks of sage brush, pushed a pot into the edge of the fire to heat water for tea, and fried some bacon and potatoes. In the tent he made a mattress from a bale of hay and, totally exhausted, fell asleep fully clothed under two blankets. He awoke stiff and cold in a lemonade-colored dawn, rebuilt the fire, made a cup of tea, and ate a can of beans.

During the first day of frenzy getting the freight car unloaded, he had paid no attention to two small buildings about a quarter of a mile to the south but on the second morning he noticed a thin blue strand of smoke rising from a shiny metal pipe in the roof of one of them. That building was obviously a homestead house because it wasn't very big and was covered with the black tarpaper that was almost a trademark of shanties scattered around the valley. The other structure with a chisel roof was probably a barn. A man, bundled up in a plaid mackinaw and cap, emerged from the house and approached Harley.

"Hello, you must be Mr. Johnston. I heard in town that you had filed on the half section next to mine. I'm Tom Bentley. I see you are hauling stuff from Lund that I'll bet you had shipped here on the railroad."

"Glad to meet you. I'm Harlan Johnston but most people call me Harley. Yeah, I'm hauling my stuff from a freight car. As you can see I'm ready to build and start farming real quick. I'm from Los Angeles.

My wife will come up here as soon as I get a house built for us. Her name is Mary. She'll be real glad to know we'll have neighbors."

"And my wife is sure happy to see somebody show up here. Some of the people that file claims never come back after they see what the desert looks like. Right now, our nearest neighbors are a couple of miles south, down close to Zane. My wife, Lorraine, and I are from Ohio where we wanted to farm but couldn't save any money so I went to work in a farm implement business. A few years ago, we had some friends who heard about a new homestead law, and they talked so much about it Lorraine and I decided to give it a try."

"I know what you mean," Harley responded. "I grew up in Nebraska and worked on farms there and in Missouri as a hired hand for twenty years before I came out to California. I got tired of working for wages there. I've always wanted my own farm, so here I am."

"I came to Milford last fall," Bentley continued, "I filed on this claim and returned in November to build the house before really cold weather started. Lorraine joined me a few weeks ago. I built a barn and a corral and dug a well. Now I'm ready to start clearing some land for spring planting, but I've waited to get a team of horses or mules until I got ready to actually use them. It will be a while before you need your mules to work on the ground so maybe I can borrow them for a few weeks."

"Well, as you can guess, the first thing I have to do is build a house and then I hope to clear ten acres for planting by May first. So you are welcome to use the mules until then."

"Building a good house is tough to do alone. I can help you get started, and when you get ready to put up the roof rafters, you'll really need help. Now, let's finish hauling your stuff from Lund."

Tom Bentley was a husky man with a ruddy face and wrinkles at the corners of his blue eyes. He had a large mustache, and shaggy blond hair stuck out from under his cap. He was wearing grease-stained work gloves, and his boots were covered with mud. Harley felt comfortable with his new neighbor.

It took three wagon trips to finish emptying the freight car, and Harley was increasingly grateful for Bentley's help as they told each other more about their backgrounds and how they came to be homesteaders. When they finished stacking the last pieces of lumber, Bentley told Harley, "Well, I'm tuckered out. And you must be pretty tired and hungry for a hot meal so why don't you come over for dinner about sundown? You can meet Lorraine and tell her about your wife. And we'll see about maybe you bunking at our house for a few nights. I'll bet that tent is not real comfortable."

"That sure is nice of you and your wife, and you can bet your life I'll come. I don't have to dress up, do I?"

Bentley laughed, "Not tonight. See you at sundown."

Harley spent most of the third day clearing brush with axe and shovel off what would be the yard for the buildings. The next day he explored his homestead acreage and the land to the west across the railroad tracks.

He traced the perimeter of his 320 acres and, after extensive searching, found metal markers at the corners. The upper half of the gently sloping land was covered with sage brush three to four feet high and with what Harley learned later was called rabbit brush up to three feet high. The lower half of the property was mostly covered by what Harley learned was shadscale, a foot high, that indicated a less desirable soil streaked with alkali.

Harley walked to the railroad tracks and was spellbound by the sight of the shiny parallel rails disappearing into a hazy infinity at the south end of the valley. To the west, the nearly barren gravely ground appeared to be a fan-shaped alluvium of probably 400 acres spreading out from the delta-like mouth of a very wide but very dry river bed. As Harley learned later, the river bed was called the Four Mile Wash that carried the runoff of major thunderstorms down from the distant foothills. Storms sufficient to send flood water the full length of the wash were very rare, separated by decades, but the erosion they caused remained starkly visible.

Back at the southwest corner of the homestead, Harley decided on the exact location of the house-to-be about a quarter mile east of the railroad tracks. The building would be 24 feet long and 12 feet wide with half of it for the bedroom and half for the living room and kitchen. The barn would be about 100 feet away and would be 16 feet long and 12 feet wide with a 12-foot-high hay loft.

After his explorations, Harley decided he had better write a letter to Mary and get it to the post office in Lund by riding one of the mules there. His grammar continued to require careful reading, and his dull pencil in the tent's dim light didn't help.

Dear Wife

Well I am located on our Utah farm. Does not look very much like a farm yet. Was two days unloading the car and holling the stuff out. Have put up the tent and am starting things up some. Our neighbor Mr. Bentley has been very good. I'll stay at his house a week and have the mules in his stable.

Am going to build our house about 4 or 5 block from them so it will be handy for you and his wife to visit. He wants me to build closer but there was no good building spot without being too close to the railroad.

Am going to [be] building the house in the morning. I guess I will have Mr. Bentley help me build and dig a well. Have had two chances to hire the mules out but I will let Mr. Bentley use them for a couple of week so I will not get to Lund very often for I will have to walk.

Well dearie it is pretty windy up here but I like it fine although I have my cough yet taken on quit a cold coming up and my lips are so sore I can't even smile. I have not shaved so now you ought to see me. Have a nice brown beard and am going to let it grow. I favor a Vandike. I can't locate any thing, can't find any towels.

Things are not much higher up here than in Santa Barbara. Butter is 30c# Bacon 23c# and spuds 1.75 per hundred and they sure are good spuds to eat.

Well sweetheart I am anxious to get things so you can come. Am lost without you. Mr. Bentley wants me to send for you and have you stay at their house. They are the kind of folk that will divide their last cent with any one.

Well darling I am going to Lund this afternoon to mail this to you and I will write you just as often as I can get to the [post] office. Must get some salve for my lips.

Well I have lots more to tell you but will haf to stop for this time.

To my darling Wife from huby with World of Love and Hugs and Kisses

XXXXXXXXXXXXXXX
OOOOOOOOOOOO
Harlan

Mary's first letter to Harley after he left was addressed "Harlan Johnston, General Delivery, Lund, Utah" and was dated March 6.

My Dearest Harlan,

You've been gone only a few days, and it seems like a year. I pray that you are taking care of yourself, staying warm up there in the winter, and not working too hard. I bet its not nearly as much fun being in a tent there as it was in Goleta that time.

Since I'll be coming to Utah pretty soon, I thought I'd visit Mom and my brothers a time or two since once I get up there I may not get to see them for a while. They are doing fine but Mom keeps asking why I want to leave. Quil got a job as an iceman delivering big blocks of ice so he has to be careful about his back. Alf and Walt are worried about the war in Europe and are afraid the United States will end up getting involved.

I will quit my job at the school district when you tell me the house is ready. I should probably get some warm clothes. You have mentioned the wind a lot, and I bet it is a lot colder there than it is here.

I am a little worried about living on a homestead out in the country but I will do my best. I miss you so much and dream about hugging you. Please write to me every day.

With all my Love. XOXOXOXOXO

Mary

In his first two days of work on the house, Harley set out concrete blocks for the foundation and bridged the blocks with floor joists to form an almost-level grid on which to nail the one-inch-thick floor boards. Bentley then showed Harley how to construct eight-foot-tall sections of wall framing. One section had framing for the single door into the kitchen, and each of the end walls had framing for a window. When all the wall sections were framed up on the ground, Bentley spent a day helping Harley hoist the sections upright and nail them to the floor and together at the corners.

At sundown, Harley wrote another letter.

Dear Mary

Have had dinner and am going to see if I can get this to the office this evening. Had bacon corn potatoes bread butter tea and fig jam. How is that [?] Have an appetite for anything. I get my bread from Mrs. Bentley quit[e] handy.

Well dearie I will be ready for you to come the last of next week or the first of the week following if you have had your visits out by that time.

You had better bring $40 or $50 with you when you come. I have not spent but 75 cents since I arrived at Lund. How is that [?] Will haf to buy some hay when the mules get home. If you will go to the New

York store there in S. B. and see if they have any more of their 48c gloves with black gauntlets. If so get me a pair.

Wish you were here right now.

With Love and regard to all
Harlan XXXXXXXX OOOOOOOO

Bentley showed Harley how to cut angle notches on the roof rafters and then helped him put the rafters in place. With the walls and roof framed up, Harley spent several days nailing boards on the roof and walls and installing the door and the two windows.

With the house enclosed, he put the stove in the kitchen, ran the stove pipe up through a hole in the roof, and tacked waterproof tarpaper on the roof. He then moved the few household items he had brought with him into the house and placed the bedstead and mattress in one corner. Although chilly wind whistled through cracks in the siding and around the door and windows, the house with heat from the stove was far more cozy than the tent especially when a light snowstorm swept over the desert a few days later.

The ramshackle quality of buildings put up by some homesteaders, who knew little about carpentry and who had no help from a neighbor like Bentley, contributed to the frequent disenchantment of newly arrived wives.

The Johnston homestead, circa 1916

The evening after moving into the house, Harley wrote another letter.

> Dearest Mary
>
> Well I have just finished my days work and I wish you were here to look at and talk to but things are not very fine yet. Am writing in our house tonight. Have the stove up and most of the stuff piled in one corner. Have been covering thing up as it look like snow tonight. The wind is blowing some but it has been just like California weather the last few day[s]. Friday the day after I moved was a windy one.
>
> How are you enjoying your visits [in Santa Barbara]? The house will be ready for you in a week or two so you can start thinking about coming.
>
> Well dear I am pretty tired so I will end now. Will try to get to Lund to mail this tomorrow.
>
> Your loving husband XXXXXXXX OOOOOOOOO

Mary's reply letters hinted that she remained worried about moving to an isolated farm in a desert but she was thrilled to know she would have a next door neighbor. She asked about wild animals and snakes. She vowed her love for him and missed his hugs.

With the house enclosed and cracks around the windows and door filled with tar, Harley decided the next priority had to be an outhouse, also known as a privy or toilet. Going out into the brush to relieve himself day and night was cold and tiresome, and he had to watch out for visitors in daylight. The prevailing wind was from the southwest so he located the soon-to-be-smelly outhouse about sixty feet downwind from the house. He dug a narrow pit four feet deep and put a makeshift shed over it with two-hole seating. The holes in wood planking were a foot in diameter and had splintery edges. The door sagged on strips of leather for hinges.

Although the privy was an absolute necessity for a homestead, Harley thought it best not to talk about it in his next letter.

> My Dear Wife
>
> Well I am through for the day and wish you were hear. Have the house pretty well along. Am cooking me a pot of beans. The stove is a sonofagun it gets so hot I burn every thing. Well I have the oilcloth on the table tonight and the lamp lighted for the first time. Oh I am so in style to night. Have the bed up too.
>
> Well, sweet heart, I am ready for you any time you want to come and do not put it off any longer than Saturday or Sunday for I want

> to see you. Am getting might lonesome without you. I will not have everything ready but we can be pretty comfortable any way.
>
> Write me two or three day a head so I will be sure and know when you are coming and do not forget to bring some money with you.
>
> With love and I cant hardly wait to see you
>
> XXXXXXXXXXX OOOOOOOOO
> Huby

The letter reminded him that before Mary arrived he should get a well and pump installed to replace hauling water in cans from a railroad water tank faucet in Lund.

The next day, Harley and Bentley took turns digging a three-foot-diameter pit for the start of the well. When it got too deep for the use of shovels, they used Bentley's four-inch-diameter augur. It was back-breaking work, but about thirty feet down the augur started bringing up mud indicating they had reached a shallow water table. The two men got the mules and a wagon and went to the lumber yard in Lund to get pipe and casing for the well. The next day they wrestled the casing down to the water level, built a platform over the well, and hooked up the lever-handled pump Harley had brought with him.

The first few minutes of hand pumping produced a trickle of muddy water but it cleared up to the point where Harley and Tom decided to taste it. It was cold and had a slight chemically taste. "That's pretty good water," Bentley commented. "Like most of the groundwater in this part of the country, it has some alkali that gives it that slightly sharp taste. Using it for washing will require a lot more soap than you and Mary are used to but it certainly is safe to drink."

The two exhausted men took off work an hour earlier than usual and went to Bentley's house for dinner. Tom pulled a bottle off a shelf and waved it at Harley. "Whiskey! We'll have a shot to celebrate!"

Harley grimaced and said, "We deserve it. You sure do. Without your help and knowhow, I'd still be trying to figure out what to do. I don't drink but I sure appreciate the offer."

Bentley shrugged, poured two gurgles worth of the booze into a tin cup, took a sip, made a face, and gasped, "Here's to well water but bourbon is better."

With Mary's arrival due in a few days, Harley scrambled to get the kitchen ready for her. He built some shelves in one corner for a pantry and constructed a sideboard with a big pan at one end for washing dishes. Stored under the sideboard were two three-foot-diameter galvanized metal tubs that would be used for clothes washing and for baths.

The next day, Bentley stopped by, handed Harley a letter from Mary Johnston in Pasadena, and said, "I was at the post office and knew you were waiting for a letter from Mary about when she would come here. So I asked the postmaster if I could pick up your mail since I'm your neighbor. He gave me this letter."

"God bless you!" Harley shouted, "You are the best neighbor anybody could have." He ripped open the envelope.

> March 29, 1915
>
> My darling husband,
>
> I'm coming! I am so excited I can hardly think. We will be together again, and I think all the time about kissing you.
>
> I got a ticket on Union Pacific train #27 that leaves here the day after tomorrow and gets into Lund at 9 the next morning. I hope you get this letter in time to meet me. If not, I'll find a way to get to our new home. I got $40 in cash to bring with me, and there is still about $100 in our bank account here. We will have to find a way to get a bank account in Milford or that other bigger town—Cedar?—since I suppose there is no bank in Lund.
>
> I've got all our clothes—mostly mine—in two suitcases, and I packed everything else in a big trunk to be shipped with me. I'm singing 'Springtime in the Rockies' and 'The Utah Trail' and waiting to hear 'All aboard!'
>
> So until I am in your arms again
>
> Your eager and loving wife XXXXX OOOOO
> Mary

Harley looked up, almost crying, and shouted, "She's coming! She will be here in three days. Praise the Lord!"

Bentley smirked, "Praise the Lord if you want to but I know you are thinking about something else, aren't you?" Harley rolled his eyes and kissed the letter.

Now that the house was finished and the well was in operation, the next major job was to build a barn, but Harley decided to postpone that until Mary could get settled. He swept and dusted the house and aired the bedding. He cleaned up the yard and stacked scraps of lumber into a neat pile for firewood. He got the mules from Bentley's barn and checked over the harnesses.

The day before Mary's arrival he took a bath for the first time since coming to the homestead. He heated pans of water on the stove and bathed standing up in one of the tubs, then he washed his two pairs of long-johns underwear in the used bath water. The Bentleys' hospitality had not included letting Harley take a bath in a tub in their warm kitchen, and he had not been inclined to strip down for a bath in the yard.

At 7 a.m., he cut off his beard and shaved, put on clean clothes he hadn't worn since leaving Los Angeles, and headed for Lund. He figured the shaggy hair down to his collar would have to wait for a haircut by Mary.

Down in Los Angeles the day before, Lu and Ray took Mary to the railroad station where they wished her good luck and told her to give their love to Harley. Mary checked the trunk and suitcases and boarded a passenger car.

As the train pulled away, Mary glanced out a window to the north where a hazy blue line of peaks loomed over her home town, over the sun-kissed, ocean-washed, mountain-girded, island-guarded, palm-fringed Santa Barbara that possibly she might never see again.

She fidgeted over a light lunch in the dining car and tried to read a book in the afternoon. As the train rolled northeast, the view of increasingly stark deserts revived the apprehension she had managed to nearly block out for the past month. She did not sleep much on the hard seat of the coach car, and, in the pale light of dawn after the train passed through Caliente, Nevada, she began looking out on the landscape of southwestern Utah.

"Dear Lord," Mary whispered to herself, *"Where are the trees?"* There were far vistas of barren foothills punctuated by rocky cliffs and the ochre-colored sides of railroad track cuts through ridges. Almost in a panic, she searched for the sight of a tree and finally saw a few dark clumps on a north-facing hillside. She learned later that those clumps were pinion pines and junipers known locally as cedar trees.

"Modena, Utah," the conductor bawled out. "Five minutes!" Mary looked out the window at the train station which was a converted freight car. Behind it was a "mercantile" building with a high false front that badly needed paint. Straggling up a gravel street were a half dozen shabby little houses with half-dead shrubs in the yards. *"This is a town?"* Mary thought. *"Will Lund be like this?"* She was relieved to see through the opposite window what was probably the main street with several stores, a livery stable with corrals and a Model T Ford in front of it.

First B. J. Lund general store in Modena, built in 1905.

The train continued, whizzing through Beryl and the five shanties at Zane. Mary began holding her breath for a sight of Lund. She did not notice a small tarpaper-covered house as the train passed the Ford siding. She soon discovered that house was her new home.

With a clanging of bells and whistle toots from the long black steam engine, the train pulled into the town where Mary would spend the rest of her life. She was vastly relieved to see a row of tree-sheltered houses along one side of the tracks, an asphalt-paved platform with electric light poles, an imposing water tank, a very tall, yellow, wooden tower she learned later had been used for drilling a deep water well, an almost pretty station building, and a block of business buildings. A dozen people were waiting at the station.

Five passengers got off the train, two of them obviously would-be homesteaders. Mary was the last to step onto the platform, and instantly she and everyone else realized she was very much over-dressed for life in Lund with her fashionable mutton sleeves and a button-up bodice. People stared. Oblivious to everyone else, Harley rushed to her, lifted her up, and began kissing her. The small audience cheered.

Harley pushed her back to arms length, looked her up and down, and exclaimed, "My, my, aren't you pretty!"

She rolled her eyes and patted his chest. "And aren't you the handsomest husband! Do all Utah farmers look like this?"

"Nope, I'm afraid not," he replied. He hugged her and kissed her again and then turned, waved toward the main street, and said, "Welcome to Lund. Our homestead and the Bentleys will be happy to see you but not nearly so happy as me. Now let's go see about your bags."

The train pulled out, and Mary stared to the west for a moment where a forbidding row of granite hills rose abruptly beyond a level stretch of land that looked like sunbaked mud. She shivered and turned to watch the station master. From the train's baggage car, he had loaded an iron-wheeled cart and pulled it along the platform to where disembarking passengers could pick out their luggage. She took one of her suitcases and Harley took one and with his other hand he helped the station master lift the trunk and carry it to the Johnstons' wagon parked across the street in front of the Lund Store.

In a rare display of playfulness, Harley introduced Mary to the mules which he decided on the spot to name Sharkey and Shanna. They glanced at Mary and then returned their sleepy gaze to the ground. She said, "Hello, Sharkey and Shanna," and gave them each a quick pat on their backs.

With glowing pride and excitement, Harley led his over-dressed bride into the Lund Store. He introduced her to the store owner and his wife, and they shopped for groceries and the staples Harley said they would need.

"Oh, I almost forgot," he exclaimed, "We'll need a Combinet which we can get at the lumber yard next door. " He emerged from the lumber yard side door carrying a two-gallon-sized white pot with a beveled edge and a lid. It would be their indoor toilet to be emptied each morning in the outhouse.

When the wagon was finally loaded up, Mary climbed onto the wood seat in front, and, as they headed to the homestead, she saw her first dust devil, a small whirlwind dancing across the flat gray and tan desert.

Chapter 8

Homestead Life

As Harley and Mary headed south from Lund toward their homestead on the morning of April 1, Mary studied the flat treeless desert landscape under a cloudless sky and thought to herself, *"Maybe this is all just an April Fool's joke or a dream, and I will wake up any minute now."* She jolted herself back to reality, slipped an arm around Harley's waist, and murmured, "It's such a beautiful day. I thought it would be windy and colder."

"It can get plenty cold, even down to zero, but there is nearly always sunshine to warm things up," Harley replied. "In summer, the temperature can get up to ninty-five degrees, but it doesn't feel that hot because there is always some wind. The dry heat here is more comfortable than damp heat back East."

He then launched into an enthusiastic monologue about the homestead. "The next project is a barn which won't take very long to

Brush and sand in the Escalante Desert

build, and then I can start working on a crop. I need to get the brush cleared off at least ten acres and get it plowed and tilled and planted before the first of May. The altitude here is around five thousand feet, and if you plant a crop too early you might get hit with a hard frost. Oh, and another project we should consider before the hot summer comes is a small cellar where we can keep food cooler than in the kitchen.

"Mrs. Bentley will be real happy to meet you. They want us to go to their house for dinner tonight. Lorraine has been asking me every few days when you would get here. The other nearest homesteads are a few miles south."

Mary listened and nodded and murmured a few comments such as "You must have worked awfully hard," but her gaze kept straying from the little clouds of dust kicked up by the mules' hooves to the endless sweep of the monotone desert around them. She struggled with the recurring thought, *"What am I doing here? It looks even worse than I had imagined."* But, she argued with herself, *"Harley seems so happy with the progress he has made on his dream of his own farm, I can't let him know how lonesome and dried out I feel already. Thank the Lord for Mrs. Bentley. I hope we like each other."*

As they turned off the road to the tarpaper-covered house, Harley exclaimed, "Well, dear wife, there is our new home and over there will be our fields."

Mary forced a smile as she surveyed a yard littered with construction debris, a pile of dirt from digging the well, stacked bales of hay, and farm implements and lumber awaiting construction of the barn. She turned her gaze to the house with its long backside facing the road. *"Where are the windows?"* she thought in a panic but was relieved as Harley drove around the building so that she could see a window at each end and a doorway.

"I'm afraid you will find this pretty different from your home in Santa Barbara," Harley said as he stopped the wagon near the door and lifted off the suitcases. "But look at it this way—you'll have a whole house to fix up the way you want it, no mother telling you what to do, no brothers getting in your way, just me, and I'll do anything inside the house that you want me to do."

Mary got down from the wagon, hugged Harley, and whispered, "It is our house, and I will make it our home. I'm going to work as hard as you have, and we will be happy, won't we?"

"We sure will!" Harley replied as he struggled to lift the heavy trunk. He opened the door, pushed the trunk inside, and extended his arms to Mary as if to carry his bride across the threshold.

"I'm heavier than the trunk so let's just pretend you are carrying me," she quipped. She took his hand, led him through the door, turned and hugged and kissed him.

Over his shoulder she got her first look at the kitchen. Harley felt her tense up. "Are you all right? I bet you're getting tired."

"I confess this is a bit of a shock," she replied. "It is different, to say the least. You will have to show me what to do, where things are, how to get water, how to start the stove, and so on. You will have to be patient with me while I learn about this kind of life."

Although he had tried to straighten up the house's two rooms, stacking stuff almost neatly in corners, the place was still drab and dusty. The kitchen/living room furniture consisted of two used brown captain's chairs and an unpainted table made by Harley out of scraps of lumber. The bedroom was furnished with a metal bedstead that was badly in need of paint. Mary's trunk, once emptied of household items and her meager personal belongings such as a few books and keepsakes, would hold their clothes until Harley could build a closet of some kind in the bedroom.

Mary plopped down on one of the chairs and looked bewildered. "This house is going to take an awful lot of work. I hardly know where to begin." Her gaze landed on a kerosene lamp on the kitchen counter. "Good Lord! I forgot for a minute we don't have electricity. I had just started to wonder where the light switches are. I remember lamps like that from when I was a kid on the Hope Ranch."

"They haven't changed," Harley smiled, "Now is as good a time as any to show you how one works."

He got a one-gallon can of kerosene from under the kitchen counter, carefully lifted off the lamp's clear glass chimney shaped like a long slim pear, unscrewed a circular metal device and poured kerosene into the bowl. The metal device held a woven wick that dangled into the kerosene-filled bowl. The wick could be raised or lowered by twisting a knob. Harley lighted the wick with a wooden match and placed the chimney back into clip-like holders around the wick. "If the wick is too high, it will smoke and dirty-up the chimney. And the wick has to be trimmed now and then so that it burns right," Harley told his new-bride pupil. He cupped his hand over the top of the chimney and blew into it to extinguish the burning wick.

Mary looked out the kitchen window at the barren landscape and thought, *"We'll never get electricity here. The railroad station in Lund looked like it has electricity. I wonder if any of the stores or houses have it. I'll have a look next time we are in town."* She turned to Harley and quipped, "I like an electric light much better but for right now what do we do about lunch?" Harley sheepishly took a can of beans and a half loaf of bread from the pantry and placed them on his homemade table.

After the Spartan lunch, Mary fidgeted and murmured, "I have to go to the bathroom. I guess that is our toilet out there in the yard."

"Yep," Harley replied. "It is brand new, the best outhouse that I could build. The seats are a little rough so be careful not to get slivers in your pretty little rump. Here is a newspaper page for wiping. It works best if you crumple it up good to make it softer before you use it. Sometimes the black ink will rub off on you but it won't hurt you."

Mary rolled her eyes and headed for the outhouse, thinking, *"No electricity, a well and a pump for water, and splintery toilet seats! The good Lord is going to have to help me a lot to stay here."*

They spent the afternoon unpacking and arranging the pantry and kitchen utensils to suit Mary. Shelves in the floor-to-ceiling pantry were stacked with canned meat and vegetables and Carnation canned milk, a slab of bacon in a pan, a box of oatmeal, containers of salt and pepper and coffee and tea, a large can of lard. A sack of potatoes and a sack of flour rested on the pantry floor.

One priority was making the bed with flannel sheets and a quilt that Mary had brought with her, replacing blankets that Harley had used for a month and that were beginning to smell. The three-inch thick straw mattress on wooden slats had its own particular odor.

While Mary continued with her arrangements, Harley went to the pump and filled five-gallon cans with water to use in the kitchen and for washing up before they went to the Bentleys' for dinner. When he found Mary in the bedroom, he resisted a strong urge to grab her, throw her on the bed, and make love. She knew what he was thinking but managed to focus her attention on folding clothes.

When the battered alarm clock on the table showed 5 o'clock, Harley announced, "Well, dear wife, it's time to go to dinner. Out here, we eat dinner at sundown, go to bed early, and get up with the sun."

Harley had left the mules harnessed to the wagon so that Mary, still dressed in her good clothes and high button shoes, would not have to walk through bushes even the short distance to the Bentley's.

Tom and Lorraine Bentley greeted them at the door with outstretched hands. Tom shook Mary's hand and almost shouted, "Welcome! We are sure glad to see you!" Lorraine bypassed the handshake and hugged Mary.

Mrs. Bentley was eleven or maybe twelve years older than Mary. She was rather heavyset, not as tall as Mary, and was dressed in a simple dark gray blouse and skirt. She had gray-streaked brown hair done up in a bun. Her wire-rimmed glasses tended to slip down on her nose. She was quick to laugh and was obviously ecstatic about having company.

For a few minutes before dinner, Lorraine took Mary on a quick tour of the Bentleys' 24-foot-by-12-foot house identical in size and layout to the house Harley had built. Mary was relieved to discover that such a basic structure could be made halfway livable with additions of furniture, scattered colorful pillows, and pictures on the walls.

Some weeks earlier when Mrs. Bentley returned from a visit to her former home in Ohio, she brought back with her a dozen chickens and materials for a small yard for the birds and a coop with nests of hay. The little flock seemed disconsolate over the change from the moist Ohio River Valley to the dry and windy Escalante Valley.

The dinner consisted of one of the chickens that had been roasted, fried potatoes, and a can of peas. Desert was a simple yellow cake made with two of the few eggs obtained so far. Lorraine made typical pioneer coffee by dumping big spoonsful of coffee into a tall pot of boiling water on top of the standard, wood-fired, all-purpose stove. A challenge for drinking the coffee was not to get burned lips from the hot tin cups.

During dinner, Lorraine reached for Mary's hand, squeezed it, and said, "Oh, I'm so happy you and Harley are our neighbors. I'm sure you could tell as you drove out here today that homesteading can be a pretty tough life, especially for a woman, and that is doubly true for a new wife. Tell me, what was it like in California? Harley told me you grew up in Santa Barbara."

Mary diplomatically did not comment on her first impressions of the desert. She summarized her early childhood on the Hope Ranch and growing up in the ocean-front town and her involvement in the church there. "I'll really miss the church and the music and the programs and my friends there. I guess there is no church in Lund or in the area?"

"No, not now," Lorraine replied. "But I'm like you, I would love to have church services somehow. There is going to be a new school house in Lund that could be used but everybody is so busy trying to get settled on the homesteads and getting started on farming that I think it will probably be a while before we can get some kind of a church."

Lorraine chatted about growing up in farm country in central Ohio and meeting Tom while she was a bookkeeper in a farm implement store where he worked hoping to save enough money to fulfill his dream of buying a farm of his own.

Mary nodded. "I certainly know what that kind of determination is like. I feel that you and I will have a lot in common besides having husbands with this dream even if we find it cannot come true. But we have to try and try hard, don't we?"

Lorraine patted Mary's hand and murmured, "Yes, we sure do."

The two men, deeply engrossed in talk about getting started on dry land farming, had not paid attention to the women's conversation. They particularly discussed what tools and equipment they would need in addition to what they could already share.

Harley wanted to talk about the Campbell theory of dry land agriculture, but Tom had only heard other people talk about it. Harley persisted with a summary of the "scientific method" and added, "One problem is that the book says we'd need a Campbell subsurface compactor. It is supposed to compact the soil at the level of roots and form a kind of reservoir there whenever there is rain or snow. A guy at the lumber yard said a compactor would have to be ordered from someplace and would probably cost hundreds of dollars. I can't afford that so I wonder if we can get by without it."

Tom interrupted, "I wouldn't want to mess with something like that. There can be a big difference between theory and reality. I think with the equipment we have now we can go ahead with maybe 20 acres this spring and see how we come out." He was inclined to follow traditional farm practices, but understood that the kind and size of crops would be very limited in the Escalante Valley compared with the Midwest.

The men's attention was diverted by Mary's barely stifled yawn. "Hey, it's been great having people to talk to," Tom said. "Mary, you must be pretty tired after the overnight trip. And, Lorraine, we have to remember that these two are newly-weds, and they have been apart for a month. I'm pretty sure they want to go home now." Mary and Harley waggled their fingers at him as if to hush him up. With a chorus of "Thank you" and "Goodbye," the newly-weds rode their wagon homeward under a desert sky of black velvet where there were a million more stars than Mary had ever seen in the denser air of urbanized southern California.

At the house, Harley tied the mules to the wagon and threw some hay in the open rear end of the wagon. Inside, he lighted a kerosene lamp, started a fire in the stove, and put on a pan of water to heat for washing. In a few minutes, Mary in a nightgown emerged from the bedroom and said, "I'm going to do a wipe-down bath with the water in that pan. You can go get ready for bed."

Harley headed for the bedroom and said, "I had a bath yesterday so I won't need much washing tonight." In the bedroom, he took off the long johns he usually wore day and night and got pajamas from the trunk.

When Mary came back into the bedroom, he pointed to the chamber pot, also known as a thunder mug, and said, "I suspect you'll want to use that to pee in instead of using the outhouse. You just sit on it like you would a toilet seat. I might have to use it myself before morning." Mary eyed the chamber pot skeptically but decided it was better than a visit to the outhouse in chilly darkness. Harley slipped on his shoes and hurried to the outhouse. In the bedroom, Mary tried to sit down on the Combinet and almost tipped it over before she learned how to crouch over it properly. She replaced the lid as she realized that the lid was necessary to reduce the smell.

Harley blew out the lamp and slipped into bed beside Mary. She was totally exhausted from the train trip and the frantic first day at the "farm" but she knew how pent up his passion must be after a month alone, and she knew there was no way she could postpone the love-making. She had decided to gamble on not getting pregnant so she skipped the contraception procedure, being very tired and not wanting to mess with the douche equipment and the chamber pot.

In the middle of the night, Mary sat bolt upright in bed, awakened by a sound that was surely the coughing wail of a banshee. "What is that?" she yelled. Harley sat up and put his arms around her.

"It's just one of the coyotes howling. They look like skinny dogs. Sometimes you think they may be talking to each other with that yip

yip yowl. Some people say there are packs of wolves out here but I think the coyotes are mistaken for wolves."

"Will they attack you?"

"Oh, no, they run away if they see you. Most of the time you won't even see them. Now, let's go back to sleep."

Mary lay back down and, comforted by the warmness of Harley, drifted into a deep dreamless sleep.

As dawn broke, Harley rolled over to face her and touched her breasts but she whispered, "Let's wait until tonight when we can go to bed extra early and do it twice, okay?"

"You promise?"

"I promise."

After a breakfast of bacon and two eggs that Mrs. Bentley had given them, Harley stood in the middle of the kitchen, arms akimbo, and said, "Well, now that you're here, what do we need to do first? Like we talked about yesterday, I need to put up more shelves and a closet and eventually put linoleum on the floors. You can hang those two pictures you brought, and we'll start scouting around for some more furniture."

"Well," Mary replied, "before we start decorating, I better learn more about how things work around here. Let's start with the stove."

The round stove was made of sheet metal with an 18-inch-diameter cast iron top for cooking, heating water, and heating triangle-shaped flatirons for pressing clothes although pressing clothes was the lowest priority in homesteads. Foot-long pieces of firewood were fed into a door faced with fireproof mica through which flames could be seen. Beneath the door was a narrow horizontal opening where ashes could be removed. Mary would soon learn that wood ashes, if removed in even a slight breeze, would blow around the room. A fire was started with wood kindling placed on a wad of paper or dried brush. There was a square piece of tin under the stove to keep errant sparks off the wood floor.

Mary would learn that the stove seemed to have a perverse mind of its own, either too hot or too cold, always full of ashes, and always needing another two pieces of wood. In summer, when the stove had to be fired up for cooking, the extra heat made the already-stifling kitchen almost unbearable. However, on winter days and evenings, the warmth and the orange glow through the little window felt cozy along with the smell of burning pine wood. "We'll run out of scrap wood to burn pretty soon, and the bigger pieces of sage brush don't burn very long," Harley commented, "so one of these days I'll have to take the wagon up into the foothills and get some dead trees for firewood."

Mary nodded and said, "Now, what about the well and the water and those tubs and washing clothes and dishes?"

Harley picked up a five-gallon can with a spigot near the bottom and showed her how to fill it at the well's lever-operated pump. Used water was dumped in the yard.

"As you can see," Harley smiled, "there is no running water, hot or cold here, and no sink. Someday, I may put in a metal sink with a pipe running out to a cesspool in the yard."

"You promise?"

"I promise."

Harley continued, "Washing clothes once a week will be a lot like you probably remember from when you were a kid on the Hope Ranch. On a bench just outside the door, we'll have one tub of hot water heated on the stove for the soaping on the washboard and a tub of cold water for rinsing. You'll have to ring the rinse water out by hand. Which reminds me, I need to put up a clothes line for you to hang the clothes on to dry in the wind. In winter, we'll set up the wash tubs in the kitchen."

Within a few weeks Mary learned that the "hard" alkaline water and the harsh bar soap customarily used for clothes washing would make her hands painfully chapped. She would also learn that wet clothes hung on the clothes line in winter would often freeze stiff and would have to be spread out inside the house to thaw and eventually dry out.

On the third day after her arrival, Mary wanted to go to Lund to shop for necessary items that had been forgotten or postponed, and she wanted to get a better look at her new home town which was so starkly different from Santa Barbara.

Harley took the occasion to teach her how to hitch the team of mules to the wagon with harnesses just in case some kind of emergency arose. He put padded horse collars as a form of yoke around the animals' necks pressing on their front shoulders, attached leather loops called hames with large buckles to the collars, and hooked traces (heavy straps for pulling the wagon) to the hames and to the wooden singletrees attached to the lower front of the wagon. He then draped the reins from bridles with metal bits in the mules' mouths back over the animals' rumps and up to the wagon seat. The animals could be "steered" by pulling their heads right or left with the reins.

Metal springs under the wagon seat were supposed to cushion bumps on the road but the cushioning was not noticeable. Mary remembered what it was like to ride in cars in Santa Barbara and sadly realized there was no automobile in her immediate future.

A general merchandise store, known for many decades as the Lund Store and later owned by the Johnstons, stocked nearly everything the homesteaders needed. To go shopping in Cedar City 35 miles away could require an overnight wagon trip or a long dusty drive in a roadster on a dirt and gravel road. Stagecoach service, which was bitterly cold in winter and hot and dusty in summer, had been recently phased out as the age of the automobile began. The store had most of its merchandise delivered by train.

The groceries section had gunny sacks of potatoes with sprouts poking through the burlap, big cloth sacks of flour and little sacks of sugar, containers of salt and pepper, soap, a large variety of canned fruits and vegetables, jars of hard candy, bottles of syrup, five-pound tins of lard, dried beef, slabs of bacon and haunches of salty ham, and packages of corn meal. Supplies of fresh meat, butter and eggs depended mainly on whether any of the more well-established homesteaders had brought some to town to sell.

Fresh vegetables were available in summer and fall, and some fresh fruit, mainly small apples, came in the fall from skimpy orchards in the Cedar City/Parowan area.

In the dry goods section there was a limited choice of clothes, a few bolts of floral print calico, pins and needles and thread and buttons, hats and caps and bonnets, work gloves, wicks for kerosene lamps, wooden matches, frying pans, coffee pots and pitchers.

There was a mini-drug store with pain medicines and cough syrups.

Mary discreetly learned from the store owner's wife that powder for a contraception solution was available.

In one corner of the main room was the post office, faced with a wall of numbered metal mail boxes each four inches square.

The backroom featured two pool tables, a few jugs of hard liquor, a display of cigars and chewing tobacco, a tray of hunting knives, and a rack of rifles.

Harley took Mary on a brief tour of the ten blocks of the town that had been laid out in a grid, but the pattern of streets was lost in

The town of Lund looking south, circa 1914

the informal short cuts through vacant lots. Vast patches of weeds separated the dozen small, clapboard, wood shingle-roofed houses that were not part of the railroad employee housing close to the train tracks. The few trees and bushes were small and scrawny, and there were no lawns.

Two freight cars had been joined to create the railroad station but some extra trim, a small portico, and two beds of hollyhocks with pink and white blossoms in summer almost camouflaged the form of the freight cars.

The main street paralleled the east side of the railroad line. Founders of the town had magnanimously hauled a dozen wagon loads of gravel from the foothills and spread it along the street which almost prevented muddy ruts. The gravel did not prevent swirls of dust raised by horses' hooves and every passing vehicle, whether creaky wagons, thin-wheeled buggies, or sputtering automobiles.

There was a livery stable with a barn and hay loft, corrals with husky horses and flop-eared mules, and an owner who pretended to be a blacksmith. The high clapboard false front of the almost new Root Hotel was already in need of paint. A few timid tamarisk bushes tried in vain to shade the hotel's narrow front porch.

Construction was underway on a Union Pacific roundhouse at the north edge of town. It would have a massive turntable over a pit to facilitate repairs on locomotives and also allow engines to quickly reverse direction if needed.

Herds of thousands of sheep trailed back and forth across the Escalante Valley between the winter range in the valley and the summer range on the Wasatch Mountains where snow and rain at the higher elevations provided lush grass from May to October. Because water was available at Lund, the town was on one of the main migration routes, and in spring and fall the pungent smell of sheep and their shit pervaded the community.

The raw shabbiness of the town's buildings was depressing for Mary who was accustomed to the neat brick bungalows and red tile roofs of Santa Barbara, and she noticed that only the railroad station had electricity. The early spring absence of greenery left her with a wave of homesickness. However, she said nothing to Harley about her feelings and tried to chat nonchalantly about her shopping.

Back at the homestead, life settled down to springtime days of hard work as Harley started construction on a barn, and Mary struggled to make the house habitable.

The barn had two sections, one for the wagon and tools and one for the mules. Above the stable for the animals was a loft where, hopefully, alfalfa hay from the farm's first crops could be stored and dropped down in batches into a manger for the mules to eat.

As soon as Harley finished the barn he got his mules back from Bentley, who had purchased a team of his own, and began working twelve hours a day to clear brush off twenty acres for his first field. When he started plowing, he discovered the roots of the bigger bushes were deep and tough. The soil, unlike that in Missouri, was barely damp at the depth of the plow.

By the first of May, Harley had prepared ten acres, scattered alfalfa seed by hand, and tilled the tiny seeds about a half inch deep into the ground.

By mid-May, he had the second ten acres planted with seed for a type of corn called flint corn that he had purchased in Lund after being told it was best for the desert conditions. The seeds were planted two feet apart to maximize the plants' use of the scant moisture in the soil. Flint corn would quickly mature at about three feet in height in August, months before standard field corn would be harvested in the Midwest. The standard corn seed Harley had brought with him was fed to the mules.

May was supposed to be a rainy month. Gentle rain fell on newly planted seeds, and homesteaders felt blessed for a change. From then on, day after day, Harley and Mary searched the fields for the sight of green sprouts, and by early June they found the first frail shoots of corn. However, it became clear that there would not be much of a hay crop.

While Harley toiled happily in the field, Mary was finding out that homestead life was even tougher than she had feared. The flimsy house was alternately too hot or too cold, depending on hot dry winds or cold dry winds and the perversity of the stove. Pumping water from the well regardless of the weather, carrying containers of water into the house, and dumping tubs of used water out into the yard gave her backaches for the first few months. However, she was grateful that she did not have to work in the fields as some homestead wives were doing.

She was learning why most homesteaders wore the same clothes for weeks at a time. Washing clothes—Harley's greasy or muddy denim overalls, his sweaty long johns, her cooking-splattered long dresses—was simply very hard work. On chilly spring and fall days, the hot water quickly became merely warm, and the cold water turned icy. Her hands which a year earlier had danced over piano keys became chapped and calloused.

There were days when dust storms looked in the windows and prowled around the door, trying to find an easy way inside the house. Mary almost gave up trying to prevent layers of grit on surfaces where she could write her name.

She hung one of the two framed pictures she had brought with her in the bedroom and one in the kitchen/living room. One print was of an ocean surf breaking on a palm tree-lined beach, and the other showed colonial Spanish-style houses on a hillside. Glances at the pictures made Mary alternately nostalgic or homesick.

Preparing meals three times a day with a very limited variety of food was not as tiring as washing clothes but it was more challenging. With the limitations of the stove, there were two choices for cooking—frying or boiling. There was no oven, and even after Mary acquired a cast iron Dutch oven, to be used on top of the stove, efforts to bake bread, cakes, and pies were frustrating. Meals got monotonous with bacon or ham, potatoes, canned vegetables and fruit, and stale bread. Oatmeal with canned Carnation milk was a standard breakfast.

Occasionally, the silence of the desert was oppressive for Mary but most of the time during daylight hours she could hear Harley working in the yard or in the fields. And every few hours, freight trains and passenger trains rumbled by. Sometimes, a freight train would pull onto the Ford siding about a mile away to let a passenger train pass.

Making love in a drafty, sometimes too hot, sometimes too cold, homestead bedroom on a straw mattress was not nearly as nice as in the bedroom in Pasadena, and Harley and Mary were often too tired to engage in a long romantic evening particularly after taking baths in a tub in the kitchen. However, they were both healthy and in love so Saturday night was still a time of revived, even if brief, passion.

As a dutiful farm wife, Mary started a vegetable garden. Harley spaded up a fifty-foot-square patch of the yard near the well so that Mary could pump irrigation water into her garden rows. With seeds from the Lund store, she planted the garden in May and got aching knees as well as a sore back. The seed packages had beautiful illustrations of huge vegetables that inspired Mary to read the directions carefully and dream of her garden harvest. Weeds that seemingly should never be found in the desert grew luxuriant in Mary's irrigated garden.

With the start of gardening and completion of the barn to house the mules, the Santa Barbara girl's memory of the smell of hibiscus blossoms was replaced by the smell of fresh mule manure when applied in the garden as fertilizer.

In June, while waiting for the first crops to materialize and pinning hopes on summer thunderstorms when cumulus clouds would roll up from the southwest, Harley turned his attention to creating a cellar. He dug a pit six feet wide, eight feet long and six feet deep with a slope for stairs at one end and then installed posts at each corner to hold timbers for a low-pitched roof. A layer of chicken wire, a layer of brush, and a one-foot-thick layer of the excavated dirt formed the roof. The dirt top helped insure that the temperature in the cellar was cool in summer and above freezing in winter. A few shelves against the dirt walls plus makeshift wooden stairs topped by a sloped, tarpaper-covered door competed the project. A cellar was the nearest thing to an ice box or a refrigerator available to homesteaders.

Also in the lull after the first plantings, Harley decided he had better go to the foothills for firewood since the supply of scrap lumber and sage brush stalks was running out. He hitched the mules to the wagon, crossed the railroad tracks at the Ford siding, and headed northwest across gravelly bench land, following a faint trail made by earlier homestead wood hunters. About four miles away behind the row of the hills that rose steeply from the desert floor west of Lund was a skimpy forest of blue-berried juniper trees, called cedar trees, and gnarly pinyon pine clutching at the rocky hillsides or lining dry arroyos.

Wood gatherers searched for dead trees that had fallen or could be pulled down. Any branches remaining on the tree trunks were axed off and piled in the wagon. A typical dead trunk was less than a foot in diameter and eight to ten feet long.

It was hard work, and loading the larger trunks was a severe test of Harley's muscles. By late afternoon, he had a wagon load that was heavy enough to tire out the mules on the long, slow, bumpy haul home. It was sundown when the modern Paul Bunyan arrived at the kitchen door to the relief of Mary who had started to worry about all the bad things that might happen such as falling trees, axe injuries, even an attack by imaginary wolves.

With the cellar job completed and the first of the year's wood hauling done, Harley began clearing more land with a goal of preparing 20 more acres for a year-long test of the Campbell theory of dry land farming.

The Escalante Valley is in a corner of what is called the Great Basin, a desperately arid region covering western Utah and most of Nevada. The valley is much less known than the spectacular red rocks country of the Escalante River and town of Escalante, the Grand Staircase—Escalante National Monument and Canyonlands National Park in Utah's southeast quadrant bordering on Colorado. The southwest end of the flat 60-mile long Escalante Valley is separated from the St. George area by a mountain range and the Dixie National Forest. The northeast end of the Escalante desert turns into the Black Rock and Sevier deserts.

The prehistoric Lake Bonneville, circa 25,000 years ago, covered more than 20,000 square miles of the Great Basin at depths of up to 1,000 feet. Eventually, raised by snow melt from the Wasatch Mountains that bisect Utah north and south on the east, the lake apparently broke over a natural barrier near the present-day Nevada-Idaho border 11,000 years ago and drained into the Snake and Columbia Rivers to the Pacific Ocean. The now-arid basin is in the rain shadow of the Sierra Nevada Mountains. There is no river outlet to a sea, and the internal streams disappear into alkaline lakebeds, also called sumps or playas, such as those scattered throughout western Utah. The largest remnant of Lake Bonneville is the Great Salt Lake which is slowly drying up, due mainly to diversions of irrigation water from streams off the Wasatch Mountains.

Sand dunes in the barren Escalante Valley

The south shore line of Lake Bonneville was about two miles south of Lund at an elevation of 5,100 feet. The lake left a layer of alluvial sediment in the Escalante Valley. The sediment would normally be good for farming, but the potential for raising crops failed due to lack of rain and the alkali concentrated by evaporation of the ancient lake. On clay soils, the white alkali salt—sodium or potassium carbonate—stays on or near the surface instead of percolating down as it usually does in sandy soils.

The floor of the Escalante Valley remains covered with a variety of bushes, some six feet high such as black sage in areas of sandy ground, and some, such as shadscale, only a foot high, in alkaline soil. The larger bushes have deep roots seeking enough moisture to survive and halt the spread of tawny sand dunes that nevertheless reach heights of ten feet in widely scattered locations. In the spring, greasewood has tiny rose-colored flowers, and in autumn, especially in years of more moisture than normal, the tops of rabbit brush turn a bronzed yellow.

Utah's state flower, the sego lily, with white petals and a lavender center, is found only rarely in foothills around the valley. Also bashful are varieties of cacti ranging from yucca with spectacular white flower stalks to the squat barrel cactus with hot pink blooms.

Areas of the desert floor with the most alkaline soil have clumps of salt grass looking like a monk's hair-fringed bald head along with very small plants that resemble strings of gray beads. On the gravelly uplands, bunch grass grows light green in spring and turns prickly tan by July.

A weather station at Modena in the southwest end of the valley recorded average annual precipitation of 10.38 inches from 1936 to 1995 although there were years of only eight inches. The average maximum temperature in July and August was around ninety degrees Fahrenheit, and the average minimum temperature was about thirteen degrees in January.

Most of the precipitation is in the form of snow, and in the desert much of that moisture merely evaporates instead of soaking into the ground. In addition to lack of rain, a problem for farming is that dry air sucks moisture out of plants not adapted to the desert.

The first "white" men to visit what is now Utah were ten Spanish explorers in 1776 with Franciscan monks Atanasio Dominguez as the leader and Silvestre Velez de Escalante as the author of a detailed journal. The Spaniards included a map maker and an amateur astronomer using an astrolabe for basic navigation. The group, accompanied by interpreters and guides, left Santa Fe, New Mexico, on July 29 seeking a route to the major Spanish mission at Monterey on the California coast. The goal was a route that would avoid the vast deserts and steep rocky canyons that earlier explorers had found as far west as the Grand Canyon and Colorado River.

The Dominguez/Escalante entourage, with a herd of horses and cattle, wandered northward through western Colorado and into northeastern Utah before turning south to present day Provo, where they made friends with a band of Paiute Indians. The Spaniards continued southward through the present day Black Rock desert, weathered a two-day snowstorm, and, on October 10, entered the desert valley later named after Father Escalante. The Indians in the region were clueless about a route to California, and the Spaniards began to sense there were only barren mountains and deserts to the west.

The route south into the Escalante desert was visibly almost flat at elevations of 5,000 to 5,500 feet compared with a possible alternative trail through the foothills of the Wasatch Mountains. Almost the same route was chosen for the same reason by a railroad company 125 years later, followed by electricity transmission lines and oil company pipe lines.

With winter approaching and California obviously far, far away, the explorers cast lots October 11 and voted to high-tail it for home, pausing at thermal mud springs south of present day Milford. They went straight south through the valley west of present day Cedar City, down what is now Ash Creek and along the Hurricane Fault past present day St. George into the northwest corner of Arizona, and then turned east past the many colorful but waterless plateaus along the north side of the Grand Canyon. All members of the original group miraculously survived a blundering search for a place to cross the Colorado River with its deep red rock canyons and, on November 7, finally found a comparatively shallow ford now labeled the Crossing of the Fathers in the middle of what is now Lake Powell. They straggled back into Santa Fe January 2, 1777, after one of the most amazing treks in North American history.

In 1826, Jedediah Smith made a round trip between southern California and northern Utah through the Escalante Valley. In 1844-1845, Army Captain John C. Frémont crossed the Great Basin and described it in detail with maps in his published journal.

In 1846, members of the Church of Jesus Christ of Latter-day Saints began fleeing from severe persecution in Illinois and sought sanctuary a thousand miles to the west. On July 24, 1847, a vanguard descended a Wasatch Mountains canyon and caught sight of the Great Salt Lake valley. The leader, Brigham Young, declared, "This is the right place!"

With Salt Lake City as their capitol, the Mormons migrated quickly southward along the west side of the Wasatch Mountains and, in 1851, established Parowan and Cedar City where streams flow down off the mountains but die in the valleys. A high grade of iron ore was discovered in hills a few miles west of Cedar, but attempts to produce "pig" iron failed as the pioneers struggled to keep from starving. However, seven decades later, ore shipments by rail from Iron Mountain and Desert Mound, with their estimated 1.7 million tons of ore, started a long-term economic boost for Cedar and Lund.

In recognition of the iron ore deposits, the General Assembly of the State of Deseret created Iron County as one of six counties in 1850.

In 1862, three Pulsipher brothers wandered over the Pine Valley Mountains from present day St. George to the edge of the Escalante Valley near present day Enterprise and reported that the barren desert they saw was useless. However, by 1872, there were two hundred Mormon settlers in that far south end of the valley, and it became an irrigated farm empire.

In several reports in the 1980s, Norman Laub, a self-styled historian with flamboyant writing skills, described the "agricultural empire" that materialized between Enterprise, Newcastle, and Beryl, claiming it had 220 irrigation wells serving 30,000 acres. The irrigation success that followed the desolation of failed homesteading was attributed to efforts of what he called the National Rural Electrification Asociation to bring power to pumps for the wells. The first well in the area was drilled by Harry Payne in 1910. The main crops were grain, alfalfa, and potatoes. After detailing the value of the crops, Laub expressed concern about some irrigation practices and possible disastrous contamination of the ground water supply.

Petroglyphs pecked onto a cliff in the Parowan Gap on the Parowan/Lund road indicate that the region was populated between 400 A.D. and 1300 A.D. The early-day residents were followed by bands of Southern Paiute Indians who nearly starved every year.

Mormon settlers took over most of the "good" land that had been occupied by fragments of Paiute bands, but generally helped the Indians continue to survive decades of failed treaties and neglect by the federal government. A reservation was established in 1915 at Indian Peaks in the Wah Wah Mountains northwest of Lund and expanded several times. However, the Indians had no dependable way of making a living and by the 1940s were concentrated in a village on Cedar City's northeast boundary. A few of them continued to trek through Lund on visits to the Wah Wah Mountains clear up to the 1950s where they gathered pinyon pine nuts, one of their staple foods.

A series of federal government programs finally stabilized the Indians' economic status by the end of the century.

Chapter 9

Homestead Worries

On the Johnston homestead in June 1915, green shoots of the flint corn were poking up a half foot high in a spotty pattern for Harley's first ten-acre crop of grain, but there was only a smattering of green leaves where there was supposed to be ten acres of alfalfa. Two weeks of 90-degree temperatures and steady wind seemed to stop any growth in the fields, but then several thunderstorms pelted the fields. The flint corn resumed growing but the alfalfa sulked.

In her first months on the homestead, Mary was so caught up in coping with her new life she hardly had time to think about the choices she had made the previous year. She walked through the brush to the Bentleys' house several times, and Lorraine visited her once a week, and their talks over a cup of tea about their families and husbands helped keep Mary from dredging up regrets about her marriage and dislocation. In the words of poet Robert Frost, she had chosen a "road less traveled," and it was certainly making all the difference in her life. Harley never wavered from the road to a farm he had chosen.

However, the pitiless sun, the relentless shadowless desert wind, and the dawn-to-dusk workload began to take their toll on Mary. She grimly remembered what her one-time good friend and counselor Flo Nelson had told her about marriage, dressing "prettily" and going out to dinner.

Mary had written several letters to her mother and brothers since her arrival, describing her duties and, in general, the atmosphere of the desert but she had managed to seem optimistic. Then one afternoon, after a particularly windy morning of washing clothes and after making sure Harley was at the far end of the fields, she sat down and wrote a letter.

> Dear Mother,
>
> I'm so tired and blue I don't know what to do. Harley has tried hard to make the house half way livable but it is really just a drafty

and dusty shack. I thank the Lord every day for the few times I get to visit with my neighbor, Mrs. Bentley, but I sure do miss Santa Barbara and you and the boys. I miss all my friends and the good times we used to have. I miss the church and the music and playing a piano. Although I have been told the weather here has been milder than usual, it is still a test of endurance compared with Santa Barbara weather.

Harley tries to cheer me up when he knows I am tired and blue but he is so determined to make a farm in this Godforsaken place that he doesn't realize what it is like for me. I wish I could come home for a while but I can't leave him. He would go crazy, and besides we can't afford the train ticket for me. We still have money in the bank but from the looks of things now we won't get a crop to sell, and the only way we get any money now is the few times Harley can rent out the mules and wagon. He is working very hard all day every day, and it doesn't seem to bother him.

I know you can tell me I made my bed so I have to sleep in it. I am not a quitter but I wish we could just have a little bit of fun somehow like we used to have at the church socials and at Goleta but there is nothing to do here, not even a Saturday night dance, in Lund or in Beryl, the next little railroad town south of us. If I can get through the summer when all the field work is done, I might try to start a Sunday school in Lund.

I love Harley and I know he loves me but I wish we could have stayed in California like you wanted us to. You will probably say I told you so but please help me not to give up.

Your loving daughter

Mary

Mary tucked the letter inside her purse, and, a few days later on her next visit to Lund, she mailed it without Harley's knowledge. A week later, the Bentleys' brought a reply letter to her from the Lund post office, and she was able to read it and hide it before Harley came in from the bush whacking.

Dear daughter,

I am very sorry you are feeling so bad. As you admitted, you did make your bed and you should sleep in it but I am not so sure you have to. I would normally be the last to advise you to leave your husband and maybe get a divorce or anything like that but I worry about what may happen to you and whether you can stay healthy in those conditions. It would be nice if everything turned out to be hunky-dory but life is not like that. If you decide you can't stand it

> any longer and have to come home, let me and the boys know, and we can help you with a train ticket. You have always been used to working hard and not having much money so maybe you can stick it out there at least for a while longer.
>
> The boys send you their sympathy and best wishes.
>
> With all our love
> Mother

Mary read the letter several times, looked out the kitchen window where bushes were rippling in the wind, and muttered, "I can be just as tough as those bushes." Nevertheless, there were similar exchanges of letters for the rest of the year, and the ones around Christmas time were especially poignant. Her sarcastically-worded description of baths only on Saturday nights with the frenzied heating of water in pans on the stove and standing naked in a tub in the kitchen amused her brothers. And in the comfort of their seaside town, they could not imagine daylong dust storms that blew across the desert and over the homestead. She received several letters from brother Quil assuring her, "Things will get better."

While Mary kept in touch with her Santa Barbara family, painful though it was at times, correspondence with Flo Nelson in Phoenix faded to zero within a year. Remembering how Flo had assumed the previous summer that Mary and Harley would stay in Santa Barbara, Mary's initial letters to her downplayed the rigors of homestead life and the desert desolation. Nevertheless, Flo's responses made it clear she disapproved of the choices Mary had made, and, after a few months, she ceased writing.

As soon as Mary's garden showed signs of life, a band of long-eared jack rabbits showed voracious interest in the kind of greenery the desert did not produce even in a wet spring. The first shoots of carrots and sweet corn disappeared before Harley could get a makeshift chicken wire fence around the garden. From then on Mary proudly watched and hoed and watered her crop of corn, carrots, and potatoes but the tomatoes and their vines kept wilting in the steady wind. At the start, the Bentleys and Harley had to help Mary decide which bits of new green were weeds and which were vegetables.

In the kitchen, after Mary got a Dutch oven, she learned the mysteries of sour dough bread, a staple of pioneers and mountain fur trappers for many decades. Mary got starter dough, a remote cousin of yeast, from Mrs. Bentley who had gotten her starter from a veteran (one year) homesteader to the south. Nearly every day, cups of flour were added with water to the fermenting dough in a two-quart porcelain jar. And normally every day, a batch of the dough could be mixed with a dash of baking powder and baked as biscuits or bread or fried as thick pancakes. Too much baking powder produced a bitter taste. The jar stayed in the family for twenty-five years, including fifteen years in a sheep camp.

Another lesson Mary learned was that any liquid took longer to boil at the mile-high altitude than she and many homestead wives from sea-level towns were used to. They discovered that an egg took four minutes instead of three minutes to become soft-boiled.

Homesteaders did not routinely get newspapers or mail order catalogues, for example, that could be used for paper to start fires in the stoves. Sometimes, Harley would buy a pile of unsold newspapers at the Lund store to be used for toilet paper and fire starter.

Harley and Mary usually visited Lund every week—sometimes they traded off with the Bentleys—to get mail, do some pinched-penny shopping, and gradually become acquainted with a few of the town residents and other homesteaders. Their three-mile trip one way was easier than for many other homesteaders who lived eight to ten miles from Lund. For visits in good weather, Mary usually switched from her dark gray work dresses to a pink dress with a few ruffles, a shawl, and a floral print bonnet. She made Harley wear clean overalls and a clean shirt. Their appearance evoked a mix of envy and disdain among some of their peers but Mary would not be deterred. She was better educated by at least two years than most of the other homesteaders, and she often wished the people could talk about something besides the weather and farm chores.

The wagon rides were cool, windy and dusty in the spring months, hot, windy and dusty in summer, almost pleasant in fall when the rabbit brush turned deep yellow, and often bitterly cold in winter requiring mittens, heavy coats, and ear-flap caps. Mary wore earmuffs because she did not want to hide her wavy brown hair. Snow storms were infrequent, and snow depths rarely exceeded six inches.

A highlight of the visits to Lund was the arrival of a passenger train with many whistle toots, clanging of bells, and belches of smoke and steam from the locomotive. There were flurries of excitement as residents greeted arriving relatives and curiously examined other newcomers. Some passengers, lugging heavy suitcases, hurried to the combination livery stable and automobile garage to arrange transportation to Cedar City and Parowan. Some wanted to talk about free homestead farms.

In July, Harley and Mary splurged on a rented automobile trip to Cedar City to open a checking account at the Bank of Southern Utah where they were customers for 40 years except for a lapse in the depths of the Great Depression. Money from Harley's bank account in Los Angeles and Mary's account in Santa Barbara were consolidated into a joint account. It occurred to Mary that the consolidation would greatly reduce her option of returning to California.

By early August, the flint corn had reached its maximum height of three feet, and the leaves began turning tan. The stubby ears had hard kernels about half the size of normal field corn but, in Harley's eyes, he had won the battle for his very first crop on his very own farm. In Mary's eyes, the corn was a sorry excuse for a crop but she kept her opinion to herself except for a few wry comments to Lorraine Bentley. Harley kept some of the corn to feed the mules and sold a wagon load each to several homesteaders.

The spotty patches of alfalfa got only a few inches high but alfalfa is fairly drought resistant and develops very deep roots so there was a prospect that hay could be harvested the second year.

Russian thistle, the ubiquitous weed that would spring up on nearly any piece of open land, competed with the anemic alfalfa. In places where it could grow unchecked, the thistle became two-foot diameter tumbleweeds—desert rovers that the wind rolled across the treeless land and piled up against any fences that got in the way.

Jack rabbits, who usually ate salt grass and weeds but could smell a garden a mile away, continued to haunt Mary's vegetable patch. Each morning, she had to check to see whether an especially resourceful and energetic rabbit had dug under or squeezed under the wire mesh fence. Some settlers

Tumbleweeds

trapped or shot jack rabbits for meat, but there was some danger in eating rabbits that might have a disease called tularemia. Homesteaders tried many ways—shooting, poisoning, trapping—to keep the pests from almost wiping out new crops but results were often frustrating. A standard joke was: "If you kill twenty rabbits, forty will show up at the funerals."

Mary could cope with the rabbits, and she gradually lost her fear of coyotes and sometimes enjoyed their nocturnal concerts. However, she remained fearful of other wildlife on the desert. Although rattlesnakes mostly frequented the gravelly uplands and foothills, one could sometimes be found on the desert floor along with non-poisonous bull snakes. Mary was in no hurry to learn the difference despite the custom of some homesteaders to kill rattlesnakes and keep the rattles as souvenirs. Long-tailed gray lizards up to ten inches in length scurried through the bushes along with gophers and long-tailed kangaroo rats. Mary never saw a badger, and, after hearing descriptions of their long teeth and claws, was glad she did not have to go walking where she might stumble on a den.

Bird life was sparse except for occasional flocks of small brown sparrows. The doleful songs of a few mourning doves drifted from railroad telegraph poles and the roofs of farm buildings. Occasionally, on spring mornings, a meadow lark's warble interrupted the desert silence. A variety of hawks rode updrafts and soared on silent wings.

To the surprise of most homesteaders, there were many insects in the desert including grasshoppers, black beetles called stink bugs, and, to Mary's horror, a few scorpions.

Occasionally a band of wild horses could be seen on the horizon with a stallion making sure his mares did not stray. Homesteaders sometimes discovered their mares were missing, lured away by a stallion. In one or two cases, the wayward mares found free range life was tough, and they returned to their corrals, rations of hay, and troughs of cool water.

In September Harley had to decide what to do with twenty acres he was clearing of brush. He planned to continue with the first twenty acres in corn and alfalfa and experiment with barley on the newly-cleared land. The choice was whether to wait until spring to plant the grain or go for winter barley with planting in the fall so that it would sprout quickly, go dormant through the winter, resume growth in the spring after winter snow moisture, and be ready for harvest in mid-summer. He decided to try the winter program, and, after that, he would test the dry land farming technique of leaving land fallow for a year to allow moisture to build up in the soil.

After the barley planting in October, Harley put thin wood shingles on the house roof. He also began installing quarter-inch thick, cardboard-like, paneling on interior walls and laying the cheapest kind of linoleum on the floors to cover cracks and provide some insulation against winter weather.

As winter approached, Harley hauled several more loads of firewood from the foothills. Mary accompanied him on one trip but felt uncomfortable in the forbidding terrain beyond sight of any house or the railroad. To make matters worse, she caught sight of a small animal that appeared to be covered with long black-tipped spikes. Harley told her it was a porcupine and warned her to stay far away from it. He thought it best not to mention that there might be a few bobcats and mountain lions in the foothills.

In December Mary missed her period, and by January it was clear that she was pregnant. She had been fairly diligent in the contraception douches after love-making, but she recalled that the doctor in Los Angeles had warned her there was no guarantee that the procedure would prevent pregnancy. The rigorous challenges of desert homestead life made it seem unwise to have a baby, certainly not while the whole farming venture was tenuous. Also, having a baby would greatly reduce the possibility that she could leave Harley and return to Santa Barbara. Nevertheless, now that she was pregnant, she was determined to make the best of it, and, anyway, she and Harley wanted children so they might as well get started. The improvements to the house interior made it more hospitable for a family.

Mary waited until the third month to be absolutely sure before telling Harley. But she immediately confided in Lorraine Bentley and was eternally grateful for the support she found there. Lorraine had, from time to time, quietly strengthened Mary's basic inclination to stick with Harley.

The two women were well-educated by the standards of the day. Lorraine had graduated at the head of her class in high school. Both were energetic, gregarious, and in love with their farm-loving husbands. The two took turns as dinner hosts every few weeks. At first, Mary was afraid her cooking would not measure up to that of the older woman but it was soon clear that neither had an opportunity for gourmet meals. They teased each other about who had the best or the worst dinner.

Over a cup of tea, Mary told Lorraine about being pregnant and about her emotional conflicts.

"As you have guessed by now," Mary said, "I've been struggling to cope with this desert homestead life that is so totally different from the life I had in Santa Barbara. I confess I have thought more than once about leaving and simply going back home even though my home is supposed to be here with my husband. Now that I'm pregnant, I wonder about going back to California to have the baby, probably in a hospital there with a doctor, instead of gambling on a delivery here in the desert so far from medical help. Of course, if I went back, it might mean the end of my marriage. Harley would be unhappy."

Lorraine reached across the table to take Mary's hand. "I have a good idea of what you're going through. As I have mentioned only a little bit before now, I had two children. The first one, a boy, died of scarlet fever at the age of five, and the second one, a daughter that I wanted so badly, died at birth. That left me with complications so I can't have children any more. The second death made me very upset so when Tom started talking about coming west to find a free homestead farm, I thought a major change might help me get over the blues."

Mary asked, "Now that you've had a good taste of desert homesteading, have you thought about going back to Ohio?"

"Yes, I have thought about that quite a few times but since both Harley and Tom are so set on having their own farms, I believe we have to chase the rainbow for a few years and see what happens. I realize how worried you might be about having the baby here but I've had experience with being pregnant and with births, and I'll be a good midwife if you decide to stick it out here. Frankly, you might as well start having a family now."

"Oh, bless you, Lorraine. It's such a comfort to talk to you, and I know I can depend on you to help with the baby. And the more I think about it, the more I realize I better stay here with Harley. It's a hard life but I am glad I got married."

"We do have good husbands, better than a lot of women have and better than we would probably find if we went looking for something else!"

Mary wrote to her mother that she would soon become a grandmother and to her brothers that they would soon be uncles. Mother King congratulated her but, as might be expected, expressed concern about her only daughter having a baby in a desert far from a doctor and hospital. The brothers got together and sent her a box full of diapers, little blue nightgowns, and blue blankets on the blithe assumption the baby would be a boy.

Over dinner on Valentine's Day, Mary told Harley.

"You are about to become a father."

"What are you talking about?"

"I'm pregnant. We will have a baby, probably in August."

"Well, I'll be darned. Hallelujah!"

Harley reared up from the table, knocked over his chair, hugged and kissed Mary when she stood up with tears in her eyes for the moment.

"I will do the clothes washing from now on," Harley shouted.

"That won't be necessary for quite a few months. But do you promise?"

"Yes, I promise."

The winter of 1915–1916 was unusually severe with several storms of up to six inches of snow and thermometer readings near zero. The road to Lund remained passable but became slick and muddy after each of the snows melted as they did within a few days. When the desert sun glared down, mid-day temperatures soared to 50 degrees. Each snow, regardless of the inconvenience, was hailed with prayers of thanks for the moisture that provided a special benefit for Harley's winter barley.

At dawn on winter mornings, Harley scrambled out of bed and hurriedly started a fire in the stove before getting dressed. Mary was allowed to stay in bed until the stove started to warm the kitchen.

In April at the start of the couple's second year on the homestead, Harley resumed field work, replanting ten acres in flint corn. Soil moisture from the snow storms helped the corn get a good start, produced enough growth on the first alfalfa field for one cutting of hay, and enabled the winter barley to be six inches high by May 15. Thereafter there were only a few scattered thunderstorms, the corn crop was meager in August, and the field of alfalfa remained anemic. However, the barley did well enough to warrant renting a small threshing machine and was the first significant cash crop for the Johnston farm.

It provided a half dozen wagon loads for sale as feed for farm animals in the area plus feed for Harley's mules for the coming winter. The income only partly replenished the couple's bank account which was steadily dwindling.

When the heat of summer arrived, Mary was very big with child and was increasingly uncomfortable. She had to turn over much of the work in her garden plus clothes washing on Mondays to Harley. One saving grace of the mile-high desert weather was that, although afternoon temperatures could reach into the 90s, the nights were always cool enough to require a sheet over the bed.

Mary had obtained a manual on child birth and care from a mail order house, and, with advice from Lorraine, prepared to become a mother. With a crop that produced a significant amount of cash, with the baby on the way, and with continued good health, Mary wrote her mother that she was "settling in" and was not considering a return to Santa Barbara. That euphoria wore thin within a year and was replaced by sorrow and despair within two years.

On August 9, 1916, Harlan King Johnston was born in the dusty homestead house. He was a husky seven pounds with blue eyes and red hair inherited from his grandfather King. Lorraine Bentley was the official midwife. She made Harley stay outside until he heard Harlan squalling. The new papa burst into the bedroom to find Mary exhausted, covered with sweat and hoarse from stifled screams of pain. Lorraine bathed the baby, wrapped him in a blue blanket, and laid him in the cradled arms of mother and father. Harley was ecstatic about having a son, and Mary was resigned to waiting for a daughter.

Lorraine had knitted two pairs of little booties. Used flour sacks supplemented the diapers that the Santa Barbara uncles had sent. Mary sewed a few other garments from a worn-out shirt. Harley had built a makeshift crib and had stuffed rags in a pillow case for a mattress.

Mary breast-fed Harlan, and he grew fast and chubby and loud-mouthed. She had to wash his stinky diapers by hand on the washboard. It was the task she disliked most about having a baby but for the rest of the time she reveled in being a new mother, not even greatly minding the early morning feedings and diaper-changing.

After the skimpy harvests on homesteads around Lund ended in September, the residents found time to lighten up with a Thanksgiving Day potluck dinner at a new one-room grade school in the town and started scheduling Saturday night dances there. Mary and Harley

Lund school house

bundled up Harlan and joined the Bentleys in their wagon for trips to the Thanksgiving festival and to a Christmas time dance, returning home near midnight while coyotes howled in the darkness. When severe winter weather came, the dances were postponed until springtime.

Mary especially missed her Santa Barbara church activities so she and Harley helped organize Sunday School programs that were held for several years at scattered homes in the homestead neighborhood of the Ford railroad siding. In the spring of 1917, Harley, who had participated in many isolated farm area social events in Nebraska and Missouri, was elected to serve six months as superintendent of the Sunday School program. The sessions were more about simply socializing than about religion.

World War I was raging through farm fields in France and continued to raise speculation that there would be a sharp increase in the price of grain everywhere, even in the Escalante desert. With a total of about 40 acres under cultivation, Harley had met the legal requirement that at least one-eighth of a 320-acre homestead be cultivated within three years. The speculation about grain prices added to the challenge for him and all homesteaders to get improved production.

In the fall of 1916, Harley made an agonizing and gambling decision. He would continue growing ten acres of flint corn and ten acres of alfalfa in the coming year, but the twenty acres that had been used for winter barley would be left fallow until the spring of 1918. Under some recommendations for dry land farming, land left fallow for up to two years would accumulate enough moisture to produce a crop much better than an annual planting. Harley, who unfortunately was still remembering fields of tall regular corn in Missouri, thought the fallowed twenty acres might produce that kind of a high value crop.

A snow storm in April 1917 and some showers in May got the flint corn and alfalfa fields off to a good start. The flint corn harvest was adequate in August, and there were two cuttings of alfalfa, enough to provide some hay for sale and plenty of wintertime feed for the mules.

While one-year-old Harlan, happy and healthy, snoozed in a shaded box nearby, Mary worked nearly every day in her garden which produced gratifying yields of a sack of potatoes, piles of sweet corn, other vegetables, and even a few tomatoes. The cool slightly damp cellar allowed some of the garden produce to be kept for several months along with a bushel of tangy Jonathan apples purchased at the Lund Store. Harlan had learned to like oatmeal gruel with the inevitable Carnation canned milk.

After Harlan passed his first birthday and the farm production reached a survival level, Mary began planning for a second child. If she ceased the contraception procedure in October, she could expect a baby in June which would seem to be a timely event in the fourth year of marriage.

She brought up the subject at dinner one night and caught Harley off guard.

"You sure you want to do this? I know it has been pretty tough on you out here after the good life you left in Santa Barbara. A second child will mean a lot more work and worry."

"Yes, I'm sure. Harlan is doing so well, and we both enjoy him. I think we should have several children, and, who knows, you may need more boys to help with the farm. Having a baby is a burden on me, not you. You have the easy part."

"Well, I have to admit that I'm not getting any younger. I won't have to work hard on this easy part, will I?"

"Oh, poor you, worrying it might get hard!"

Harley laughed, and Mary blushed at the unintended double entendre.

Mary followed her plan, Harley happily cooperated, and by mid-December she was sure she was pregnant. She told everybody and spent the winter looking forward to the family addition.

On April 6, 1917, the U.S. Congress declared war on Germany, and patriotic fervor swept the nation. World War I was supposed to make the world safe for democracy, and the wars thereafter were supposed to make other countries safe for democracy.

Involvement in the first world war had little effect in and around Lund where newly-arrived homesteader families seldom included young single males of draft age. There was a surge in the existing speculation that war-ravaged Europe would badly need foreign grain which would be a boon for even the minimal products of the Escalante desert.

Harry, Earl and Harley Johnston.
Harley's two brothers visited the homesteaded land in Lund, circa 1920.

At Christmas time, the Doolittle merchandise store and warehouse in Lund gave candy and popcorn balls to children and handed out cigarettes to soldiers on troop trains that stopped for water.

Earl G. Johnston, the youngest of Harley's brothers, was 23 years old, single, and working for the Union Pacific railroad in Nebraska. He was drafted into the Army and slogged through mud in several of the final battles prior to the Armistice on November 11, 1918. When Earl wrote to Harley about being drafted, Mary wrote a letter to him, wishing him good luck and a safe return to civilian life.

Earl survived without harm, returned to the states, married a beautiful and strong-willed woman named Evelyn Pattersfield, June 22, 1919, and went to work for the Union Pacific at Lynndyl, Utah, about 80 miles north of Lund. Evelyn was not happy in the little town, and when she and Earl quarreled, he would visit his older brother in Lund for consolation. They had three children who, in later years, would sometimes visit their cousins in Lund using Earl's Union Pacific pass. Eventually the couple split, and she took the kids to southern California.

Although Harley's and Mary's bank account was slowly dwindling, the couple agreed Mary should take Harland and squeeze in a few Yule days with her mother and brothers (Harlan's grandmother and uncles) in Santa Barbara. Since Mary was pregnant and expecting a baby in six months, it was unlikely she would have a good opportunity to "go home" again in the next few years.

Chapter 10

Elizabeth and the Dream's Ending

Right on schedule, June 15, 1918, Elizabeth Lorraine Johnston was born in the still dusty and drafty homestead house where Harlan had arrived. Mrs. Bentley, flattered to have the baby partly named after her, was again the midwife. Again the birth was strenuous but successful, and Harley and Mary were delighted to now have a son and a daughter. Elizabeth was slightly smaller than Harlan had been at birth. She had Harley's blue eyes and blonde hair. With Mary's breast feeding, she grew rapidly, and two-year-old Harlan showed signs of jealousy over the attention she received.

In late April prior to the birth of Elizabeth, Harley planted the 20 fallowed acres in standard field corn but hedged his bet by continuing with 10 acres of flint corn. The alfalfa field appeared to promise two meager cuttings of hay. The winter of 1917–1918 had been fairly mild with less snow than the previous winter. However, light rains in late spring had gotten the crops off to an encouraging start. Harley spent long days hoeing the rows of sprouting field corn.

Then, for six weeks, the sky remained brassy blue every day, the sun glared down, and the implacable dry wind from the southwest seemed never to cease, not even at night. The 20 acres of field corn shriveled and the alfalfa drooped. Only the sturdy flint corn showed any life although stunted. Harley fretted, and Mary prayed. In painfully tantalizing fashion, billowing thunderstorm clouds with flat pewter-colored bottoms and whipped cream tops rolled over the valley several times with streaks of lightning, but only one stopped to pound the area for a few minutes in late July. The moisture was too little and too late, and the violence of the storm beat down the already tired alfalfa.

All around Lund and Beryl, other homesteaders had gambled, like on a roll of the dice, on a bumper crop for one last time, but the dice came up snake eyes.

At the Johnston place, the fields yielded enough food for the mules and chickens for a few more months, but the human beings were facing a return to sour dough biscuits and bacon for dinner after the produce of Mary's garden was gone.

The Bentleys' fields were no better than Harley's, and the couples sadly compared notes over dinner on Tom's 40th birthday. They discussed whether they could last another year. If they spent their last dollar trying to salvage the men's dreams, they would not have enough money to move back to where they came from or to try something someplace else. The railroad and the few businesses in Lund and Beryl offered very few employment opportunities, and the many homesteaders who were going broke would compete for a job of any kind. The dinner ended on a note of sadness and uncertainty.

For thousands of years, long-term droughts changed the course of human history from the time a Biblical Joseph gave a warning to an Egyptian Pharaoh to the sudden disappearance of the Anasazi from Colorado cliff dwellings to this experiment with dry land farming in the American dust bowl of the 1930s. A summer drought in the Escalante desert would not be even a blip in the history of the world or of the desert, but it was a life-changing event for dozens of families.

Harley took his book about the Campbell method of dry land farming to the outhouse and used its pages for toilet paper.

By September, he had cleared the fields of what grain and hay he could salvage. He began visiting other homesteaders to see what had happened to them that summer, whether they planned to stay or leave, and what the prospects were for selling his farm implements and mules.

In the fall of 1918, Harley and Mary made their final sacrificial offerings to the unforgiving god of desert homesteads.

In the middle of the month when Elizabeth was four months old, she began to cry unusually long and often and sometimes writhed as if in pain. She began rejecting even liquid food and appeared to be bloated. Mary was frantic and tried all the home remedies, such as Paregoric, she and several neighboring women could think of, but nothing seemed to help. Then the baby ceased crying and became listless.

Finally an anguished Mary told Harley they would have to get her to a doctor in Cedar City. A two-day round trip there by wagon was out of the question. They took Harlan to stay with the Bentleys and then drove the mule-drawn wagon to Lund where Harley persuaded Jim Lunt to use his new Model A Ford to drive them to the hospital as a medical emergency for two dollars. Mary bundled up Elizabeth and set off with Harley and Lunt for the two-hour dusty and bumpy ride to Cedar City.

At the hospital, a doctor quickly examined Elizabeth who was now colorless and quiet. The doctor came out of the examination room and faced Harley and Mary, shaking his head. "I'm so sorry. She's dead. I can't be sure of the cause without an autopsy but there is really no need for that. My best guess is that she developed a blockage of the big intestine. That would of course cause bloating and be very painful. I know you live out in the desert and it's difficult to get to Cedar, but if I had seen her a few days earlier I might have been able to save her with an operation. At her age and in her condition even an operation might not have helped."

Mary began to sob and clung to Harley for a few minutes. He was unable to say anything except, "There, there."

Mary stood up, wiped her eyes, and said, "Let's go home." She turned to the doctor and said, "We will take her home and bury her there."

Harley picked up the tiny bundle, and they went out to the car where Jim Lunt could tell from their faces what had happened. Without a word, he started the car, and they headed back on the long painful journey to Lund followed by the wagon trip back to the homestead in late afternoon. Mary wept quietly most of the way, and Harley stared stoically out over the gray-tan desert.

At the house, Mary told Harley, "You go tell the neighbors. We'll have a funeral in the morning." She bathed Elizabeth's cold little body and dressed her in a white gown on which Mary had embroidered pink roses. She put the body in the crib and went to the kitchen to fix dinner.

Harley went to the Bentleys, told them what had happened, and they agreed to help provide a very simple funeral at 11 o'clock the next morning. Harley took Harlan home and struggled to explain to him that the baby was going away. Harlan, who was just learning to talk, did not understand but he soon sensed that his mother and father were very upset.

Tom Bentley rode to several homesteads where the residents had become friends of the Johnstons and told them what was happening. He returned home and immediately constructed a little box of pine boards for a coffin.

Mary and Harley ate supper and did the evening chores in painful silence. A totally exhausted Mary went to the bedroom and lay down on the bed. Harley could hear her sobbing for half an hour. They went to bed and clung to each other through a long night, made more heartbreaking by the mournful wails of several coyotes.

Tom Bentley came over the first thing in the morning with the tiny coffin. He and Harley put the body in the box and nailed a lid on it. They then dug a narrow grave three feet deep in a strip of brush about 100 yards north of the house.

At 11 o'clock the neighbors arrived and gathered around the grave. While Mary and Harley stared into the distance, Tom served as a minister.

"We are gathered to bury Elizabeth Lorraine Johnston, a sweet and beloved baby who God decided to take away too soon. She will be waiting in heaven for her parents, Mary and Harley, and her brother, Harlan. May God grant them peace and strength to continue on." Lorraine read the 23rd Psalm from her family Bible, and Tom said, "Now, let us say the Lord's Prayer."

Tom and the neighbors lowered the coffin into the grave, shoveled dirt over it, and placed a foot-high cross made of sticks on the mound while Harley, Mary, and the women trudged back to the house. Lorraine Bentley had brought a basket of sandwiches and hard-boiled eggs for lunch for the group.

The next day Harley went to the lumber yard in Lund and bought a foot-high galvanized metal grave marker in the shape of a cross with an opening in the center. He wrote on a piece of cardboard, "Elizabeth Johnston, Beloved Daughter, 1918," inserted it in the opening, and used the metal marker to replace the cross of sticks on the grave.

Mary never visited the site.

The October weather on the desert was warm and golden with only gentle breezes, but Elizabeth's death had left a gray chill in the Johnston household. Harlan continued to grow and be healthy and boisterous, but his parents were haunted by the thought that any day he, like Elizabeth, could become ill and die before they could get him to a doctor. Mary knew from reading about pioneers, and Harley knew from his years on Midwest farms, that childhood deaths from disease, illness and injuries were a fact of life in isolated rural areas but such knowledge offered little solace. Both parents thought it but didn't say it—if they had stayed in Los Angeles or Santa Barbara, Elizabeth would probably still be alive and they would not have to worry about Harlan.

For several weeks after Elizabeth's death, Mary was almost catatonic. She went about her household chores as if in a daze and spoke only when spoken to. Harley didn't know what to do. He didn't have the temperament nor communication skills to comfort her beyond pats on her back and platitudes such as "It will be all right." Lorraine Bentley was worried but she too could not help much and could only assure Harley that time would heal the hurt.

Mary wrote a letter to her mother and brothers describing the death and funeral in a facts-only manner, but she did confess she wished she were back home in Santa Barbara among family and old time friends and in a setting she loved. Mother King and the boys replied with letters of condolence and tactfully refrained from any version of "I told you so." They wished she would come home at least for a visit.

Mary said nothing to Harley about going back to California for a visit because she knew as well as he did that they simply couldn't afford it. However, the death of her second born and the near total failure of the crops intensified her dislike of the desert and homestead farm life and enhanced her nostalgia for the golden days in California. Her despair reached a level she had not felt since the second and third months after her arrival when the novelty of the new life had worn off and reality had set in.

Now, however, quitting was even less of an option. If she left Harley now and took their son with her, it would be a very bitter end to their marriage, an embarrassment over the failure of the move to Utah, and a challenge to find a way to support herself and Harlan. If she could convince Harley to leave the farm and return to civilized life in California, he would probably never be happy and probably never entirely forgive her for giving up. All she could do was to sit tight and see what would happen.

Harley was at least sensitive enough to have an idea about the struggle she was undergoing. However by his nature and from his many years on farms he had a more fatalistic attitude toward life and death. He hurt but not nearly as much as she did, and he was soon ready to simply move on to whatever they had to do next.

The fields he had cultivated and the "improvements" he had made on the half section met the homestead law requirements for issuance of a patent as a form of title. Harley, quietly determined to come out of the experience with at least ownership of some land, hired Jim Lunt to take him to the county courthouse in Parowan where he filled out papers for the patent. It came in the mail a few weeks later.

On a cold and gray early November afternoon, Harley came in from the barn an hour earlier than usual, put a cup of cold coffee on the stove to get warm, and waited for Mary to get Harlan up from his nap. She came into the kitchen, holding the thumb-sucking little boy, and Harley motioned for her to sit down beside him.

"Well, dearie, I guess I have to give up on this darn farm idea and go get a job some place. I've tried my hardest to grow enough stuff here that we could at least make a living but, as you well know, it hasn't worked out. Dry land farming may work in other places but not in this darn desert. We should be able to hang onto the homestead land, and maybe someday we can come back here with enough money to put in a deep well for irrigation but I'm afraid that will be quite a while."

Mary hugged baby Harlan and looked out the fly-specked window so Harley could not see the relief and joy on her face at the prospect of leaving. After a moment to compose herself, she turned to Harley. "I'm sorry we have to give up. I know how much you wanted to have a good farm of your own, and I've worried about you working so hard from sunrise to sunset. But I certainly agree that we can't keep on going here. Right now, we still have enough money in the bank that we can move and try to rent a house somewhere else."

Mary was careful to stop short of suggesting that somewhere else might be in southern California, even Santa Barbara. Her relief at hearing they would not remain on the homestead was stunted by his reference to possibly returning someday to start an irrigation farm where her life probably would not be a lot different than on the dry land farm. Nevertheless, she felt the occasion was cause for what, in her mind, would be a celebration dinner with the Bentleys as guests.

They came the next day as the sun became a red ball slipping behind the dark lavender horizon. Lorraine sensed that Mary had changed from her mourning mood and was a little excited about something.

The hostess had fixed a roasted chicken dinner that reminded all of them about their first dinner together three years earlier.

Midway through dinner, Mary could wait no longer for Harley to bring up the news. "We have decided to give up on the homestead and move someplace else where Harley can find work. The events of the last few months have been so heart breaking we can't see spending another year here."

Tom put his fork down, looked at Lorraine, and said, "This is really a coincidence. We've been debating for the last few weeks about the same thing, and we are probably going to go back to Ohio. We hope to be able to move in about a month so we can be back with our families for Christmas and not have to spend another winter here. Lorraine has been ready to leave any time in the past few months the way the weather was. I hate to quit, and, Harley, I bet you hate to quit too but the party's over."

"Yeah, I guess so," Harley mumbled. "We sure can't eat dirt, and that's all there is out there in the fields. We could go back to California but as I told Mary, I want to hang onto the homestead and maybe someday I can put in irrigation here. But for now, I guess I'll look for work in Lund or maybe in Cedar."

Lorraine glanced at Mary and knew that the prospect of staying in or around the Escalante desert was disappointing. However, Lorraine had come to know the Johnstons well, and she knew that Mary would stay with Harley.

The talk turned logically enough to what was happening to homesteading in the whole Escalante Valley. Several couples a few miles to the south had already left abruptly, abandoning their tarpaper shanties without even a goodbye to neighbors. George and Martha Collard who had filed on two half sections west of the Ford siding in 1915 and who had made several attempts at farming there told Tom they were returning for good to California.

Harley said owners of businesses in Lund had told him the homestead boom was ending as rapidly as it had begun, and a lot more people were leaving on the trains than were arriving. The departures meant fewer farm-oriented customers for the businesses, but warehousing and the freighting of goods was steadily increasing between the railroad at Lund and Cedar City which was the gateway to most of southern Utah where new small towns were springing up.

Harley and Tom dejectedly agreed they would probably get only a few dollars for sale of their animals, wagons, and farm equipment, and there would be a lot of competition. They guessed that half the homesteaders in the Lund and Beryl areas would try to stick it out for maybe another year and might be willing to buy stuff at panic-motivated prices.

The homesteaded half sections of land would not be worth anything, although an optimistic homesteader who was going to hang on might pay an immediate neighbor a few dollars for an adjoining 320 acres. Otherwise, the sites would simply be abandoned, brush would reclaim the land, and thousands of acres would revert to federal government ownership.

In 1918, the deadly epidemic of influenza that swept the nation and the Escalante Valley escalated the exodus from homesteads that the lack of rain had started. The desert landscape slowly became dotted with abandoned houses—desiccated, hollow-eyed, cadavers accompanied by wagons and a few cars left to rust when they could not help their owners flee. Feeble windbreaks, even those with drought resistant and alkali-resistant Russian olive trees, lost their fight with the dry winds. Lund never had a cemetery because most of the residents never stayed long enough to die but, in some respects, the whole desert bracketing the railroad line became a graveyard.

Most of the people who left their Escalante desert homesteads would leave with broken dreams and only the clothes they were wearing. One of them getting on a train at Lund commented to no one in particular, "We just starved out."

Chapter 11

Conoco Era

The morning after the "we-give-up" dinner with the Bentleys, Harley put on his Sunday-best clothes, hitched up the mules, and headed for job-hunting in Lund. He didn't have a résumé because he didn't know anything about résumés. He would just have to talk around town. As he climbed onto the wagon, he told Mary, "If I find a job, we can move to Lund, and I'll be able to keep an eye on the homestead. If we ever get irrigation here, we can still live in town where you will be a more comfortable."

He bent over from the wagon seat to kiss Mary's upturned face. She continued to hide her disappointment over his determination to stay in Utah, but she was at least glad to know with some certainty that she would never again live in a lonely shanty. In her bravest and most cheerful voice, she told him. "I sure hope you find some work. If there's nothing in Lund, maybe we can go to Cedar City for a day or two and see if there's anything there. The homestead land here won't go away even if the wind tries to blow it away."

Harley returned late in the afternoon and reported that he would have to go back to Lund tomorrow to talk to a guy who would be coming from Cedar City.

The next day at noon, Harley returned to the homestead and unhitched the mules, whistling "Onward, Christian Soldiers." He burst through the kitchen door and shouted, "Guess what! I'm going to be an oil man. You know that company store with the big gasoline storage tank out by the stockyards on the railroad spur? One of the Lunt brothers who has a deal with the company called a franchise needs help because more and more people are getting cars and needing gas and oil.[1] He said my bookkeeping experience at the store in Los Angeles is better than several other guys he talked to about a job as a clerk. So, anyway, I go to work in two weeks, and we'll have to scramble to get moved so I won't have to use the mules every day. I'll be working about ten hours a day. The pay is good enough that we should be able to rent or even buy a house in Lund with no trouble."

Mary grabbed Harley, hugged him, and kissed him again and again. "Bless you! Bless you! I knew you could do it. We're saved. Hallelujah! Let's go over and tell the Bentleys, and if Tom still has that bottle we might even have a drink—but just one mind you!"

They went to the Bentleys, who congratulated them warmly but the joy was dampened by the neighbors' preparations to load their belongings in a freight car and return to Ohio. They had sold their horses and chickens, and Tom decided to take his farm equipment with him. The Bentleys would catch a train in two weeks, leaving on the very day Harley would start to work in Lund. That would be a day of sad good-byes especially for the two women who would never see each other again.

The Johnstons found a one-and-a-half-bedroom clapboard house for rent in Lund a block east of Main Street. It was the middle unit in a group of three houses, plus two barns and three ramshackle structures for livestock and wagons, all surrounded by a wire mesh fence. There was a long wooden gate and two small metal gates in front.

Flanking the house Harley and Mary rented was a two-story two-bedroom house and a one-story one-bedroom house. The two-story house was occupied by the family of Ed Townsend who worked at the lumber yard. The third house was vacant and for rent. Each dwelling unit had its own outhouse. The complex had been built five years earlier by a developer whose expectations that Lund would grow into a city were dampened by the fadeout of homesteading.

The Johnstons' house was square with a windowed front door and a back porch with a screen door and a screened window. Near the back porch was a sloping hinged door over steps to a cellar excavated under the house. The kitchen was long and narrow with a sturdy sideboard, a window, built-in cabinets, and a large wood-burning kitchen range. The "front" room was a combination dining room and living room with two windows and a pot-bellied stove. The main bedroom had a small walk-in closet and one window. Squeezed into a rear corner of the house was an eight-foot-square room that would serve initially as a nursery and later as a regular bedroom.

Three scraggly trees and an unkempt row of tamarisk stood in the front yard. A one-car garage in the middle of the yard was to be used by the first family to own a car.

This was to be Mary's home for the next thirty-five years. Compared to the homestead shanty, it was heaven but still a far cry from the cozy home of her childhood and youth.

Although toilet facilities continued to be a two-hole outhouse and a Combinet in the bedroom at night, there was, wonder of wonders, a sink with a faucet and cold running water in a corner of the kitchen. The sink drain led to a small cesspool behind the house, but it could be easily overloaded so water from dish washing, clothes washing, and bathing had to be thrown out into the yard.

The kitchen water faucet and the large kitchen stove with an oven were two of the major blessings for Mary in the move to Lund. Another blessing was merely the proximity of neighbors and stores.

When the Union Pacific company drilled a deep well and installed a water-softening system and a fifty-foot high water tank to serve steam locomotives, a pipeline network was added to provide free water to railroad facilities and employee housing. Lund promoters and the railroad cooperated in providing water pipelines to other properties within the platted town site. The softened water was easy on Mary's hands compared with the alkali-laced "hard" water from the homestead well.

An outdoor faucet served an eight-foot-long livestock watering trough just outside the front gate. Mary would eventually resume her

The Johnston home from 1919 to 1957.

annual vegetable gardening in a corner of the yard, thankful that all she had to do for irrigation was hook up a hose to the faucet instead of laboring over a well pump handle and pails of water.

In the kitchen, the cast iron stove top had space for four pans. Two round lids could be lifted with a special tool to feed wood into the fire box. Under the fire box was a removable container for ashes. The oven adjacent to the fire box had a drop-down front door. Two small warming ovens could also be used for utensil storage. To Mary's delight, the stove was decorated at the corners with chrome-plated scroll work.

The screened porch became Mary's clothes washing room with the tubs lined up on a sturdy bench. The tubs were only a few steps from the kitchen faucet and from the pans of heated water on the large stove so doing the laundry was almost a pleasure compared with the homestead, and there were clothes drying lines in the back yard.

While taking a bath in a tub in the kitchen was not much different from what it had been at the farm, the proximity of the faucet and the hot water on the stove was another blessing.

Within six months, Russian thistle began to reclaim the homestead fields. Wind continued to moan around the Johnstons' empty shanty-house and barn.

Harley had managed to sell his farm implements for enough money to make the initial monthly rent payments. He could walk the quarter mile from the rented house his job at the Continental Oil Company (Conoco) complex but he kept the mules and wagon for transportation and firewood hauling until purchase of a truck was possible.

Gasoline was delivered to the Conoco facility by railroad tank car and was pumped into the 1,000-gallon storage tanks there. From the tanks, barrels were filled for deliveries to Cedar City and other towns in the region to meet the growing demands of the emerging auto age. New models of trucks would soon totally replace commercial wagon hauling.

Harley worked an average of ten hours weekdays and generally a half-day on Saturdays, making $18 a week, which was a good wage at that time in Lund. Although smaller than average in stature, he was as capable of physical labor such as moving barrels as anyone else. His even temperament and wry sense of humor made him popular with customers and his half-dozen fellow workers.

The Continental Oil Company (Conoco) facility in Lund, circa 1920.

At Mary's suggestion, he agreed to buy a new set of clothes since he was now dealing with customers instead of mules and a plow. They hired Jim Lunt to take them in his Ford touring car on a shopping trip to Cedar City where Harley tactfully decided that Mary should get a new dress for two reasons—in celebration of the move to Lund and because he was getting some new clothes.

Some homesteaders who were abandoning their dreams and "going home" were willing to almost give away their furniture. Before long, the Johnstons had a round oak dining table and matching chairs, a battered sofa and overstuffed armchair, a vanity table that doubled as a desk in the living room, and a chest of drawers for the bedroom.

Although the family finances were still iffy, Harley and Mary felt they could they live it up a bit more at Christmas time than they did on the homestead. Unlike several of their homestead neighbors, they had never thought it worthwhile to make a Christmas tree of tumbleweeds. On the third Sunday after starting to work in Lund, Harley went to the foothills for firewood and returned with a five-foot high pinyon tree that Mary decorated with pieces of colored paper and a lopsided star made of used tinfoil. On Christmas Eve, they exchanged presents—a tiny bottle of perfume for Mary and a new shirt for Harley. Harlan got a new teddy bear. Their neighbors, the Townsends, invited them to Christmas Day dinner, and Mary made a lemon-flavored cake with cooked sugar frosting.

During the winter of early 1919, Mary spent much of her time just getting settled but she did so at a leisurely pace that left more time and energy for love-making than the homestead life. Thoughts about returning to Santa Barbara faded.

Sunday was supposed to be a time of rest for Harley, but he usually spent the day on some improvement project around the house or the yard or the outbuildings, one of which became a chicken coop with a row of hay-filled nests.

At the wood pile behind the house, he chopped logs from the foothills into firewood and stacked some of it in a shed to keep dry. The preferred firewood for heating was pitch-filled gnarly pinyon that burned longer and slower than kindling from juniper trees which were best known locally as cedar trees. But cedar logs were easier to split up, and Mary needed thin pieces to produce an extra hot fire in the kitchen stove for baking pies.

Harley surprised Mary on her birthday, January 25, with her choice of patterns for new linoleum for the kitchen and living room floors to be ordered from Montgomery Ward. When the shipment arrived, Harley had to spend a Sunday figuring out how to measure, cut and lay the linoleum without creasing it.

For the first time since her marriage, Mary found a few hours each week to get back to reading books which had long been one of her favorite past-times. She had brought a few books with her including a cherished copy of *A Girl of the Limberlost* by Gene Stratton Porter. It was bound in brown suede leather with gilt lettering on the cover. There was always a clothbound Bible on the vanity table, and Mary turned to it occasionally to seek solace from some new worry.

Lund was certainly no substitute for Santa Barbara where the gregarious Mary had many friends and many social activities. Nevertheless, compared to the homestead, the small town offered daily opportunities to meet and talk with people next door or at the businesses and post office. The one-room school house was the center of social life, and it was only a block from the Johnstons' new home.

In addition to their immediate neighbors the Townsends, Harley and Mary gradually became well acquainted with other Lund residents such as David Leigh who ran the lumber yard, Harry J. Doolittle who owned a wholesale and warehouse business and was considered the richest man in town, the Jasper Cartwright family that operated a small hotel, Bob and Betty Couch who had given up on a homestead ten miles north of Lund, and Bill and Corda Stafford who had also homesteaded north of Lund. The Johnstons' longest-term friendships were with

General Store in Lund owned by J. David Leigh, circa 1915

the Arlie Fourman and Oscar Frahske families, both of whom stuck with their homesteads for three decades.

The Couches came from Arkansas and started their homestead in 1913. They had a deep well, some irrigated crops, and a landscaped yard that was an oasis in the desert. But the desolation and hard winters took their toll, so the Couches moved to Lund. Their shingle-covered home had a half-acre backyard where they "stored" old farm equipment. The implements sat rusting among springtime waves of purple stinkweeds until they were sold for scrap metal during World War II. The Couch family included a daughter, Jewel, who was one of the prettiest young women ever in Lund, and sons Verle who had a penchant for mechanics and Wallace who liked carpentry.

Corda and Bill Stafford were from Missouri. Corda married Bill at age sixteen and followed him to California. In 1916, he decided to try homesteading in Utah so they loaded up a freight car with equipment and livestock in Los Angeles early that year and set out for the middle of the Escalante desert. In their first year, they built a shanty, dug a well, sold their cow for lack of hay, ate their chickens and geese, and planted flint corn. In the corn field, Corda fought jack rabbits with a rifle and corn bait that had been soaked in strychnine. She recalled, "The rabbits would eat anything we planted except spring squash, and we didn't like that either!" The Staffords stayed on the farm summers and in Lund during the winter until 1921 when they got title to the homestead. They ended up back in Missouri.[2]

Many years later Corda reminisced about living near Lund: "One of the worst things about the desert was the wind. It would come up, and the sand would blow. Then there would be some perfect days, the well water would be sweet and cold, and the country would grow on you so you didn't want to leave. The mirages on the desert were amazing like visions of lakes . . . Even yet, I still miss the howl of the wind and the coyotes and the smell of the sage. I would like to relive those days if I had the opportunity."

Also among the homesteaders who bailed out after only a few years was the Lee and Ethel Wright family, parents of Calvin E. Wright and other siblings. The Wright family had moved from Kansas to Los Angeles and then to a homestead in 1916 in the Latimer area north of Lund.[3] Calvin later wrote about the sight and sound of trains, the desert air, the quiet, the wind, the views of distant buttes, and "all the fond memories" such as getting his first ice cream cone at the Lund store, selling newspapers on the street, buying shoes for a day's wages of $2.50.[4]

A few other short-term homesteaders wrote nostalgia-filled letters about the days of their youth in the Escalante desert. Gladys Wolfe wrote about homesteading in 1917–1918, saying "I do get lonesome for the desert . . . I think it was a sad disappointment for the men who tried to make something out of it [homesteading]. They tried!"[5] Roy Bessler recalled that fried jack rabbit tasted like corn-fed rabbit probably because they had eaten his flint corn crop! George Collard wrote about "the effort just to exist in the desert" and about the trains, saying "I could see and hear them from a long distance until they disappeared in a mirage of heat waves."[6]

Such memories of childhood and young adult days often cancel out the pains of reality but there is something about deserts such as the Escalante Valley that evokes in some people a sense of freedom, of bitter-sweet loneliness, of time and space and distance and infinity not found in noisy, traffic-congested, people-jostling urban places. In the desert, lonesome comes with a whisper of wind or the howl of a coyote in the darkness or no sound at all, with a feeling of tranquility tinged by undefined sadness, with the expectation that tomorrow will be the same as today. For the more thoughtful desert homestead settlers, some may have felt they were a part of something greater than themselves if only for a little while, sensing that everything was temporary and that eventually a plowed field would be reclaimed by Russian thistle and rabbit brush.

Arlie and Ottie Fourman were the long-term best friends Mary and Harley had in the valley. The Fourmans came from Ohio where, as a child, Arlie suffered from severe asthma and eczema. In 1910, he and several relatives boarded a train to Los Angeles, lured there like tens of thousands of others in the Midwest by reports of good jobs. On the train, Arlie met Ottie, and they got married September 20, 1911.

Much like Harley Johnston, Arlie found steady employment in L.A., but got restless and, when his health greatly improved, he decided late in 1914 to try homesteading. In March 1915, he rode a loaded a freight car to Beryl and built a typical homestead house. Ottie and daughter Alice joined him a few months later. Arlie dutifully cultivated 20 acres but he and Ottie decided the family could not survive on dry land crops so he began on-again-off-again work for the Union Pacific railroad on section gangs at low pay for long hours.

Unlike her friend, Mary Johnston, who was stuck in the desert regardless of the temptation to return to California, Ottie was able to persuade her husband to return to Los Angeles for two years. In 1921, over Ottie's strenuous objections, they returned to the homestead and to Arlie's work on the section gang which paid fifteen cents an hour.

The high dry climate was good for Arlie's health, and, like a few other unusually stubborn homesteaders, he was determined to have some kind of a farm or ranch regardless of how long it might take. He traded 120 acres of his homestead land for 80 acres where ground water was more accessible for irrigation. He moved the original homestead house there and built up a herd of fifteen to twenty head of cattle on his "ranch."

Ottie and Alice moved into Lund in the fall of 1921 so Alice could attend school. She was four years older than Harlan and was like a sister to him. In 1926, while continuing to be a part-time farmer, Arlie became the foreman of the railroad section gang that maintained five miles of track south of Lund. The Fourmans got one of the three houses with bathroom tubs and flush toilets that the Union Pacific built for its local leaders.[7]

Other notable homesteaders in the area west of Beryl were Joseph and Mary Del Vecchio and their children who had immigrated from Italy in 1903, and Aram Boghossian who had received a medical education in his native Armenia before immigrating to New York City in 1913. When he contracted tuberculosis, he sought a high dry climate by homesteading near Beryl in 1920. For many years, he was known as "Doc" as he treated both human and animal ailments among the area's residents.[8]

A record of eighty years for tenure in the middle of the Escalante desert was set by the Frahske family. The saga began when Oscar E. Frahske, who was born in Buchfelde, Germany, homesteaded six miles north of Lund late in 1912. He and Alma August Hunt, a German woman whose brothers were also homesteaders, were married in Lund in 1917, a year after he became a United States citizen.[9]

Oscar emigrated from Germany at age 16 and set out on an odd jobs odyssey that took him to melon fields in California where he began dreaming of having a farm of his own. He was joined in the Escalante Valley by Hugo Hunt, also a German immigrant, and they filed homestead claims on Section 9, Township 32S, Range 13W.

Hugo borrowed $2,500 at eight percent interest to create an irrigated farm after he got title to his 320 acres in 1917. Oscar was very frugal all his life, and he and his family scratched out a hand-to-mouth living for fifteen years on his half of Section 7 depending on two windmills for water for crops and livestock. Toward the end of the Great Depression in the 1930s, Hugo got discouraged and sold his place to Oscar who was then able to grow more and better crops and expand his assortment of livestock.[10]

The Frahske children, Eddie and Fay, rode horses, and sometimes bicycles for a few years to attend school in Lund until Oscar's work at a variety of jobs in the region permitted the family to buy a Model A Ford pickup truck. He then began years of driving every week to work on railroad section gangs operating out of Lund. Fay and Eddie would ride with him and hang out with other kids, including the Johnstons, after school until Oscar got off work.[11]

In February 1922, Lund was flooded with muddy water that was 18 inches deep on Main Street and lapped at the edge of the Johnston yard. Everyone, from the townspeople to a *Salt Lake Tribune* reporter, was flabbergasted over a flood in the middle of a desert where average precipitation was ten inches per year.

Residents on the south side of town were the first to notice a sheet of water moving along a brush-bracketed dirt road from the southeast. People gathered on the embankment of the north/south railroad tracks and soon concluded the sight was not a mirage as the water piled up against the embankment and began flowing into the center of town.

There was speculation that an irrigation dam at the base of mountains twenty miles to the south had collapsed, but telephone calls soon squelched that rumor. Thereafter the consensus was that

Water tower and homes in the flood of 1922

Union Pacific Railroad houses in the flood.

Lund Main Street underwater.

an unusually heavy snowstorm was followed by unseasonably high temperatures, and snow melt water flowed down the gradual slope of the valley floor toward the usually dry lakebed just west of Lund.

Apparently no one in authority in the region at that time realized that the lakebed was at the lowest point in the middle of the valley and was one of several usually dry but sometimes wet, alkali-laden, lakebeds scattered along western Utah as remnants of the vast ancient Bonneville Lake. About thirty miles east of Lund is the Little Salt Lake near the town of Parowan where runoff from the Wasatch Mountain is trapped against foothills.

Engineers and constructors for the Union Pacific tracks' four-feet-high embankment south of Lund may not have realized that the embankment crossed the nearly imperceptible valley floor flow line toward the lakebed. The railroad company hurried to pierce the embankment with a temporary culvert to allow the flood water to flow to the lakebed and drain Main Street. A permanent bridge was later built over the flow line.

The few homesteaders still left in the south end of the Escalante desert wistfully thought about how welcome some of the flood water would have been on their dusty fields.

After almost two years of the "good life" in Lund, with the transition from homestead to town completed, and with the memory of Elizabeth fading, Mary decided it was time to add to the family. Harlan was now running instead of toddling and was showing signs of being a very bright kid. Mary figured he should have a brother or a sister or two.

In the balmy days of May 1920, Mary began a routine of coming to bed wearing only a gauzy chemise instead of a flannel nightgown and skipping contraception procedures. Within a month, Mary missed her period. She was hoping for a baby girl but she would have to wait several years for that wish to come true.

The pregnancy went well, and on January 15, 1921, Mary gave birth to William Kent Johnston. Going to a hospital 35 miles away was still out of the question for mothers in Lund. So, with the experience gained in her two previous birthings and with help from her neighbor, Mrs. Townsend, Mary brought Harlan's little brother into the world in the bedroom with only the usual pain and no complications.

Harley and Kent, 1921

Kent, as he was to be called by family and close friends all his life, had brown hair and blue eyes and looked more like his mother than his father. Even as a baby, he showed characteristics quite different from Harlan, being cranky and crying for a time, then lying quietly for hours in his crib in the main bedroom. But he was strong and healthy and quick to learn to play with the few toys in the crib.

A few months after Kent was weaned from breast-feeding, his parents bought a cow which could forage in daytime on vacant land east of the barnyard and provide fresh milk for their growing family.

Harlan turned six years old in August 1922 and entered first grade in the one-room schoolhouse, joining fifteen kids sprinkled through eight grades.

The south side of the frame school building was lined with sash windows that were stuck tight. The north side of the one room was covered with the traditional "blackboard"—actually dark green—fitted with a narrow shelf for pieces of white chalk and fist-sized felt erasers. A door on the east end of the building led to a woodshed, to two small outhouses, one for boys and one for girls, and to the barren dirt playground where clumps of salt grass could be used for second and third bases in softball games. A wood-burning pot-bellied stove provided heat. On the roof was a classic little cupola housing a brass bell that was rung by a rope from inside the west end of the room.

The school was part of the Iron County School District headquartered in Cedar City. Finding a teacher willing to tackle eight grades in a very isolated desert town was always problematic. Teachers usually rented a small house from the Johnstons for nine months and returned to their home towns in the summer. In the thirty-five-year history of the school, only two or three teachers lasted more than one year.

Shortly after the move from homestead to town, Mary announced, "I want to see about getting some kind of church service started on Sundays."

Harley, who was basically an agnostic whether he knew it or not, replied, "I'm sure the town will welcome your effort."

There was a battered old pedal pump organ in the lumber yard office on which Mary, with her piano skills, could play hymns. She persuaded the lumber yard owner to let her use the office and the organ for impromptu Sunday church services to which everyone in town was invited.

Religion was a minor part of life in the community where mere survival was uppermost in the minds of the eclectic and mobile residents. Nevertheless, up to a dozen people would attend services where Mary read scriptures from her Bible and led singing from a few battered hymnals she borrowed from the Presbyterian Church in Cedar City. One attraction was that a collection plate was not passed around. The services continued sporadically through the 1920s until the Great Depression began in 1930.

Mary was not overtly or evangelically religious and was seldom preachy, but she believed deeply and personally in an all-seeing God and a benevolent Jesus Christ. She often said silent prayers at bedtime but did not make a ritual of praying. One of the most used books in the family over the years was an illustrated collection of stories from the Bible's Old and New Testaments. Her children absorbed her quiet faith.

A major economic development occurred in 1923 with construction of a railroad track southeastward straight as an arrow for about 25 miles across the desert from Lund to Iron Springs and then 10 miles into Cedar City. Construction of the line was driven by the need for iron ore shipments to steel-making plants in southern California and later in central Utah, as well as the opening of tourist facilities at the national parks and monuments of southern Utah and northern Arizona.

At plants in the Provo, Utah area, the iron ore met up with shipments of coal from Carbon County mines on the east side of the Wasatch Mountains. Near the end of the 1920s, an average of 231,000 tons of ore per year were shipped from open-pit mines near the town of Iron Springs to a new Columbia Steel plant near Provo.

At the south end of Lund the new tracks formed a "Y" to facilitate switching of railroad cars between the Cedar line and Union Pacific's

Union Pacific train carrying
President Warren G. Harding through Lund.

main line. Freighting on the new track replaced use of wagons and Model T Ford trucks between Lund and Cedar. President Warren G. Harding's train rode over the tracks June 27, 1923, to the new Cedar City depot accompanied by a large entourage to visit Zion National Park.

The federal government's designation of national parks at Zion Canyon south of Cedar City, Bryce Canyon northeast of Cedar, and Grand Canyon to the south in northern Arizona spurred the Union Pacific railroad to create a subsidiary, the Utah Parks Company. It built and operated facilities at the parks and provided transportation through the Lund depot for tourists from around the nation to the parks and to a national monument called Cedar Breaks that looks like a mini-Bryce Canyon. Tourism with Lund as the railhead gateway feeding tour buses grew steadily through the 1920s, peaking at 51,000 visitors in 1929.

The first railroad depot in Lund had consisted of two railroad freight cars, one for a passenger waiting room and the station master's office and one for freight and baggage. In 1924, the cars were replaced by a beautiful Colonial Spanish-style building with red tile roof, tan stucco walls, and planters with white, pink and red hollyhocks. Designed by noted architect Gilbert Stanley Underwood, it was the most modern building in the entire life of Lund. The waiting room with rows of massive, high-backed, oak benches had two white globe chandeliers. Men's and women's restrooms had hot and cold water, flush toilets, and the only vertical urinals within a thirty-five-mile radius. A wall with ticket windows separated the passenger room from the station master's office with its telegraph equipment that was then the key to railroad communications. The south one-third of the building was a baggage

The national parks sign in Lund for 20 years.

room equipped with large sliding doors and ten-foot-long, iron-wheeled, carts for transporting baggage. Narrow asphalt platforms stretched north and south to serve people and their baggage getting on and off passenger trains and to facilitate movement of sacks of mail.

Near the Lund depot where all railroad passengers could see it was a ten-foot-by-twenty-foot billboard with full color photos of the three parks and the headline, "Lund, Utah. Gateway to America's Most Colorful National Parks."

The first half of the Great Depression slowed the tourism business, but by the end of the 1930s up to 60 tourists per day were getting off trains at Lund and getting on buses for tours of the national parks. Later, Pullman passenger cars were switched off the main Union Pacific line and taken on the track to Cedar City. Unfortunately, tourists catching the buses or riding the Pullman cars did not have time to shop at the Lund Store but there were no souvenirs there anyway!

Tour bus drivers had long, joke-filled, monologues to entertain their passengers on boring stretches of the trips. A sample of the jokes: "It's so dry out here the trees chase dogs, and jack rabbits kick prospectors to death in order to steal their canteens."

Bracketing the town for a half mile were several siding tracks to allow trains going in opposite directions to pass each other and also to allow freight cars containing consumer goods and materials to be sidetracked next to warehouses for loading and unloading. Heavy freight, gasoline tankers, and livestock shipping docks were located on a spur rail line on the west side of the town.

An eight-foot-square "jail" with weather-beaten board walls around an iron cage stood for almost 40 years near the stockyards. No one in Lund could remember whether the jail was ever used by the Iron County sheriff. By the 1960s, the board walls and shingle roof had blown away, and the rusty iron cage stood naked and lonely on a barren patch of cracked hardpan like part of a Salvador Dali surrealist painting. The cage was eventually moved to a museum complex in Cedar City. There was a legend that the only prisoner ever housed in the jail was a bear that wandered into town from the foothills and was lassoed and put in detention where it died.

Through the "Roaring Twenties," the character of Lund changed as the automobile age replaced the brief era of the homestead boom and freighting by team-drawn wagons. The first automobile in Iron County had been delivered by train in Lund in 1907. Model T Fords were replaced by Model A Fords and by competition from other car makers such as Chevrolet and Packard. Teams of manure-dropping horses and mules disappeared. Liveries and their bales of hay for animal fuel were replaced by garages and gasoline pumps. Two wagon trails were consolidated into a graveled Utah Route 91 that provided improved access to Cedar City and the Iron County seat of Parowan. The "highway" was minimally paved later for a few decades, then reverted to gravel as usage plummeted.

Ollie Norris established a full-blown new and used auto sales business and built a cinder-block garage for motor vehicle repairs. Ollie sold the Frahskes their first Ford. While autos became the choice for personal transportation, the railroad remained the basic economic reason for Lund's existence.

Harley's job with Conoco went well as the business expanded with the increase in motor vehicles in the region. Harley, in keeping with his basic theory of self-sufficiency, saved every penny he could toward purchase of the house and cessation of rent payments. By the end of 1921, he and Mary were able to buy all three houses on the fenced lot. The Johnstons found themselves in the real estate business, renting the two-story house to the Townsends and offering the third and smaller house for rent. With Harlan ready to start school, Mary began taking an interest in the Iron County School District and called the attention of the district office to the small house that would be suitable for school teachers. In 1922, she and Harley began a 17-year tradition of renting to teachers.

With home ownership achieved and with rental income, the couple felt they could afford to buy a Model T Ford truck for $400. They sold the old wagon and mules, and Mary delighted in speeding off at twenty miles per hour in the truck for shopping in Cedar City.

Mary was well pleased with her two sons and with the circle of friends and activities she cultivated in the town. But, in keeping with the times when large families were common, she decided in March 1923 to have another child who she was sure would be a girl to provide a mother-daughter relationship and a complete family circle. She stopped the contraception procedure and warned Harley about her plan; he agreed with wholehearted participation, and conception was virtually automatic.

As delivery drew near, the Johnstons were affluent enough to allow Mary to go in the new vehicle to the hospital in Cedar City and have a doctor in place of a midwife. On November 9, 1923, Mildred Evelyn Johnston was born, fulfilling her mother's determination to have a daughter. Millie, as the family and friends soon began calling her, was a baby doll with blond hair and blue eyes like her father but her face was more like her mother's face. Mary kept a more detailed record about this daughter than she did for her sons, listing Millie's first visitors and gifts and dates of her first laugh, word, tooth, steps, etc.

Harlan, Kent and Mildred

Harlan was a surprisingly mature seven-year-old who quickly became proud and protective of his little sister. Kent at almost three years of age didn't much care about the fuss over the new addition to the family.

While awaiting the arrival of Mildred, Harley and Mary faced the imminent need for a bigger house. The exodus of homesteaders left a variety of buildings abandoned out in the desert. The structures

Millie, Harlan and Kent, circa 1924

became free game for permanent residents who needed used lumber or could move all or part of a vacated house into Lund where it could be occupied by the mover or rented. In most cases of abandoned buildings, the absentee owners could not be located or the homestead had not qualified for a title and ownership of the property reverted to the government.

The moving of "free" or cheaply-purchased, one-or-two-bedroom, homestead shanties to as far away as Cedar City became virtually a cottage industry in the 1920s. The comparatively light weight frame structures, usually twelve feet wide, could be jacked up and loaded onto heavy duty wagons for very slow transport to new locations.

Harley, starting to show the brazen attitude toward use of abandoned homesteads that he exhibited for many years, carved a 12-by-16-foot room off a vacant house a half-mile from Lund and added it to the south end of the Johnston family home. It became the "boys' room" for two generations. The addition had sash windows on two sides and a never-used door on the third wall that opened onto the side yard. A door was cut through the south wall of the house for access from the added room into the screened porch and thence into the kitchen.

The windows allowed cooling ventilation in summer, but the room had no heating, and the boys learned how to exchange clothes and pajamas in a few seconds in sub-freezing winter evenings and mornings. The preferred technique was to leave shirt and trousers attached to their long johns. The clothing assemblage could be unbuttoned and peeled off as a unit at bedtime and be slipped back on and rebuttoned in the morning.

Well in advance of Mildred's arrival, Harley reluctantly agreed to allow Mary to return by train with the two little boys to Santa Barbara for two weeks. The visit allowed Mary to rebond with her aging mother and the brothers who were easing into middle age, to show off the two boys, to reminisce with old friends from school and church, and to visit her father's grave. She returned to Lund and contentedly settled down to raising a family and the prospect of a life of comfort compared to the homestead hardships.

With the family economics in good shape and with Harlan, Kent and Mildred all doing very well, Mary took the next steps necessary to round out the family at four children in a decade, hopefully with two boys and two girls. During the Christmas season of 1925, Harley and Mary enjoyed carefree love-making, and Mary quickly became pregnant.

On August 12, 1926, just ten years and three days after Harlan was born, Richard Sterling Johnston came into the world in the Cedar City hospital, weighing seven pounds. He had sandy-colored hair and blue eyes like his oldest brother and his Grandfather King. He inherited his mother's round nose. Dick, as he was to be called most of his life except in legal documents, was not the girl Mary had hoped for, but she happily resigned herself to a family of three boys and a girl and was prepared to help Mildred cope with three brothers as she had learned to cope with her own three brothers.

Life was good, but a drastic change in Mary's life was coming as the 1920s waned.

---

1. The company was a predecessor to Conoco—the Continental Oil Company.
2. Corda Stafford, "The Corda E. Stafford Story of Lund, Utah, circa. 1916–1921," March 1960, Fay Frahske Burns Collection, Special Collections, Southern Utah University.
3. As an adult, Calvin Wright became probably the most prominent former "desert rat" from the Lund area. His basic career as an accountant led him to be elected the Idaho state auditor three times. In 1950 he lost a race to become governor of Idaho.
4. Letter, Calvin E. Wright to Fay Frahske Burns, 22 October 1976, Fay Frahske Burns Collection, SUU.
5. Letter, Gladys Wolfe to Calvin Wright, Fay Frahske Burns Collection, SUU.
6. Letter, George Collard to Calvin Wright, Fay Frahske Burns Collection, SUU
7. Alice boarded in Cedar City while in high school, graduating in 1930. She married Wally Couch who was a foreman on Union Pacific construction gangs until he got laid off in 1933, and they moved to Montebello, California. Arlie and Ottie joined them there after selling their expanded ranch to the Mormon Church for $20,000 in 1950. Ottie died in 1978; Arlie died in 1989 at age 100.
8. Hankins, Esther W. "Beloved Escalante doctor was exiled." *Nevadan Magazine*, 22 April 1984. Copy in Fay Frahske Burns Collection, SUU.

9. Oscar and Alma had a son, Eddie, and a daughter, Fay. It was Fay who kept in touch with three generations of residents of the area and left her personal and community history in the Special Collections of the Sherratt Library at Southern Utah University.

10. In the Depression years of 1932–1933, taxes on the Hunt and Frahske properties were $12 each per year.

11. As described later, the Frahskes purchased the Johnston family property in Lund in 1957, and Fay was a resident there off and on until 1990.

Chapter 12

Sheep Era Starts

In the first quarter of the 20th Century, western Utah deserts were a Mecca for huge herds of sheep trailing back and forth across the valleys between winter and summer pastures. Millions of acres of public (federal) land were available for open range. At one time, it was estimated that more than 200,000 sheep were sheared of a million pounds of wool in one year in just the Escalante Valley. Lund was one of the focal points for sheep shearing, for railroad shipping of big burlap bags of wool to cloth industries in the East, and for shipping carloads of lambs in the fall to markets for fattening and slaughter.

Wool and cotton were the standard for most clothes from long john underwear to business suits and high-style dresses. Also, at that time, lamb chops and roast legs of lamb were highly popular menu items, a popularity that would slowly fade over the coming decades.

After about eight years at Conoco, Harley began to chafe under the routine of working for wages. With the steady departure of homesteaders from the desert, and with the memory of hard work that produced crop failures, it had become clear that he could not be a dry land farmer. The forty acres of the homestead that Harley had cleared were overgrown with new bushes and weeds but he would not give up on his hope that someday it might, it just might, be an irrigated farm. For now, however, he began to think about being a rancher, being his own boss, being independent. The sheep business appeared to be prosperous, and Harley figured a herd could survive on the open uplands west of Lund and on abandoned homesteads checkerboarded around the town.

The Conoco facility was near the stockyards and rows of concrete troughs where migrating herds of sheep would fill up on railroad water. Harley began taking his lunch break to talk with hired sheep herders, and sometimes the herd owners, about their business, their experiences, trends in prices for wool and lambs, how much a herd of 500 to 1,000 animals would cost, the amount of land needed for grazing such a herd, the life of sheep herders living year around in canvas-covered wagons, and how long a herd could be left alone while a herder went home for a visit with a wife and family.

He also started driving around the area south and west of Lund to pin down which homesteads had been vacated and whether the few abandoned windmills might be used to water a herd of sheep. Land not covered by patented homesteads was public land, and no federal or state government agencies were paying much attention to how it was used or not used, especially for livestock grazing. Many of the patented but abandoned homesteads could be acquired by paying probably less than $100 each to the owners or paying a few dollars in back taxes. Most of the tracts were 320 acres but a few were 640 acres. By acquiring title to some of the sites and by knowing which homesteaders had left without caring whether someone used their land, Harley figured he could put up to 700 head of sheep on 5,000 to 6,000 acres of land near Lund with very little capital investment and without paying land leases.

The legality of what he planned to do was not questioned.

The focal point for the envisioned livestock ranch would be Homer Green's place—320 acres about a mile southwest of Lund in Section 19 Township 32S Range 14W. It had a one room "house," a fairly large barn, several fenced corrals, and a windmill over a dependable well. The site was roughly in the middle of the open lands west of Lund and the railroad tracks. A herd could be watered there and then could go off in all directions for one to three miles to graze. Harley would have to buy and install a 500-gallon galvanized metal tank to store water provided by the windmill and three 10ten-foot-long metal troughs for watering the sheep. A sulphur-tainted spring a mile north of Homer Green's and a sporadic spring in hills two miles to the northwest could also be used briefly for watering a herd.

For a few months in late summer and early fall when the uplands had turned tinder dry, sheep could find some grass and weeds on the desert floor east of the railroad tracks and be watered at a pond of railroad water at the north edge of Lund or sometimes at thunderstorm pools in the area.

Harley was a vigorous conscientious employee at Conoco and was earning pay raises nearly every year. But after Dick was born, Harley began saving money to buy a sheep herd and fix up watering places. He discussed the sheep ranch idea vaguely and sporadically with Mary. However, she was busy raising four children, and the implications of Harley leaving Conoco and becoming a sheep rancher did not sink in for a year until decision-making time arrived.

In 1927, Harley began quietly acquiring some abandoned homesteads both east and west of the railroad tracks. Homer Green had moved to California but returned each summer to check on his place. Harley caught up with him in August and expressed a seemingly casual interest in buying the property. There was virtually no market demand for desert homesteads and Green agreed to sell for $110.

Harley would also eventually acquire the homestead of Hiram N. Inman immediately north of Homer Green's place. The Inman family, who had hoped to have a chicken ranch, left stretches of fences and rusting barbed wire around the tract.

Mary began to get nervous as she sensed that Harley was increasingly serious about the sheep business. She was aware that he was buying up homesteads and talking to sheepmen. However, he slowed down on the acquisitions for half a year and quietly let the family bank account build up. He kept the family "books" but Mary was happy to have more leeway than many wives to buy groceries, clothes, and things for the house.

Early in June 1928, ten years after he started the final effort to raise crops at the homestead, Harley told Mary he wanted to buy 700 head of sheep, quit his job at Conoco, and become a rancher. For the first time, with him and Mary sitting in the living room on a Sunday afternoon, he reviewed assembling enough land for a ranch and described his plan in detail to be carried out that summer. He concluded that by fall he would probably be a fulltime sheep herder living in a sheep wagon.

As he talked, all the fears that Mary had had about coming to Utah in the first place and all her memories of good times in Santa Barbara and of bad times on the homestead came flooding back. The security and steady income provided by the Conoco job would be replaced by what seemed to her to be a risky gamble on a bunch of smelly sheep with no assurance they would survive on the desert any more than farm crops had survived.

She had seen the thousands of sheep meandering back and forth across the Escalante Valley and the horse-riding herders in greasy pants and sweat-stained hats that lived in wagons covered with dirt-streaked canvas. She had idly wondered whether those men had wives and families somewhere, and, if so, what the women did when their husbands were away, probably for months at a time. She knew that the owner of a sheep herd had two choices about caring for the herd—hire somebody or do it himself. Mary knew Harley well enough to be sure that he would do the job himself. Also, the income from the comparatively small herd would not normally warrant paying a salary to a hired hand.

Mary had survived homesteading to find a relatively comfortable life in town, and now the good life was about to revert to another time of hardship. She sat biting her lip as Harley enthusiastically described his plan. He was talking about the timetable when she jumped up and started pacing around the living room.

"Those other herds get fat on grass in the summer over on the Wasatch Mountains and come over here in the winter when there's some snow on the ground. What makes you think sheep can get enough to eat around here in the dry summer to live through the winter?" Mary asked.

"Sheep don't need much grass. They also eat brush and weeds, and there will be enough grazing on the foothills at the start of summer and then later down on the flat land. And our sheep will have places all within a mile or two to get water, and they won't have to walk 40 miles across the desert twice a year to get to winter and summer pastures," Harley replied with a sigh, sensing that the transition from a Conoco worker to sheep herder would not be easy.

"And you are going to be gone all the time living at the sheep camp, leaving me here alone with four kids, a house to take care of, and a cow to milk twice a day winter and summer. Why can't you stay home and drive out to take care of the herd every day? The sheep won't run away, will they?" Mary asked.

"No, dear, they won't run away but they have to have someone with them on the range to herd them to different areas for grazing and teach them where the water holes are and scare coyotes away, especially when there are lambs. Unlike most of those herders you see who may be gone for months, I will be only two or three miles away at any time. I will be home at least every Saturday night, and I can come home for lunch once in a while especially in the summer and for part of a day like when we need to go to Cedar City."

"Okay, so you will be near but you will still be gone. I want the car here with me. You can ride a horse to and from your sheep camp. And what about the chores here?"

"Harlan is old enough now to milk the cow and chop wood for the stoves," Harley replied. "Kent is getting old enough to take care of the chickens and gather the eggs. And if something has to be done around the house, fixing something, I'll have time to do that."

"You've been keeping the books and handling the bank account so I assume you feel you have enough money to buy a herd and a sheep wagon and a horse and whatever else you'll need. Are you going to take the records to the camp and should I save the mail for a week until you come home Saturday night?"

"No, dear," Harley said, "you will decide what to do about the mail each day, and you will be in charge of the bank account, and you already know more about the household expenses than I do. You can tell me each week how things are going and whether I need to sign something. And, remember, you've been handling the rents from the two houses all along."

"Well, I sure hope you've thought this thing through enough so we won't go hungry next winter," Mary went on. "The rent income is not enough to pay the bills. As I understand it, we'll have two main sources of income—sale of lambs in the fall and sale of wool in the spring—so we'll have to get enough money at those times to tide us over through the year."

"That's right. The herd I want to buy this summer will include lambs that will be a half year old in the fall and can be sold so we'll have money for the winter."

Mary could tell she was not going to dissuade Harley but she could not resist one more jab. "So, we will both be sleeping alone in cold beds except for Saturday night when you will want something special, right?"

Harley felt that was hitting below the belt (no pun intended), but he kept his cool and murmured, "We've had something special for quite a few years now, and I hope it will continue. Besides, we both know I'm getting old enough so that doing it every week may become more than I can handle."

Mary laughed, "Let's hope that doesn't happen soon!" She tugged at Harley's sleeve, and he stood up and kissed her.

She decided to forego one more complaint about how she would have to roust out of bed six mornings every week to fire up the kitchen stove year around and to stoke the living room stove early on cold weather mornings. Harley had always done those chores.

There were a few more talks about the change including the step-by-step schedule for implementation. Mary grudgingly resigned herself to the determination of her husband, just as she had overcome earlier fears and married him. She was, in last analysis, back to the choice she had the first year on the homestead: staying with her husband and loving him through thick and thin or quitting and going home to mother. The decision to stay was easier this time, especially when she tucked four tousled heads into bed each night.

Harley's conversations about where and how to buy a herd led him to a Parowan-based owner of several thousand head of sheep. A few days after his "discussion" with Mary, he began haggling with the owner for a week, finally agreeing to pay two dollars each for 700 ewes.

Under the timing of the deal in June, the seller would have sheared the sheep and sold the wool two months earlier. The buyer would avoid the extra hard work of the six-week springtime lambing season and the castration, called docking, of the male lambs, but would still have the year's crop of lambs to sell in the fall.

The owner of the big herd helped Harley find and buy a used sheep-camp wagon, a nondescript bay horse, a used saddle and bridle, and a part-Collie dog. The presence of a large dog at camp would keep coyotes away when the sheep were bedded down for the night. Equally important was the role of dogs as companions for lonely sheep herders.

On June 15, 1928, Harley gave a two week notice to his Conoco employer who expressed deep regret at losing Harley and shook his head over what he thought was a big gamble.

On July 1, Harley and Mary left the children with the Townsends and drove to Parowan to get their herd of sheep, or, as Mary would have put it, Harley's herd. This was the start of the Johnstons' two decades in the sheep business.

Mary drove the Ford truck hauling the sheep wagon over gravel roads from Parowan to Lund followed by the herd and Harley on horseback averaging 12 miles a day. The couple slept in the wagon two nights and ate cold food for most meals. The first watering stop was on a thin creek in a canyon called The Gap west of Parowan, and

Typical sheep herd

the second watering place was a rancher's windmill east of Lund. By sundown of the third day, the entourage reached the corrals at Homer Green's place.

Harley stayed home that night, and the next morning before he left the house he kissed Mary brusquely and commented that everything was working out exactly as planned. She went to the bedroom and cried.

He scrambled that first day to get organized for the life of a sheep herder. He filled a ten-gallon milk can with water and went to the Lund store to get the first basic supply of food for the sheep camp—mostly canned meat and vegetables, oatmeal, flour, salt, bread, bacon, tea and coffee. He drove the truck out to Homer Green's, moved the sheep wagon to the first, and ultimately the most used, camp site at the base of a rimrock hill. On horseback, Harley began "teaching" the sheep to graze as they moved that afternoon to the camp site for their second night on the Johnstons' "ranch."

In the house in Lund, on that first night of being alone at the start of the sheep era, Mary tucked the kids in bed and explained why Daddy would not be home very much from now on. She did not sleep well that night.

Within a few days, the herd of sheep learned what became a standard routine on most warm weather days of each year—get "kicked off" the bed ground at dawn, graze for a few hours, stroll to Homer Green's for noontime water and rest, return to the camp site in the afternoon grazing along the way, and bed down at sundown. Typically, from then on, Harley had a sandwich lunch and took a noontime nap in Homer Green's homestead shanty. Sometimes, especially in the summer, he went home for lunch and napped on the living room floor.

Loneliness was, of course, inherent in the life of a sheep herder, and some men found they could not cope with that but Harley didn't mind. He was more fortunate than most herders to be comparatively close to his home and family. Also, he didn't mind the bareness of the desert because, as he wisecracked once, "Out here you can see if someone is sneaking up on you." There was no need for binoculars.

The sheep wagon, like thousands of others in the Mountain West, many of them made by Henry Mitchell of Salt Lake City, was merely a wooden box, seven feet wide and twelve feet long, mounted on a chassis having wood-spoke wheels and rubber tires. An eight-foot long wooden tongue attached to the front allowed the wagon to be pulled by a team of horses or by hooking onto a truck. The wagon was usually moved monthly to spread the grazing out from different camp sites.

Canvas was stretched over an arched framework to allow a maximum headroom of seven feet inside. The ends of the enclosure were framed in wood.

The front door was a Dutch door which allowed the upper half to be opened for ventilation in warm weather and closed in cold weather. The front half of the wagon was the combination living room, dining room, and kitchen. In one corner, a small, flat-topped, wood-burning stove with a tiny oven was used for both cooking and heating. It was vented by a metal pipe through the canvas roof. In the opposite corner was space for the ten-gallon can of water replenished on visits to the Lund home. Along the sides of the "room" were two-foot-high lockers for storage and seating.

Typical sheep camp

The back half of the wagon was the "bedroom" with a thin-mattress bed two feet below the canvas ceiling and spanning a storage space underneath for a bale of hay, saddles, and tools such as an axe and shovel. A one-foot-square sliding window in the back wall above the bed allowed some ventilation in summer. Bedding consisted of wool blankets and gray flannel sheets that did not show dirt between semi-annual washings.

A table top slid out from under the bed into the "dining room." The "living room" floor was dirt-gray linoleum plus a piece of tin under the stove. The "toilet" was anywhere outside at least fifty feet from the wagon. Going there was a test of will in winter.

Cooking utensils were few and basic including a frying pan, a pan for baking sourdough biscuits, a coffee pot that Harley also used as a tea pot, and a pot for boiled potatoes, soups, stews, and cooked oatmeal. A porcelain jar contained carefully-tended sour dough. Cooking provided welcome heat in winter but very excessive heat in summer when the temperature inside the wagon would soar to 100 degrees.

Each evening Harley put leather-and-chain hobbles on the horse's front feet so the animal could go grazing. In winter, the horse got a sheaf of hay at the rear of the wagon and in very cold weather was bundled in a horse blanket. The dog's "house" was boards propped against a bale of hay.

In winter, Harley lighted a kerosene lantern and read the *Saturday Evening Post* and week-old newspapers until bedtime. In summer, when daylight lasted until 8 or 9 o'clock, he skipped use of the lantern and went to bed at dark. Wakeup time year around was at dawn. A watch or a clock was superfluous. There was sunlight, moonlight, and starlight but no flashlight.

For Harley alone in the sheep camp after sundown, there were two common sounds that usually made him listen for a moment—the ratcheting howl of a coyote on a hillside and the intolerably lonesome wail of a steam locomotive whistle in the valley. From some campsites, he could see the powerful headlights of trains stabbing through the black velvet of desert darkness. Also, in the clear night air, he could see millions of stars that were seemingly touchable and unknown as constellations. Each morning the rising sun caught the night by surprise and forced darkness to retreat under the hills, replaced by a palette of dawn colors.

The Escalante desert and its fringe of rocky hills seemed at first glance to be devoid of color or anything sensual or pleasant. But a sheep herder could smell a few drops of rain on summer dust and grey-green sage brush or catch the elusive scent of a spindly Mormon tea bush. He could delight in the rare brief and precious glory of springtime flowers—the hot pink petals and fuzzy yellow stamens and pistils of a rock-surrounded barrel cactus in bloom, the startling white petals of desert poppies with deep green sharp-spined leaves, the surprise of an orange Indian paintbrush peeking bashfully from under a squat, blue-berried, juniper tree. On the valley floor, yellow-topped rabbit brush fought to contain the spread of tawny rippled sand dunes. When a bush died, the wind exposed and scoured the skeleton-like roots.

And there was no cure for tension equal to the sigh of a breeze in the boughs of a piñyon tree above a sheep herder snoozing in a patch of sunshine on a bed of pine needles.

Chapter 13

Sheep Ranching

"Harlan! Kent! Stop it! Stop it this minute! Just wait 'til I tell your father!" Mary yelled at her sons fighting in the middle of the hardpan yard, scuffing up puffs of dust.

Harlan, five years older and fifteen pounds heavier than Kent, was winning as usual in this the latest of their frequent scraps. He held his brother in a headlock while Kent twisted and turned and flailed out with both fists. "Say uncle!" Harlan kept shouting.

Kent's muffled reply was "Go to hell!"

After a moment of circling the boys and wringing her hands, Mary grabbed their overall suspenders and tried to pull them apart. Harlan released the headlock and stepped back, but Kent resumed the stance of a prizefighter. Mary jerked him around and pushed him toward the screened porch door, bypassing a patch of mud where the dishwater from breakfast had been thrown out. "Go to your room and stay there!"

Little sister Mildred, wide-eyed, had been watching the fight from the cracked concrete stoop at the porch door and held onto little brother Dick when Kent stormed past them and slammed the door. Dick looked up at her as if to ask a question. "Kent sure seems to get mad easy," she whispered.

Mary turned to Harlan. "What did you do?"

"I didn't do anything. I was just teasing him about the way his hair is usually messed up."

"Well, stop teasing him!"

Harlan's red hair was always combed in a smooth pompadour in the fashion of young men in 1930 while Kent's brown hair always seemed to stand on end to signal defiance and add to his frequent fist-waving stance.

The threat about telling their 55-year-old father had no effect on the brothers who knew from past experiences that by the time he got home from the sheep camp near sundown that summer Saturday evening he would be more interested in dinner time than in punishing them. Since Harley, despite Mary's concerns, had purchased the herd of sheep two years earlier, Mary had learned the hard way about raising the family's four children alone. Harley stayed with the sheep except for Saturday nights when he came home for dinner, some loving, and Sunday breakfast.

After dinner as Harley helped Mary wash dishes, Mary said, "I don't know what to do about the boys. They had another fight this afternoon and one of these days Harlan is going to lose his temper and give Kent a broken nose or worse."

"What started it?" Harley asked.

"As usual nothing serious. Harlan was just teasing him about his hair. They need more discipline. It's embarrassing when the neighbors see them fighting so often. Kent usually starts it, and if I try to spank him that makes it worse. You should at least talk to them."

"Well, I don't think the problem is very bad. I can't just come home and spank them. Harlan is almost as big as I am, and I agree spanking won't change Kent. And, anyway, Harlan is away at Wasatch Academy most of the year, and Kent will eventually learn to get along with people. Harlan won't stick around here long after he gets out of school. He'll go to Salt Lake City and get a job. Kent is a loner, and I bet that he will stay here on the desert with us and maybe help me get an irrigated farm to go with the ranch."

Mary took a deep breath but said nothing more and put the dishes in the cupboard. Harley returned to the dining area table and began scanning the week's accumulated editions of the *Salt Lake Tribune*.

Since the sheep herd purchase in 1928, revenue from the sale of lambs in the fall and wool in the spring had been more than enough to cover expenses and tide the Johnston family over the winters, especially since a couple of fat lambs were held back for butchering and a no-cost supply of meat. Harley felt good about the change from the Conoco job to ranching but Mary remained skeptical, especially when she pondered her dawn-to-dusk duties of taking care of the kids, the milk cow, and the finances.

When the summer waned, buyers from livestock commissions based in Cedar City began visiting the Johnston ranch to inspect the crop of four hundred six-months-old lambs and submit offers to buy.

Harley sold the 50-pound little woolies for $1.50 each. They were rail-shipped to market and ended up in dining rooms around the nation.

The production of lambs had begun when Harley purchased rams to impregnate the ewes in late fall 1928 and start the gestation periods that would yield lambs in the spring. The Merino breed of sheep was the standard for herds in the eastern United States, but the Rambouillet breed was preferred in the Mountain West because of its heavier wool and because of its ability to withstand severe weather and to survive on rough forage.

Harley purchased a dozen Rambouillet males from a producer of purebreds in Pine Valley south of Cedar City. The rams, much larger than the ewes, were impressive animals with pugnacious faces and huge horns in half circles around the sides of their heads. Conventional wisdom was that one sturdy ram could service more than 50 ewes during the breeding season.

Harley hauled the rams in two truckloads to Homer Green's and turned them loose in the herd of ewes who eyed the big males like school girls sizing up boys at a dance. The rams saw no need to fill out a dance card and immediately began a two-step on their hind legs behind any ewe ready to be impregnated. When all the ewes had been satisfied, the rams were kept the rest of the year in a fenced pasture and fed hay.

It was a life that Mary pondered occasionally—males who did not have to really work to earn their keep, did not have to nurse babies, change diapers, worry over medicines for ill children, or keep house or cook or wash and iron clothes. However, she admitted, men were supposed to "earn a living", something the rams did not have to worry about.

Rambouillet rams

The productive life of a ewe was five to seven years, and when worn-down teeth and loss of teeth revealed her age she

was sold off for slaughter and was replaced by a one-year-old female. Some of the ewes emerged as leaders and were fitted with bells so that if one of them led a flock out of sight a herder could hear the bell tinkle.

In the spring of 1929, Harley and Mary had learned about the hardest work season in the sheep business—shearing time and lambing time.

In April, Harley hired one of the itinerant shearing crews that roamed the region. The crews were composed of five to eight mostly young men from small towns who could earn "good" money and three meals a day for eight hours of back-breaking labor for three to ten days depending on the size of a herd. Some big sheep spreads provided bunkhouses but for the most part the men pitched tents or slept in campers and makeshift trailers as they did in and around the Johnstons' yard in Lund. They used the cold water faucet in the yard to wash up each day.

The shearing was done with a scissors-like tool having super-sharp wide blades attached to a half-circle spring that kept the blades open until closed by the hand and arm strength of the operator. The shears could cut a three-inch-wide, inch-and-a-half-thick, swath of fleece off a sheep, leaving about one-fourth inch of wool covering the skin. A ewe was held in a sitting position between the knees of the shearer who started on the stomach and rotated the animal between his knees to clip the sides and back. A top hand could shear a sheep in four minutes, stopping for four or five minutes now and then to sharpen the blades on an oilstone.

The factors of speed and strength were critical for each shearer who was paid by the number of fleeces shorn. Important to the owner was the uniformity of the fleece depth and the number and size of nicks and cuts inflicted on an animal's skin because the injuries could become infected.

Each morning, part of the Johnston herd at Homer Green's was put in a corral with a chute from which shearers would drag sheep on to the barn's plank-floored shearing room. When a shearer finishing clipping a ewe, he would bundle the fleece into a ball weighing up to ten pounds and throw it out a window onto a ten-foot-high platform. A burlap bag two and a half feet in diameter was suspended from a circular hole in the platform. A worker—Harley in the first year or two, the Johnston boys thereafter—on the platform would fill the bag with the fleeces and stomp on them much like an old time winemaker stomping a tub of grapes. When an eight-foot long bag was full of tamped wool, the top was sewn closed, and the bag, looking like a huge sausage, was dropped to the ground and rolled to a truck for hauling to the railroad freight yard in Lund.

In the barn, the greasy wool, fresh sheep manure, drops of blood, and sweat of the shearers made the stinking and dirty work a daily test of endurance for the crew.

A sheared ewe was released into a corral with others in the chilly mid-spring weather. The experience may have been like a person being sent outside in pajamas.

Just prior to the start of the shearing season, wool buyers would tour the region, inspecting herds and offering purchase contracts to herd owners. In the first year, Harley agreed to a price of twelve cents per pound of wool with payment made after the big sacks were weighed at the Lund stockyards.

By late April each year, grounds near the stockyards were covered with pyramid piles of the sacks from herds in the center of the Escalante Valley. Children delighted in playing on the piles. When the stockpiles were large enough to fill one or two freight cars, the railroad station master would arrange for shipments to textile industries in the East. There, grease and dirt would be washed out of the raw wool to prepare it for spinning into cloth for many uses.

Mary had to cook and serve three big meals a day to the always-famished crew of shearers who started work at eight o'clock, returned to the house at noon for lunch and naps, then worked until 6 p.m. The living room was turned into a large dining room where the men ate first and the Johnston children, always excited by the activity, ate second.

Mary got up at six o'clock and by seven o'clock served a typical breakfast of bacon, eggs, fried potatoes and pancakes or fresh bread or cinnamon rolls, fresh butter, homemade jam, and gallons of coffee. Her meals and her rolls especially were praised by shearing crews for many years. She spent the mornings and afternoons preparing lunch and dinner that included fried lamb chops, roasted leg of lamb, fried, baked or scalloped potatoes, gravy, corn bread, Navy bean soup, canned fruit and vegetables, and sometimes, if time and energy allowed, pies and cake for dessert.

By the time the dishes were washed each evening with help from the kids, Mary was as exhausted as the shearers but she reveled in praise for her cooking. On the final day of shearing, most of the men paused to thank her and offered compliments such as "You make the best damn cinnamon rolls in the valley!"

For a thoughtful sheep herder, the lambing season starting in early May was both a time of hard work and a sense of fulfillment and comfort in the continuity of life. As the spring days lengthened with pink and saffron sunrises over violet-hued mountains, the bleating of lambs seeking out their mother's teats for breakfast was pastoral music. And later in the cool mornings, the spindly-legged little creatures would frolic up and down the arroyos, seemingly propelled by tails spinning like miniature propellers.

One of the mysteries for humans watching sheep in the lambing season was how each ewe and her lamb knew each other. To people, the sheep all looked the same and smelled exactly the same, but obviously each animal had a distinctive smell and sound.

The ewes would drop their lambs wherever they were when birth time came. A herder had to watch out every day for ewes having trouble giving birth and, sometimes, he would have to be a veterinary obstetrician, pulling a slimy little lamb free and helping it to start breathing. Dogies, whose mothers had abandoned them and refused to let them suckle, could be saved by feeding from a nipple-equipped bottle of milk, but for herds on the range that was not likely. A few might be saved by giving them to families with kids. The Johnston children tried that chore for a few years until the novelty wore off. There was no 4-H program in Lund.

In the first four to six weeks of their life, the lambs were not able to trail with the herd the one or two miles to the water at Homer Green's so water had to be hauled to the herd every day with a hundred-gallon tank mounted on the Ford truck and on later-model trucks over the years. Three metal troughs from Homer Green's were set up within a half mile of the sheep camp and were filled several times around noon from the truck tank after it was filled from the windmill-fed storage tank.

By mid-June the lambs were strong enough to walk to Homer Green's learning from their elders to eat grass and brush along the way and then to drink water. Their long tails were doomed, as were the futile efforts of little boy lambs to mount little girl lambs.

The days of "docking"—cutting off all tails and castrating the male lambs—were the hardest and nastiest of the sheep business year. Castration was necessary so the males would develop into fat docile yearlings preferred for eating.

At the corrals, a docker man would grab a male lamb and prop it up facing him on a high bench while a helper held the animal still for castration. The tip of the testicles sack was sliced off with a sharp knife, the two testicles were pushed upward until they could be pulled out by teeth or a tool, and then severed. In his first experience with docking, Harley hired a veterinarian to do the procedure and show him how it should be done. Thereafter, Harley was assisted by Harlan and Kent as each one grew old enough for the work. They used sharp pocket knives and their teeth for the castration of hundreds of lambs each June. Severed tails and testicles were treated as trash.

In later years, stockmen learned that castration could be accomplished by wrapping rubber bands tightly around the base of testicles which would then atrophy and drop off in a few weeks.

The tails of all the lambs were cut off at their rumps because the tails tended to get clotted with diarrhea when the animals ate Russian thistle. More importantly, leaving the tails on would inhibit rams' efforts to impregnate the females.

Mary could not watch any of the docking work and dreaded the effort to soak out and wash out the spattered blood on the men's overalls.

A final springtime ritual was branding. Harley carved a ten-inch high J from a block of wood and dipped it in a shallow pan containing a mixture of oil and lamp black to stamp a brand on the back of each of the adult sheep herded through a narrow chute.

At the start of the sheep era, Harlan reached the age of twelve and replaced Harley for milking the cow each day. A constant priority chore for Mary was taking care of two or three quarts of the fresh milk. It was poured into several flat round pans and left for cream to rise to the surface. Mary skimmed the cream off with a large spoon and stockpiled it in a square jar until there was enough to be churned into butter by turning a crank on the jar for at least twenty minutes. The skimmed milk was kept in pitchers and jars for consumption at all meals.

In the early years in Lund, Mary did clothes washing every Monday for six people. It was the same back-breaking labor over a washboard as she had done at the homestead. But she finally made it clear to Harley that a washing machine with a gasoline motor and a ringer was a priority on a par with the Ford truck. The Maytag machine they purchased seemed to have a mind of its own, being especially stubborn about starting on very cold mornings in the screened porch. While Harley was working at Conoco, he would start the machine on Monday mornings before going to work. However, when he became a sheep herder, Mary had to get the engine started by herself. Occasionally, wash day was postponed until Harley could come home and do battle with the machine.

Early Maytag wringer washing machine

Another appliance that Mary pressured Harley into buying on grounds it would save the family money was a pedal-operated sewing machine. The spindle mechanism and sewing deck was table-high on top of an ornate metal frame. Fold-out wooden wings on each end extended the deck for long lengths of fabric. Mary had learned about sewing in home economics classes in Santa Barbara, and she started making curtains and simple dresses.

On Tuesdays, when the kitchen stove had to be fired up to heat flatirons for pressing clothes, Mary usually put a pot of beans on the stove to simmer.

Other days of the week were spent cleaning house, wiping away the little sand dunes that often appeared at each window and door seal, mending clothes and darning socks that were never allowed to wear out, baking bread and pies and sometimes cookies and cinnamon rolls, limited shopping at the stores, and constant close monitoring of the school children's homework done by kerosene lamp light in the evenings. On Saturday evenings when Harley came home, Mary fixed an extra big dinner of mutton, potatoes, and gravy, and for Sunday breakfast, she prepared fried eggs, bacon, and pancakes in place of the usual cereal.

In mid-summer, Saturday dinner was sometimes a special treat that the Johnston children would remember throughout their lives. Mary would fry one or two young roosters accompanied by heaps of mashed potatoes and chicken gravy and followed by fresh whipped cream on fresh strawberry shortcake made with baking powder biscuits that could never be found in a restaurant.

Mary became the household's secretary and bookkeeper, handling all correspondence, collecting rents, mailing deposits to the bank in Cedar City, and balancing the checkbook.

Her main entertainment was gossiping with neighbors or reading books. The family finally got a battery-operated radio in 1930.

Mary loved her three sons dearly, but Millie was the apple of her eye and eased Mary's hidden pain over Elizabeth's tragic death.

Despite the benefits of family and friends, there were many times when Mary collapsed into a cold bed alone and wondered about how other husbands treated their wives and families, about man-and-woman love, about the extent of sacrifices and compromises required in married life, about what she might be doing if she were still in Santa Barbara and if she had not married Harley, and about an uncertain future in the sheep business. Each time, she concluded that she loved her teetotaler husband and was thankful for beautiful children.

After successful wool and lamb sales in their first two years in the sheep business, Harley and Mary splurged on the purchase of a Chevrolet passenger car which could be used for shopping trips to Cedar City and for Mary's use as needed. The Model T Ford truck was still needed for hauling lambing-time water, firewood, hay, and livestock, and could be kept at Homer Green's place for Harley's use, mainly to and from home. Mary was delighted with "her" Chevy that started with a key instead of a crank.

However, the good times were short-lived. The United States stock market crashed in October 1929, and prices for lamb and wool slid steadily downward until the mid 1930s.

On August 9, 1929, Harlan turned 13 years of age and, after being advanced a year, had finished the eighth grade in school. So, early that summer, Harley and Mary faced the question of what to do about high school. It was a question they would face successively for each of their four kids. The Iron County School District would not provide bus transportation for daily seventy-mile round trips to Cedar City for the few high school age students each year in Lund. The time and cost of driving a personal car on each weekday trip was out of the question for parents. The choice of most Lund area parents of fourteen-year-olds for several decades was to pay for board-and-room five days a week in Cedar City, delivering the students there on Sunday afternoons and picking them up on Fridays after school. For a few youths, especially during the 1930s Great Depression, the alternative was to quit school and try to find work.

Mary particularly did not like the alternatives and was determined to provide a better education for her children than she thought they could get in the public high school in Cedar. There had been a small Presbyterian Church in Cedar for many years, and from friends there Mary learned about Wasatch Academy, a boarding school in Mount Pleasant in the center of Utah. Harlan became the Johnston family's pioneer there.

Wasatch Academy (WA) was founded in 1875 by Dr. Duncan J. McMillan, a messianic Presbyterian Church minister from Illinois, as a Presbyterian mission school. In the first year when payment of $1,000 on a mortgage was due, Dr. McMillan received a check for more than that amount from a Presbyterian ladies club in Cedar Rapids, Iowa, which had heard second hand about the school in Utah. It was the first of several instances over a half century in which contributions from individuals and organizations saved Wasatch Academy from closing down. It evolved into a boarding school for students in grades 7 through 12 with strong financial support from, and some supervision by, the Presbyterian Board of National Missions.

Dr. McMillan named his school after the Wasatch Mountains, declaring, "Let it endure like the mountains." The ridge line of the

Wasatch Academy football field. Gym building – right.
Dormitories – center and left behind trees.

mountains to the east with its Bishop's Chair formation formed a backdrop for the academy in the Sanpete River valley, elevation almost 6,000 feet. Rows of tall Lombardy poplars were a WA campus trademark.

By 1930, WA was like a small college with boys and girls dormitories, a two-story-high gymnasium with a large kitchen and dining room in the basement, an administration and classroom building, a wood-working shop and home economics classroom building, an infirmary, several old Victorian-style residences, and two tennis courts. Catty-corner across a street intersection was a small Presbyterian church. The campus buildings surrounded a half-block quadrangle used for football and later for soccer.

Three meals a day were prepared by hired cooks in the large kitchen and served in the dining room, assisted by students. Students were supervised and taught "table manners" by a faculty member at each table of ten people. Each meal began with a blessing. At the semi-formal Sunday meal at noon, boys had to wear coats and ties and girls dressed accordingly.

The academy became a magnet for an eclectic mix of children from communities and Indian reservations in isolated parts of the Mountain West which, like Lund, were long distances from public high schools. There were a few students from cities such as Salt Lake City and Denver and even Honolulu, Hawaii. Some families developed intense loyalty to WA, sending second and third generation sons and daughters there. Some Mt. Pleasant families sent their children to Wasatch rather than to the local high school.

Wasatch operated on a tight budget, and student labor plus contributions from the Presbyterian Missions Board kept the cost of tuition and board-and-room reasonable for parents like the Johnstons. All students on-campus had daily "institutional" duties such as washing dishes. Some students who needed financial assistance could get jobs that paid for their tuition. All the Johnston children got such jobs. Blue jeans could be worn only for work or outings. At all other times, girls had to wear dresses and boys had to wear "proper" shirts and slacks.

The reputation for good education was based on such factors as small classroom sizes of ten to twelve students, dedicated teachers from around the nation, and two hours of homework time every school day evening. The course work was in effect a college-preparatory curriculum. About half the faculty members stayed for twenty to thirty years, some of them teaching all four of the Johnston children.

A major attraction for many parents was the strict Presbyterian ethic discipline. Smoking tobacco or drinking liquor of any kind was cause for immediate dismissal as was sexual activity between students. "Making out" was virtually impossible because, it seemed, there were faculty eyes everywhere all the time. Kissing was allowed in the town's movie theater, on hayrack rides, and for a few minutes after dinner under lilac bushes at the girls' dorms. Church attendance was required every Sunday. Students were allowed to leave the campus for only a few hours at a time and had to sign out at their dormitories. For Wasatch Academy's first 75 years, no dancing of any kind was allowed. There was no overt pressure for students to join the Presbyterian Church. A required course of study was the Bible taught as history not church dogma.

The strict regime was lightened by hikes in the hills that were close by or up 13,000-foot-high Mount Timpanogos, homecoming events, off-campus picnics and outings of many kinds, sports team contests both on and off the campus (Wasatch mascot were the Tigers), junior/senior banquets, Halloween costume and horror shows, and small group overnight visits to Wa-Sat-Ka Lodge, the school's rustic cabin built in 1933 on a creek two miles up a canyon. Students went home only for two weeks at Christmas time.

In 1933, when Harlan graduated in the depth of the Great Depression, enrollment had declined from 200 to less than 100, and Hungerford Hall, the administration and classroom building, was destroyed by fire. A Presbyterian woman from Illinois made Wasatch the beneficiary of her estate which financed the replacement of Hungerford Hall and a new dormitory for girls in 1934-1935.

Hungerford Hall, Wasatch Academy, circa 1920

When the U.S. stock market crashed on October 29, 1929, followed swiftly by the crash of financial markets around the world, the people in Lund, like those in most of the nation, did not sense it was the start of the Great Depression and what, for millions, would be the most difficult decade of their lives. Few, if any, of the Lund residents had stock market investments, the railroad kept operating as usual, and the cycle of livestock life continued. When big money moguls lost their fortunes and began leaping out of tall office buildings, the "little guys, the working guys" could care less.

Within a year, however, the meaning of the newspaper headlines began to sink in.

Prices offered for wool and lambs dropped thirty per cent. By 1931, Harley and Mary were getting increasingly nervous about the needs of their four children. As prices continued to decline, the Johnstons' sheep business income barely covered expenses. Thankfully, rent payments from the two houses continued to provide at least some money for groceries.

As the Depression deepened, Lund lost one of its two railroad section gangs in 1933, causing a one-third reduction in the town's work force. Arlie Fourman was reassigned to a section foreman position in Zane. That "town" was a dreadfully desolate place with half a dozen railroad worker shanties and a few sheds but the job allowed Arlie to keep a small herd of cattle on his nearby "ranch." The change took Ottie Fourman, Mary's best friend, ten miles away from Lund. Mary felt sorry for Ottie who for several years was the only woman in Zane. Mary made sure to visit her now and then for a few hours even though each visit meant a twenty-mile round trip over a rutted road.

On one visit, Mary told her friend. "I get pretty discouraged sometimes with Harley at the sheep camp all the time, but it's hard to imagine how lonely you must get here in Zane."

"It is tough but I manage to survive because there are always chores every day and that keeps me from losing my mind," Ottie replied. "I don't do much housework but I usually go out nearly every day to check on the cows and the windmill. Arlie's usually too pooped after nine or ten hours on the section gang to visit the ranch on week days. One thing I hate most here is going out to the ranch in wintertime to break ice in the water troughs so the cows can drink."

"I remember you telling me how you hated to leave Los Angeles and come back to the desert and the homestead so many years ago. But you're still here, and things haven't gotten any easier, have they?"

"No," Mary answered, "but I guess I've kind of gotten used to it. I have to hand it to Arlie, he's managed to keep expanding the ranch and our little herd of cattle. He's sure that when the Depression is over we'll be on easy street. I hope I can hang on that long."

"You two found a way to get a deep well and irrigation. Harley was so darn stubborn about dry land farming and that dumb Campbell theory. He still thinks that someday he will have an irrigated farm on our old homestead. The way our sheep business is going nowadays, we'll be too old and too poor to start a new farm."

"Did he ever think about going to work for the railroad like Arlie has and a lot of the other homestead men have done?" Ottie asked.

"No, not really," Mary replied. "When we bailed out of the homestead effort, he was lucky to find a good job at Conoco. I really thought he should have stayed there instead of getting the sheep, but if he had stayed at Conoco, he'd be out of a job today in the Depression, and we might be worse off than we are now. Sometimes I think he has an easy life at the sheep camp while I have to take care of four kids pretty much by myself."

"I would like to have had more kids but that wasn't possible after Alice was born. But, anyway, I can't imagine that Arlie and I would be here in Zane if we had had more kids."

"Someday next winter, you should simply tell Arlie you are going to sleep in, and he can go break the ice."

"Ha! Ha! That would be the day that we might split. But I've stayed with him this long there's no use quitting now."

"Yes, that's true for both of us. We've got the kind of husbands we can't change. And I guess that really means we can't go home again."

Standing: Kent, Harley, Mary, Ottie Fourman,
Alice Fourman, Sitting: Harlan

Chapter 14

Depression Era

The national economic recession triggered by the October 1929 stock market crash quickly sank into the Great Depression, and by 1932 thousands of banks were failing, unemployment was edging toward twenty-five percent, and factory production was slashed for lack of product buyers. The nation's staunch Republican president, Herbert Hoover, insisted that the free market economy would soon recover on its own without government interference.

The United States, regarded by some older nations as being a smart-ass upstart, had nevertheless become the major economic force in the world so that in 1929–1930 when the U.S. market sneezed, the rest of the world caught a cold. Disillusioned by the outcome of World War I, the U.S. had become strongly isolationist, withdrawing behind the protection of the oceans. With the coming of the Depression, the U.S. paid little attention to the culmination of a violent revolution in Russia, the unrest in Germany and the rise of Nazism, or the drive of militaristic Japan to create an Asiatic empire.

In Lund, one of the two small hotels burned down, and the other closed as the flow of transient railroad employees ceased. The lumber yard was in bankruptcy. The Doolittle and Ballard stores and warehouses closed. The Conoco facility moved to Cedar City, leaving Sam W. Johnson's Lund Store and gasoline pump as the only viable business remaining in town.

The Union Pacific railroad's business in Utah was fast sliding downhill, especially as the herds of livestock dwindled and as shipments of iron ore ceased from Cedar City to steel-making plants. The railroad, mother of Lund, began weaning its dependents. It ceased using special gangs for improvements such as bridges and finally had to slash the number of track section maintenance gangs, called "gandy dancers," which hit hardest at the small towns in the Escalante Valley. The section gangs of four to six men did hard physical work for minimum pay under brutal desert sun in summer and in some zero

Lund Hotel, circa 1930.

degree winter days, but that was better than no jobs at all during the Depression.

For the remaining railroad workers, housing, stark and minimum though it was, continued to be free. Much of the housing, particularly individual units, consisted of remodeled freight cars. One building had three, one-bedroom, "apartments" with cold running water. A stinking four-hole outhouse served three families.

Ollie Norris' garage had very few customers, and his car sales had ended abruptly. The Norris family of six hungry children included Richard who was Dick's age, Amy who was Millie's age, and Tom who was Kent's age. In desperation, Ollie turned to bootlegging to take advantage of a demand for illicit liquor despite a U.S. voter-approved constitutional amendment called Prohibition. It banned the production and sale of alcoholic beverages.

Ollie hid a whiskey-making still under the floor of a hog barn and buried caches of bottled white lightning in nearby sand dunes. Richard Norris and Dick Johnston found one cache and choked on a sample drink before being caught and whipped.

Lund was too remote for lawmen to enforce federal Prohibition there. As a result, carloads of mostly young hellions that may have included some deputy sheriffs out of uniform from Cedar City and Parowan would visit Ollie on Saturday nights for rounds of buying and drinking his high quality liquor. The business and the parties ended in

1934 after Congress and most state legislatures voted in 1933 to repeal Prohibition.

On a pleasant winter afternoon early in 1932, Millie and Dick came home from the post office with the mail. Mary opened one letter, screamed, and almost fainted. It was a notice that the Bank of Southern Utah in Cedar City had folded, and the Johnstons' few hundred dollars in savings had disappeared. When Harley came home for lunch, Mary showed him the letter. In one of the few times in his married life, Harley cursed in four-letter words. He stormed over to the Lund Store and tried to telephone the bank. There was no answer. The bank reopened six months later with new capital, but no reimbursement for people's lost deposits. Rental income and about $100 cash the family had on hand when the Cedar bank closed kept the family going through 1933.

Harlan graduated in May 1933 from Wasatch Academy as the number two student in his class, second only to his true love girlfriend, Kathryn Wall, daughter of well-to-do Salt Lake City parents. Kathryn's parents regarded Harlan as too poor for her, and, although he was awarded a scholarship for one year to the Presbyterian Church's Westminster College in Salt Lake City, he never saw her again.

One major advantage the Johnstons had over most other poverty-stricken Lund residents was a steady supply of meat. The carcasses of lambs or old ewes butchered in cool and cold weather would keep for a month when hung in a barn. Part of the meat from lambs butchered in warm weather could be sold and part kept in the cool cellar for a few weeks.

The Union Pacific railroad sometimes left refrigeration cars filled with block ice on rail sidings north of Lund. On two occasions one summer, Harley and Harlan broke the locks on the cars at night and "swiped" blocks of ice that turned the cellar into an ice box for a week. Some of the ice was used to produce a rare treat of homemade ice cream.

Mary's vegetable gardening in a corner of the yard got bigger with emphasis on easy-to-grow potatoes and sweet corn as the family budgets got tighter. The mutton, milk, chickens and garden kept the family comparatively well-fed so that limited cash could be used for gasoline and for feed for the cow, saddle horse, and chickens.

Christmases in those years were the hard rock candy kind. A Yuletide tradition for a treat for Harley was a box of chocolates but that tradition was suspended. Although every member of the family got a present on Christmas Eve, the presents were always clothes. Birthday parties featured a cake and no gifts.

The boys' and Harley's shoes got half-soled several times with pieces of old tires, usually sewn on with thin wire. It was in keeping with Harley's motto, "Use it up, wear it out, make do, go without."

In the tough times, Harley had little tolerance for sentiment. The family dog, a part-Collie named Ring, was suspected of joining a pack of rogue dogs that had killed some sheep. Harley killed Ring with a rifle shot in the front yard, using a forty-year-old .32 calibre rifle that was usually kept at the sheep camp for hunting coyotes.

Mary's interest in the school plus the continuing rental to teachers of the little cottage made the Johnstons the Iron County School District's best known family in Lund. Good Methodist Mary considered herself the protector of teacher morals. She worried about twenty-year-old Harlan spending evenings with one young female teacher, and Mary let it be known a year or two later that a woman teacher, who was married but renting the house alone for the school year, should not spend some evenings talking to guys at the depot.

In 1928 when Harlan became old enough for a job the school district hired him—and later his successor male siblings—to be the janitor at the one-room school at eight dollars per month. The job involved taking a pail of drinkable water to the school each morning, starting a fire in the stove on cold days, cleaning the blackboard and erasers and sweeping the floor after school. The responsibility included having a key to the door locks.

The district also hired Harley for $30 per year for a decade to provide firewood, oil the school floor each August to hold down the dust level, and provide structural repairs as needed. In 1932, the district hired Harley for $40 to paint the school house blue-gray with white trim. It was the first and only time the building was painted after it was built.

For a decade, the Johnstons made sure there was a Christmas play, usually about the Nativity in Bethlehem, by the students. A wire framework was strung between walls at the north end of the classroom to support bed sheets to form a stage with curtains that could be opened and closed. Mary was the advisor for costumes and made many of them.

Mary also served as an unofficial "revolving librarian" for the school, getting and returning a batch of Cedar City library books on her monthly shopping trips to Cedar.

As bad as the years 1932–1933 were with the bank failure and no profit from wool and lamb sales, it seemed that things could not get worse, but they did.

On a Saturday morning in the fall, the house rented by the Townsend family burned down. Lund had no fire department of any kind to try to save the building or to investigate the cause. There was some consensus that the cause was seven-year-old Dick Johnston playing with matches near living room curtains. Fortunately, Mrs. Townsend and Mary were able to save most of the Townsends' valuables and clothing but the house and most of the furniture were a total loss. Like most buildings in Lund, the house was not insured so the Johnstons lost the value of the house as well as the rental income. The rent payments were about to end anyway because Mr. Townsend had lost his job at the lumber yard, and the family was preparing to move away.

Mrs. Townsend sat in the yard after the fire and sobbed. Mary and Harley agreed they were very lucky their own home did not catch fire.

The drought in the western half of the nation that seemed to get worse as the Depression got worse hit the Escalante Valley with a vengeance in 1933. Clouds of billowing dust 100 feet high swept over Lund like the "Four Horsemen of the Apocalypse," turning mid-day light to dusk. Children walking to school wore wet bandanas over their noses and mouths. The conditions were not as bad nor as long-lasting as in the Oklahoma Dust Bowl region but they were bad enough for the hungry residents of the valley, and they sounded the death knell for all but a few remaining homesteaders.

The Johnstons' sheep still produced wool, but the herd would stay skinny through the grass-bleaching summers, and the lambs that survived were hardly worth selling.

With each dust storm, Mary remembered Santa Barbara where the weather was always wonderful. And she would remember even more a few years later when the hot dry months were replaced by a winter of below zero temperatures and hip-high snow drifts.

In 1916, the nation's last major expansion of homestead laws, the Stock Raising Homestead Act, had been passed to encourage livestock herds in the arid and semi-arid parts of the West with no regard for the impact on fragile environments. Sponsored by Colorado Congressman Edward T. Taylor, the act allowed claims of 640 acres on non-irrigable land, and was, in effect, the final "remnant sale" of federal lands. The law was only partly responsible for the hundreds of thousands of sheep that swept over Utah in the first quarter of the century. The owners were taking advantage of free range on federal land that covered ninety percent of the state. But even before the drought of the early 1930s, livestock men themselves were beginning to sense that over-grazing on desert ranges was making them even more deserty.

The hammer fell in 1934 with a law that a year later renewed Harley's dislike of the federal government. Among the many actions of a new Democrat-controlled Congress under mandates from Franklin D. Roosevelt, elected president in November 1932, was passage of the Taylor Grazing Act, named after the same Colorado congressman who had fostered the 1916 homestead law expansion.

The Grazing Act, a landmark in public land policy, said large parts of the West had been severely over-grazed, causing erosion and damage to about 80 million acres of federal land. The law required owners of herds of cattle and sheep to obtain grazing permits for use of federal public lands adjoining or intermingled with private property used for grazing. Also, stockmen who did not have enough privately-owned property in relation to the amount of federal land needed for their grazing permits would have to reduce the size of their herds. The law was partially administered by boards of local citizens in regional grazing districts including one for southern Utah beginning in 1935.

Harley complained about dictators and bureaucrats to everyone who would listen and was foaming-mouth-furious when he got a notice that he would have to reduce his herd of sheep by killing up to 50 head.

Homer Green's place became a killing field that summer as federal agents and Harley and his sons cut the throats of ewes, skinned them, buried the carcasses in a bulldozer-dug trench, laid the wool-covered pelts out in the sun to dry and later sold them for 25 cents each. Federal officials provided reimbursement of several dollars for each of the slaughtered animals. Mary wept at the sight of the spread-out sheep pelts and of a ton of good mutton that was buried. Although normally even-tempered in the face of most hardships, Harley's mood after the killing made him difficult to live with for several months.

In 1946 the grazing district program and its rules about permits were merged into the new U.S. Bureau of Land Management which took control of almost one million acres in the western half of Iron County. Harley never got around to obtaining a permit.

The one railroad section gang remaining in Lund after 1933 was responsible for twice as much track maintenance as previously and was bossed by George Azuma. He had immigrated from Japan to California seeking work on Japanese-owned farms there but had ended up going to work for the Union Pacific. He was a section foreman in Lund for about eight years. The Azuma family included Shinichi, Harlan's age; Moriko, Kent's age; Chiyo, Millie's age; George Jr.; and Sinski, Dick's age. The two older boys attended Wasatch Academy for a time with the two older Johnston brothers.

The Azuma family's railroad-owned home was adjacent to the Union Pacific main line in the center of Lund. A big yard, shaded by huge Carolina poplar trees and silver maple trees, included a patch of lawn, flower beds, a typical Japanese vegetable garden, a dirt-roofed cellar, a two-car garage, and a thick-walled, dirt-roofed, ice house. The railroad company periodically filled the ice house with 100-pound blocks of ice from refrigerated freight cars that were unloaded by the section gang and stored in layers of sawdust. George Sr. allowed railroad worker families to get free blocks of ice in warm weather months, a privilege much envied by the Johnstons and a few other non-railroad families whose cellars were no substitute for ice boxes.

The Azuma parents continued several aspects of the life style in Japan such as ritual bathing in a huge hot tub, Japanese food, and Japanese language newspapers mailed from San Francisco. The landscaped yard and the elder Azuma's position as section gang foreman and keeper of the ice house made the family appear to be the most prosperous family in Lund despite behind-the-hand remarks about "those Japs." When the Azuma family bought a shiny new aluminum bicycle in the middle of the Depression, Harlan promptly used money he had made trapping coyotes to buy a shiny new red Schwinn bike for his siblings, admitting he did so "to get even with the Japs."

In 1934 in the absence of a second scholarship and with no family funding for more higher education, Harlan returned home from Westminster College. He helped Harley through the year, occasionally staying at the sheep camp to give his father a few days off. Harlan also set out lines of traps on the range to catch coyotes and make a few dollars from government bounties and sale of pelts.

The ubiquitous coyotes lived mostly on jack rabbits, gophers and kangaroo rats, and, although usually very cautious, they liked to find, kill and eat a lost lamb or an ailing ewe. Sheepmen, as well as cattle herd owners, claimed without much documented proof that coyotes killed a lot of expensive livestock and should be eradicated. Environmentalists' concerns about endangered species were two generations in the future, and governments at all levels in the 1930s offered bounties as payments for dead coyotes.

Trappers hid steel spring traps under thin layers of dirt. A scent made of putrefied entrails was dabbed on nearby bushes or fence posts to lure the animals to step on the traps which were tied to sturdy stakes in the ground. A coyote pelt typically dried on a wood board A-frame, or the ears of a pup, was worth one or two dollars which was attractive to unemployed victims of the Depression.

A coyote with a leg caught in a trap would usually not be found by a trapper for a day or two. The animal would try to wrench free of the trap until the skin of the leg wore off exposing white bone and tendon. By the time the trapper approached to kill the coyote with a rifle shot to the head, it would be exhausted, crouching or lying down, watching its executioner with malevolent yellow eyes showing as much hatred and defiance as fear.

At a time when unemployment reached almost twenty-five percent, Harlan, with his one year of college and above-average IQ, scored high on a U.S. Post Office Department examination and won a job as a delivery man in Salt Lake City in the fall of 1935. He took a tiny apartment in the city and began developing a circle of close friends out of the Presbyterian Church there. He was on his way to becoming a successful "urban" man but that ended in 1942.

Despite the Johnston family's minimum income, Kent entered Wasatch Academy in September 1934 as Mary remained determined that her children get a good education.

One of Millie's most vivid memories was about Paiute Indians who wandered through Lund from Cedar City in the 1930s in old trucks or horse-drawn wagons to harvest piñyon nuts in the godforsaken Wah Wah Mountains west of Lund. The Indians would stop at the store, sometimes to buy gasoline and usually to try to buy vanilla extract as a substitute for liquor. One summer day when Millie was nine or ten years old, some Paiutes, including a huge old woman, made themselves at home in the Johnston yard where they could get water at the outdoor faucet. Harley was at the sheep camp, the boys were away, and Mary and Millie were afraid to ask the Indians to leave. At one point, the big old woman beckoned to Millie and gave her a little beaded bracelet. The next day, the Indians filled their water barrels at the faucet and headed for the hills.

Nuts from piñyon trees were a staple of the Paiutes' diet for centuries and harvesting them was also a cause for autumn outings by Lund residents. Extracting the thin-shelled nuts from fist-sized cones was tedious work made worse by sticky resin that had to be cleaned off hands with kerosene or gasoline. The nuts could be eaten raw but were best when lightly roasted.

School picture. Top Row: Kent Johnston, Moriko Azuma, Eddie Frashke, Tommy Norris. Next row: Amy Norris, Fay Frahske, Raymond Nodel. Bottom row: Mildred Johnston, Chiyo Azuma, Ola Norris, Charlotte Nodel, George Azuma

Dick had entered the mysteries of first grade in 1932 and competed for the next few years with Sinski Azuma and Jimmy Holyoak. At the beginning of the Depression, Jimmy's parents left the tiny town of Paragonah to try to find work with the Union Pacific. Del Holyoak started on a section gang at Clear Lake, a "town" of a few houses in the middle of the Black Rock Desert. After Del injured his back, he won an assignment as custodian at the Lund depot in time for Jimmy to start the third grade. Jimmy commented later, "After living in Clear Lake, I thought Lund was a metropolis. It had a store and a depot and a bunch of houses!"[1] Dick and Jimmy remained friends for seventy-five years.

Through most of 1935–37, with Harlan gone to Salt Lake City and Kent at Wasatch Academy, Mary once again had to resume the chore of milking the cow twice a day. When Dick reached eleven years of age, he followed in his brothers' footsteps as the milker, and Mary never again had to balance a pail between her knees under a cow.

While the Depression years were tough for everybody, they were devastating for the Ollie Norris family. Ollie's bootlegging business died when Prohibition ended in 1934. The family subsisted for two years on income from a few car repair jobs and government handouts of beans and what was called salt pork. During the summer, all the kids went barefooted. The family's well dried up in the fall of 1935, and Ollie started filling barrels with water from an unofficial public faucet at the Union Pacific's water tank. Then there was the heartbreak over the death of six-year-old Billy when a windstorm blew down a part of the garage wall on top of him.

As soon as school ended in May 1936, the family packed up and left Lund to join relatives in Monroe, Utah, where there were few jobs but at least there was water. Ollie loaded up an old Ford car with as many family belongings as could be crowded around the family of six, and they set off at dawn one morning, looking very much like the Dust Bowl Okies who were filling highways to California. Dick got up in time to say goodbye to his best friend, Richard Norris, and they shook hands for the first time like men.

For the Johnstons, however, the summer of 1936 was like emerging from a dark and fearful tunnel into the Promised Land.

Some late snows and spring rains produced green grass and a summer of good grazing. The sheep herd recovered from the trauma of the Taylor Grazing Act. The wool clip and lamb crop were better than average, and prices for them were slowly rising under the economic impetus of the avalanche of "New Deal" programs that President Franklin D. Roosevelt, a Democrat, started in 1933 after routing the Republican president.

With the first glimmer of prosperity, Harley magnanimously decided the family could afford to visit all the relatives in California in July.

At age 16 Kent was left in charge of the sheep herd, the duty of feeding the chickens and milking the cow and giving most of the milk away to neighbors. It would not be the only time that he got the short end of family trips. However, getting to drive an almost new Chevrolet boosted his ego and his prestige among the town's younger set.

Harley, Mary, Millie and Dick caught a train to Pasadena where they spent a week visiting Harley's three sisters and their families. Harley returned to Lund, and Mary and the two kids spent two weeks in Santa Barbara with Mother King, the three brothers (who had gotten married), and assorted nieces, nephews and cousins. Millie and Dick learned about the "California dreaming" laid-back life style that featured afternoons on the beaches in stark contrast to life on the Escalante desert. Mary, feeling more relaxed than she had felt in almost a decade, relished renewing old acquaintances, showing off her freckle-faced children, and enjoying familiar Methodist church services.

With the family back home in August, thunderstorms nearly every afternoon for about ten days north of Lund provided the next exciting event for 1936. The storms sent sheets of muddy water down a previously imperceptible drainage channel west of the Union Pacific railroad tracks to the lakebed west of Lund. Like the flood of 1922, the flow showed once again that the lakebed was, and is, the sump for much of the valley.

Nearly every day, a troop of kids from town would hurry to the north side of the lakebed to watch a one-foot-high wall of chocolate shake-colored water deepen and widen the previously shallow wash leading into the lake. The churning torrent tore bushes loose and sent them like ghostly little pirate ships out into the lake. Water in the 200-acre lakebed reached knee high to the delight of children who could wade for a hundred yards with mud squishing between their toes.

When the Depression began to ease up, railroad section foreman George Azuma and his family moved to Japan, probably sensing the rising anger in the United States about Japan's brutal empire-building wars against Manchuria and China. The Azumas also probably had saved enough money to feel they could live comfortably in their native land. Moriko and his family were somewhere in Japan when his one-time good friend, Kent, was in B-29 bombers that devastated Tokyo and Yokohama in the first half of 1945.

The winter of 1936–1937 with its huge snow storms was apparently the worst ever experienced in the Escalante Valley. It began with the first storm on December 31st that dumped one to two feet of snow on parts of southwest Utah including one foot in the valley. Thereafter, for three weeks, a series of storms dropped two to three additional feet of snow on the region in what the *Iron County Record* declared was the "heaviest snow in many years and possibly the heaviest in history." Strong winds created drifts five feet high. Most highways and roads were closed for at least several days, and hundreds of motorists were stranded in Cedar City and St. George. The only Iron County snow

Snow in the Johnstons' front yard in the winter of 1936–37.

plows ever seen on the desert opened the Lund/Cedar highway after two weeks of closure.

In the second week of January, temperatures dropped as low as minus 26 degrees Fahrenheit for six nights and seldom rose above freezing for almost a month. The high temperature on January 13 was five degrees. The *Iron County Record* on January 21 said the snow and cold made conditions "perilous" for livestock owners and "threatened a terrific loss of livestock" especially sheep.

Harley was a staunch Republican all his life, dedicated to self reliance that did not need government interference. But that winter, the federal government saved the Johnston family from disaster.

On the range, the snow was so deep the sheep herd would not move very far from the bed ground to graze so Harley spent days tromping spoke-like paths outward from the camp to expose some brush and weeds. He literally kicked most of the sheep off the bed ground to feed in the paths each morning. But it was clear most of the herd would die within a few weeks from exposure and nothing to eat. Harley could not afford to buy hay even if he could find some to purchase and get it hauled to Lund.

The federal Agricultural Adjustment Administration, created in 1933, launched an emergency program to buy cotton seed cake in pellet form from the cotton-growing regions of the South and distribute it free by rail shipments to livestock owners in blizzard-swept parts of the Mountain West. The cotton seed cake was not very palatable, but it was nutritious and could be eaten by sheep and cattle who washed it down with bites of snow. When a railroad freight car load arrived in Lund, Harley made a sturdy wooden sled that could hold several sacks of seed cake and be pulled over the snow by the saddle horse fitted with an old harness. Bundled up like an Eskimo, Harley and the blanket-covered horse struggled nearly every day for several weeks to haul loads of cotton seed cake out to the snow-bound sheep who ate it like candy.

Fortunately, when the blockbuster storms began, Mary had sacks of potatoes and beans, jars of canned fruit, a big crock full of eggs preserved in a gel, and a bushel of carrots, all stored in the cellar. And there was the frozen carcass of an old ewe in the barn.

Railroad workers' families cleaned out food supplies at the Lund store and started going hungry while the store owner scrambled to get rail shipments to replenish his stock.

Mary wrote letters to her mother and brothers describing the hardships and wishing she were back in sunny Santa Barbara. Their replies expressed amazement at the scope of the snow and cold, but their letters to Mary said, in effect, things are tough all over; your brothers are out of work much of the time and your relatives can't help you.

Early in February, the severe conditions eased up, typical desert weather slowly returned, and the snow began melting, showing there were about 50 dead sheep. The winter's silver lining was the six inches of precipitation in the snow that made the desert bloom in the spring, providing grass and succulent bushes for the sheep to eat. Harley was quietly thankful for the federal government assistance that meant survival of the herd.

In 1937, as wool and lamb prices continued to rise, Harley pleased Mary by hiring a down-on-his luck carpenter to install half-inch-thick textured paneling in the living room of their house to cover up the thin warped cardboard walls. He also agreed to the purchase of a new overstuffed chair and sofa in brown tweed fabric with blond wood arms. Mary's ego also got a boost when her canned fruit won prizes at the annual Iron County fair.

The visit to Santa Barbara and the improved economy left Mary happy, and finally, she gave up thinking about leaving. However, another big change in her life was just a year away.

Chapter 15

The Lund Store

In the middle of a beautiful September afternoon in 1938, Mary noticed out a window that Harley, who would normally be with the sheep herd at that hour, had driven up to the front gate, parked the pickup truck, and used his right hand to open the gate while his left arm was crooked against his stomach. Mary met him at the back door, grabbed his shoulders, and asked, "What happened?"

"Well," Harley replied, "We have to go see the doctor in Cedar. I think my arm is broken."

"Oh, Dear Lord, how did that happen?"

"Well, I pushed the sheep out of the corral and went to saddle the horse. I must have forgotten to tighten up the saddle cinch so when I started to get up on the saddle it slipped sideways, and I fell on my arm."

"Does it hurt?"

"It hurt bad when I hit the ground but doesn't hurt now if I don't move it."

"We better get to the doctor quick. I'll go change my dress and shoes—just take a minute—and I'll drive."

They went to the school house to tell Dick to wait at home after school (Millie was in junior high school in Cedar City that year) and then set out on the highway to Cedar in the Chevrolet passenger car. After a few miles, Mary looked sideways at Harley and said, "My dear, this confirms what I've been a little bit worried about for a year or so. I think we have to face the fact that at your age you should not be out there alone."

"I'm only 63, and you know as well as I do that farmers and ranchers don't retire at that age."

"So what will we do—wait 'til the day I have to come looking for you and find you dead because there will be no one around to help you if you have a heart attack or fall down the well or something?

Remember when you got a sunstroke changing tires on the sheep camp and you barely made it home? And remember what a close call it was two years ago when Kent was using the truck to pull you up out of the well where you had to fix something. A pulley came loose and hit you on the head, and you almost fell back down into the well. You had a gash in your head, and we had to rush you to the doctor then. Remember that?"

"Yeah, but that was an unusual accident."

"And what was it today, a usual accident?"

Harley sat quietly for a few minutes, gazing out the window at the stark desert scenery.

"Well, I hate to admit it but you might be right. And I have to admit I am getting tired of the sheep camp life. It gets a little bit harder every day to get up and out at sunrise, especially in the winter. The way things've been going the last two years, I guess we can think about hiring a sheep herder. You remember meeting Jewel Couch's husband, Lyle Applegate, last summer when they visited Lund? He said something then about needing work and said he'd done some sheep herding."

"They were living in Milford, weren't they? When we get back this afternoon, let's see if we can telephone him and see if he can come to work now. You shouldn't stay out at the camp with a broken arm."

"The sheep know about going to the bed ground at night and going to water at noon, and we can go out and check on them every evening and every morning for a few days 'til we can hire Lyle or somebody."

They got to the doctor who set what fortunately was a simple break in a bone in the forearm. He put a plaster cast on the arm and showed Harley how to use a sling. The couple got home, had dinner, drove in the dusk to Homer Green's, fed the horse and put him in the barn, took the dog to the camp and left him to hopefully scare away coyotes. They herded a few straggling ewes onto the bed ground, went home, and went to bed where they didn't sleep very well.

The next morning they telephoned Lyle Applegate who said he could come to Lund the next day and be in the sheep camp that night. Harley helped him for a month thereafter to get a small house moved to a lot just north of the Johnstons' yard where Jewel and their baby daughter could live.

Hiring Lyle proved to be timely. Two months later when Mary had to spend a week in the Cedar City hospital for a hysterectomy, and

Harley was able to stay home with Dick and with Millie when she was home for weekends.

Harley was now retired, at least for the time being, and Mary enjoyed the leisurely time with him at home. Her days of loneliness and extra hard work raising the family by herself while he was at the sheep camp had ended. He relieved Dick of the chore of milking the cow, leaving the boy with the duty of chopping firewood and taking care of the chickens. Harley was in bed with Mary every night and was up in his pajamas each morning to start a fire in the kitchen stove and in the living room stove if necessary, leaving her to luxuriate for an extra half hour in bed. They were able to visit their good friends, the Fourmans, in Zane more often.

But Harley was not really ready to retire.

The surviving store in Lund had started out as the "J. David Leigh Store: Everything for Camp and Farm." Sam W. Johnson owned and operated it as the Lund Store and adjacent Conoco gasoline pump from 1918 through the prosperous time of the Twenties. However, he watched the business steadily decline as the Great Depression continued. Some families begged him for credit so their children could have something to eat. He and his wife wanted to retire but they could not afford to unless they could sell the store.

In 1937, despite the lingering Depression, a young couple from Parowan, Paul Carpenter and his wife, thought they would like to have a little business of their own so they bought the store for about $400 dollars. The Johnsons moved to California. The Carpenters had more personality and enthusiasm than business sense and within 18 months were ready to abandon the store.

Harley thought strongly that the town should have a store and a gasoline station, mainly so he would not have to set up a gasoline tank—a safety hazard—to assure that he, and others, did not get stranded for lack of gas. The nearest other stations were in Cedar City.

Harley bought the store property for half price after a brief consultation with Mary who could only sigh at the prospect of another hard work scheme. Thus, the Johnstons started the store, restaurant, and "hotel" phase of their life.

Harley's jobs in Los Angeles and at the Continental Oil Company had given him good experience about operating a business. And Conoco officials, remembering Harley's work for them, were willing to keep sending a truck out to Lund periodically to fill the store's gasoline tank in the ground underneath a round, nine-foot high, pump fixture. A hand-operated lever, secured by a lock, pumped gasoline from the tank up into a ten-gallon glass cylinder. A scale on the glass showed a user how many gallons he would get through a hose to a motor vehicle.

About once a month Harley would leave Mary in charge of the store and drive to wholesale businesses in Cedar to stock up with supplies, especially cases of bottled beer. In the next decade, beer sales (Harley didn't bother to get a state license) at a 100 percent markup produced almost as much annual income as the sheep business.

The store property included the main building, a storage shed mainly for firewood, and a sprawling structure at the rear that housed three bedrooms for rent, served by a common bathroom.

The front wall of the main building had two large windows looking out on to Main Street and the Union Pacific's handsome depot. Along one side of the front room was a ten-foot-long, marble-topped, soda fountain-style counter in front of a hand-operated cash register and a large mirror framed in ornately carved golden oak. On the other side of the room were shelves and display cases for canned food and some goodies such as cookies and candy bars including Snickers and Baby Ruths. A wood-topped counter was equipped with a roll of brown wrapping paper. The Depression era merchandise was very limited compared with what the store had offered in the homestead boom.

Ice cream service was not feasible so the marble counter was the bar for beer and Coca Cola customers. A propane gas-operated refrigerator chilled the beer and soda pop.

In one corner of the rear half of the main room was the post office and Lund's only public telephone—a four-party line housed in a booth paneled in golden oak. In the other corner was a full kitchen with a white linoleum floor, propane gas stove, cold running water, and a sink that drained to the property's large septic tank. Near the door to the kitchen was a

Lund Store and Post Office, circa 1938

dining table and chairs. In the middle of the back half of the room was a typical wood-fired stove for heating. As was the custom in country stores, visitors gathered around the stove in cold weather to smoke and tell old stories and new lies.

A singular feature of the store was an old nickel slot machine. It was technically illegal in Utah but, as in most other matters of law, the county sheriff in Parowan paid no attention to Lund. The slot machine was a lightly-used device of amusement for Lund's poor people. Harley had a key to it and made sure that were never enough nickels inside to pay off a big jackpot.

In the rear half of the main building was a pool hall with two massive, green-felt-covered, pool tables and complete equipment for playing pool. The most popular game for the few players who could afford a dime a game was simple rotation. Dick and Jimmy Holyoak learned to play pool "on the house." The room, with a door in the rear, also served as the store's main storage area.

That rear door, which routinely was not locked, was the pivot point for two escapades involving Dick. When he and Richard Norris were about seven years old, they loaded a little wagon with two cases of soda pop from the storage area and hid the booty in the Norris' barn. Within a few hours, Sam Johnson noticed that some soda pop was missing and followed wagon tracks to the barn and the two boys. Richard got spanked, but Dick escaped a whipping. By this time, Harley was tired of spanking four children and appeared to be more amused than angry about the incident.

The Lund Store building in 2010.

Years later, members of a special railroad gang were playing pool one evening, and Dick was supposed to be the watchdog in the back room. One of the men gave a very naive Dick a handful of nickels and suggested he go "have fun" playing the slot machine in the front room. In the few minutes he was gone, the men formed a chain to carry cases of beer out the back door to a hiding place in the darkness where they could make off with the contraband at store closing time. The next morning, Harley noticed a lot of beer was missing, and, after questioning Dick, quickly figured out what had happened. Dick was too old to be spanked but his feeling of stupidity was punishment enough. Harley, all of five-feet-seven-inches-tall and 150 pounds, grabbed a pick axe handle and set off to find the gang at work, determined to beat the hell out of the men. Fortunately, he could not find them and escaped getting himself beaten up.

Within a month after the store was purchased, Mary was serving as postmaster, running a cafe for itinerant railroad employees, and sometimes renting rooms for a dollar a night.

The bathroom serving the three bedrooms for rent had a wash basin, flush toilet, and regular bathtub. A hot water tank was fitted with a smelly kerosene-fired heater that had to be lighted a few hours before anyone could take a hot bath. Each bedroom was equipped with a table, a chair, and a small wood-fired stove that renters had to take care of themselves in cold weather. Mary changed the bed sheets after each rental and washed sheets and towels in the aged Maytag washing machine at home.

As things turned out, the business operation provided several treasured perks for the Johnston family. Foremost was use of the hot water bathroom which ended Saturday night baths in a galvanized tub in the home kitchen. The family use of the bath tub, usually on Saturday afternoons, had to be coordinated with use by the occasional renters. Another benefit of the business was that purchases of many kinds of food, drinks, and materials, even gasoline, for the family were made at wholesale, rather than retail, prices which meant significant savings on the family budget.

The children and Harley could help themselves without payment to a candy bar or a Coca Cola whenever they felt like it, but Harley soon found he had to set a limit. Nevertheless, the poverty-level kids in town were very envious of Dick's and Millie's prerogatives. For somebody other than Harley, "free" beer could likely have meant no profit and maybe even alcoholism. But Harley, a teetotaler by nature, sipped briefly on only a half dozen bottles of beer in a decade in the store, and those were times when partying friends insisted they buy him a drink.

A year after buying the store, Harley, nudged by Mary, built a white picket fence around a 200-square-foot patch of land on the south side of the main building and planted it in a bluegrass lawn with a fringe of hollyhocks. It was the only lawn the Johnstons ever had in Lund and was a favorite place for family photographs.

In the restaurant operation, Mary served balanced meals of meat and potatoes, vegetables, sometimes salads, desserts, and coffee or tea. As might be expected, the menus often included mutton in one form or another—roasted, fried, or stewed. One of the most frequent customers was a telegraph system maintenance man who, at the first meal, declared he did not like mutton. Mary tried unsuccessfully four or five times to fool him, even disguising mutton with barbecue sauce. He would take one bite of whatever was mutton in any disguise and would push it aside. Mary gave up and thereafter served him chicken or beef even if it had to be out of a can.

Mary and Harley relaxing in the yard at the Lund Store, circa 1945.

Harley, being the hard worker he always was, opened the store about 8 a.m. every day of the week and closed at 6 or 7 or 8 p.m. The family had lunch and dinner there every day.

Mary had qualms at first about the demands of the business, but within

Lund looking north over the depot, circa 1944.

a few months found herself relishing the role of her and Harley as the area's best known couple. She enjoyed the flow of customers, a few of whom came in merely to have somebody to talk to, and Harley loved to argue about politics. In small rural towns in Utah, the Mormon church bishop was often more important than the mayor. In Lund, some residents started calling Harley "bishop." The store and the depot, which was open 24 hours a day, were the town's social centers.

However, the post office became the most important non-personal aspect of Mary's entire life in Lund. It was a fourth class post office, the lowest level in the U.S. Post Office Department, but it served a vital function in the Lund area. If not for it, mail service would be available only in Cedar City. The wife of the Lund Store owner usually became the postmaster (the title did not recognize gender differences). Postmaster General James A. Farley sent Mary a framed certificate, dated April 1, 1939, saying, "Know ye, that reposing special trust and confidence in the intelligence, diligence, and discretion of Mary D. Johnston, I have appointed and do commission her Postmaster at Lund, in the County of Iron, State of Utah, and do authorize and empower her to execute and fulfill the duties of that office according to the laws of the United States and the regulations of the Post Office Department, and to have and to hold the said office with all the rights and emoluments thereto legally appertaining . . ."

Mary, with her better-than-average education, was well qualified to be the postmaster. The pay was only around $25 a month, but the money was strictly hers, and she set out to save most of it for a sense of security. She would never admit to being a snoop, but she did like the opportunity to know more about most Lund residents' affairs than anyone else simply by paying close attention to names and addresses on incoming and outgoing mail.

Her office, about ten feet square, had an old roll-top oak desk and a counter cluttered with rubber stamps and other tools of a postmaster. A wall facing the main room of the store was stacked with four-by-four-inch-square metal boxes with numbered doors and combination locks. When small bags of mail arrived daily off the trains, Mary would sort the letters into the open back ends of the boxes and leave notices about any packages to be asked for. She quickly became well-versed in the lengthy post office regulations.

Kent graduated from Wasatch Academy May 25, 1938. Despite his somewhat sullen personality, he was ranked fourth in his class of 37. "Honor students" at W.A. were chosen by the faculty on a basis of grades, athletic achievements, and extracurricular activities including student leadership positions. Kent would never win a popularity contest, but he lettered in football and track. His grades were close to straight A's, a sign of his intelligence.

For three years, Kent held a Wasatch "paying" job as a member of what was called the "Black Gang" that took care of the buildings' coal-fired furnaces. The crew unloaded coal from Sanpete Railway cars, distributed it in wheelbarrows to furnace rooms, and removed ashes from the furnaces. Crew members were often covered with coal and ash dust and were regarded as the "Untouchables" of the student work force. Kent seemed to enjoy the exclusive comradeship of the gang and a feeling of "belonging."

Comments scrawled by classmates in his 1938 Orange and Black Wasatch yearbook revealed conflicting attitudes toward him:

> I've really admired you even if you did get mad at my calling you 'Vinegar Puss.' Hope we can come back and meet at W.A. again. Congratulations on your work here.
>
> Weren't we two silly as freshmen? Glad you seem to have changed your mind about me and don't hate me so much. I hope I'll see you again.
>
> Well, Kent, You darned old sour puss you. I didn't get to know you until this year but I have really enjoyed going on athletic trips with you and scuffling with you. Remember me as a pal.
>
> Well, you big bully, we must part. Wish you all the success in the world.

There was no evidence he had a girlfriend, and his only dates were probably those required on the annual Sadie Hawkins Days when the girls could ask boys.

Mary took twelve-year-old Dick with her to attend Kent's graduation. Because there was a shortage of motel rooms in Mt. Pleasant at W.A. graduation time, Dick spent the night in the infirmary. The son of the desert was intrigued by the sound of irrigation water gurgling through ditches on the campus in the twilight. He went to sleep with the sound of several young men somewhere in the darkness singing a then-popular ballad that in its sadness seemed to fit the mood of seniors leaving the campus womb. The song was about Old Pappy who got caught messing around with a neighbor's wife. When a posse found him, "By the neck they strung him, by the neck they hung him from a branch of the old apple tree. Now my dear Pappy lies in the orchard out of his misery. If my Pappy had of knowed it, he never would have growed it 'cause he died on that old apple tree."

Like Harlan before him, Kent received a one-year scholarship to Westminster College in Salt Lake City where he had to work hard part time for board-and-room. There was no money for Kent to continue in college so he returned to Lund in June 1939 and replaced Lyle Applegate as the family sheep herder.

The week that Kent graduated from Wasatch was also the week that Harlan married Lucia Dawson in the big Presbyterian Church in Salt Lake City. It was a modest ceremony followed by a modest reception for family and a dozen friends. Mary, Kent, and Dick went straight from Wasatch to Salt Lake for the wedding. Lucia was not pretty in face or form but her face and her large luminous eyes were always animated and radiating warm. She and Harlan were very much in love but they would have only a few precious years together.

Harlan, circa 1935-36

Millie finished the eighth grade in Lund in May 1937 and would normally have gone on to Wasatch to be a freshman while Kent was a senior. However, Mary missed the deadline for getting her enrolled at Wasatch, so Millie had to attend the ninth grade in Cedar City, getting board-and-room with a single woman and her teenage daughter in an apartment. Mary, usually accompanied by Dick, drove two 70-mile round trips weekly across the desert to pick up Millie after school each Friday and return her each Sunday afternoon, rain, shine or snow.

The summer of 1939 was highlighted by the visit of a crew of denim-uniformed young men who were in the Civilian Conservation Corps, one of the "New Deal" programs. The CCC constructed at least 4,000 public projects around the nation including forty-two in Utah. The Lund area project was a small dam at Mountain Springs about fifteen miles west of town. One of the leaders was an especially handsome and well-mannered young man with a Southern drawl who visited the store each week. Mary treated him like a son.

Despite its isolation, the Lund area benefited from the federal Public Works Administration as well as the CCC. The PWA, using local labor and equipment, constructed an elevated and graveled road west out of town along the south edge of the often-muddy lakebed.

For a few of the children in Lund, hunting jack rabbits with a .22 caliber rifle was a major pastime along with "drowning out" gophers. Two buckets of water poured into a gopher hole would force a rodent to emerge and face death by a rifle shot or a hungry dog. Several times, porters in Pullman cars on railroad sidings waiting to be taken to Cedar City spotted the gopher activity and delighted in helping the kids carry buckets of water.

Hollywood discovered southern Utah's color country and canyon lands in the 1930s, and it became the backdrop for dozens of western films. Escalante Valley was featured in *Union Pacific*, made by Paramount in 1938. Director Cecil B. DeMille used Iron Springs to imitate Cheyenne as it looked in 1865, and the rail spur to the iron mines for scenes of building the railroad through the West. Cedar City's Thorley Theater was site of one of two world premieres in 1939. Mormons are not supposed to drink intoxicating beverages so, to the dismay of motion picture crews from California, the small state-controlled liquor store in Cedar City stocked only the most basic supply of booze. Singing star Deanna Durban, on location in the area for a few days, got furious when she could not find a bottle of champagne.

Even in the midst of the Depression, railroads around the nation were starting the seismic switch from steam locomotives to diesel engines and by the mid-1930s were showcasing their new bullet-nosed "streamliners."

At dawn on a summer morning in 1936, many Lund residents got up and went out, some in their pajamas, to watch the first, red-striped, yellow, *City of Los Angeles* roar through town without slowing down, signaling the passing of an era and the chilling harbinger of things to come for little towns along railroad tracks. The days of smoke plumes, hissing steam, and long lonesome whistles that charmed railroad buffs for many generations, were numbered.

As is usually true in small towns, Lund had some "characters." One was Oliver Stone, a corpulent, beer-loving widower who worked at the railroad's roundhouse. The facility had indoor and outdoor hot water showers for locomotive engineers, and Lund residents could use them freely. A big diesel engine that operated the turntable for work on locomotives was Mr. Stone's nemesis. Dick and his best friend, Richard Norris, looking for pollywogs in a small pond near the roundhouse, would overhear his five-minute streams of swearing at the balky machine:

> "Goddamm/sonofabitching/nogoodpileofcrap/worthlessjunk/pieceofshit/Christcouldn'tfix/whyinthehelldoIhavetoputupwiththis/shoveituptheassoftheboss. . ."

On a typical Sunday, Mr. Stone, always dressed in greasy overalls, and a drinking buddy would stagger along Main Street from the store to his house carrying a half case of beer between them. Holding onto the beer container kept them from falling as one would zig when the other zagged. One day when Mr. Stone hadn't shown up at his usual time at the store, Harley went looking for him and found him dead in bed, apparently having suffered a heart attack. The UP did not replace him at the roundhouse.

Mr. and Mrs. Deffenbach were a "character couple." They were both white-haired, slight of build, fidgety, and precise in everything they did. He was responsible for maintenance of the system of signals along a twenty-mile section of the UP railroad tracks, operating out of his own little tool shack and riding his own little motor car separate from section gangs. Her hobby was growing flowers of many kinds in every corner of the yard of their railroad-supplied house. His hobby was making furniture in the house basement. One year, he made three nearly identical chests of drawers before the third one satisfied his desire for perfection. The couple eventually retired and moved to Hurricane in southern Utah's Dixie.

And, out on a homestead north of Lund, there was Jesse Steele trying with great determination for years to invent a new and efficient system of water-based fertilizer that could be used on any farm.

The challenge was to mix proper amounts of manure in a labyrinth stream of well water that would be automatically controlled to flow into irrigation ditches. The idea was good but making it work was something else. Although he had a small pension of some kind, he and his wife were very poor, and she died of tularemia after eating a diseased jackrabbit. Jesse gave up his dream of a patent and moved away.

A gypsy-style "medicine" show came to Lund for two days one summer with horse-drawn wagons resembling that of the mustachioed medicine man that Dorothy and her dog, Toto, met at the start of the movie, *The Wizard of Oz*. The caravan family, traveling through the back country of Utah to avoid law enforcement officers, performed skits followed by a sales pitch for a bottled "snake oil" medicine guaranteed to cure backaches, acne, catarrh, and many other ailments. Harley bought a pint out of curiosity and found it tasted like kerosene.

In 1939, Dick was the only one in the eighth grade in the Lund school. The other seventh and eighth graders were in Cedar City's junior high school, getting board-and-room with friends or relatives.

As the Depression's unemployment rate declined, the Iron County School District found it increasingly difficult to find teachers willing to face the one-room school challenge in Lund. For the 1939–1940 school year, the teacher was a middle-aged woman who lived in a tiny trailer parked beside the school so she could use the school outhouses and carry water from the Johnstons' outdoor faucet. She was so kooky that, for all practical purposes, Dick was self-taught that year, reading voraciously with Mary's support.

Dick spent a somewhat boring summer in 1940 with Kent at the sheep camp. Kent was often morose and not inclined to talk much. On several occasions, a rage that seemed latent in his personality erupted, and he beat his horse over the head with fists and bridle reins. Dick was very careful not to cross him. The younger brother was the designated cook, learning how to fry bacon and how to make sour dough biscuits and pancakes.

At Wasatch, in September 1940, Dick joined Millie who was a senior that year. She had a job in the school's bookstore, and Dick worked as a janitor.

Back in Lund, with Dick and Millie safely away at Wasatch, with Kent as the family's free sheep herder, with slowly rising prices for lambs and wool, and with the store and the post office providing both pleasant and lucrative work, Mary felt more secure and happy than she had felt since leaving Santa Barbara. The desert and Lund were now totally her home, and with a feeling of belonging, of rootedness, of knowing herself, she was content to spend the rest of her life there.

But there would be one more period of fear and heartbreak, starting December 7, 1941.

Chapter 16

World War II

On September 16, 1940, the United States' government approved the Selective Service Training Act to draft men for military service that would be required when, as it appeared likely, the U.S. became involved in wars then being waged in Europe and in the Far East. The three Johnston brothers were caught in the cross hairs. The next six years would bring death to one, a time of comradeship followed by terror for the second, and an enjoyable adventure for the third.

Nazi Germany had conquered Western Europe except for Great Britain. Japan had set out to conquer the Asian rim of the Pacific Ocean, occupying Manchuria in 1931 and invading China in 1937.

The Great Depression was ending as the U.S. began producing goods and armaments for lend-lease to Britain besieged by Germany. Roosevelt's "New Deal" flood of alphabetized agencies financed by billions of dollars of "new" federal money had kept the nation from collapse, but had not resulted in a very significant increase in permanent jobs and manufacturing production. Roosevelt was re-elected to an unprecedented third term in November 1940 as the war clouds darkened.

Business on the Union Pacific railroad was slowly picking up, and new technology was emerging in locomotion and communications. That, plus different methods of track maintenance, meant an inexorable reduction in employment, especially for section gangs in the little towns strung out in the deserts of western Utah.

Harlan Johnston and his wife of two years were living a comfortable life with modest jobs and a church-based circle of close friends in Salt Lake City. Kent was still the family's sheep herder. Dick was excitedly adjusting from being the only eighth grader in a country school to the swirl of activity and 200 students at Wasatch Academy, watched over by his sister Millie, a senior. Harley eased up on his penny-pinching ways to allow family trips to Yellowstone and Grand Canyon National Parks. In each case, Kent stayed with the sheep.

On Sunday morning, December 7, 1941, the world changed.

The Japanese Navy's sneak attack on the U.S. naval base at Pearl Harbor, on the Hawaiian island of Oahu, used carrier-based bombers that expanded the new era of airplane warfare. The United States emerged from 25 years of isolationism into a global conflict called World War II and into a future of internationalism. President Roosevelt, citing "a date that will live in infamy," called for a declaration of war and Congress immediately agreed. Frenzied radio broadcasts told the nation what had happened, and millions of people asked "Where is Pearl Harbor?"

Harlan and wife Lucia learned about the attack while at a church service. Harley and Mary drove out to the sheep camp to tell Kent, and they could only share questions about his immediate future. At the Holy Cross Hospital nurses' school in Salt Lake City, Millie heard the radio broadcasts. Dick and a dozen classmates were on a weekend outing at Wasatch Academy's mountain cabin, and they all reacted with a mixture of excitement and fear to the news on a portable radio. The outing ended abruptly without the planned lunch of hot dogs.

Mary Johnston stared at newspaper headlines and agonized over the possibility that she could lose all of her beloved sons.

Conscription of men for military service is as old as civilization. The U.S. Selective Service law, as amended several times, was somewhat unique in its democratic process. The national administration basically set policy which was carried out by county-based Selective Service Boards composed of local civilians with considerable discretion as to who got drafted and when. By the start of 1942, about 20 million men had registered for the draft. The ages for military service were 18 to 37, and duration of service was for the length of the war, however long that might be.

Within days after the Pearl Harbor attack, Japan's well-experienced military forces had swept into the Philippine Islands and European colonial countries along the Pacific Rim. By mid-1942, Japan controlled the rim, leaving Australia isolated as a bastion of the Allies fighting the Axis nations of Germany, Italy and Japan. However, Japanese Admiral Isoroku Yamamoto who had lived in the United States and was familiar with the nation's industrial capability and spirit, warned his peers after Pearl Harbor, "I fear all we have done is to awaken a sleeping giant and fill him with a terrible resolve."

The giant had indeed been awakened, and the tide of the war began to turn. American Marines won the very bloody six-month fight over a vital airfield on Guadalcanal in the Solomon Islands. It was followed by the amazing defeat of the Japanese navy at the mid-Pacific island of Midway. From then on, in touch-and-go battles in 1943 and 1944, the U.S. swept over island chain after island chain to Saipan, Tinian, and Guam in the Mariana Islands. From there, huge B-29 bombers carrying crews that included Kent Johnston could devastate the Japanese homeland.

As the war effort gained momentum, so did the Union Pacific's business through Lund. There was a notable increase in freight trains for transport of implements of war, and troop trains passed through Lund every day replacing a slowdown in regular passenger traffic. But the biggest impact came from skyrocketing demand for iron ore.

In 1941, the federal government became concerned that most of the steel needed for ship-building on the West Coast to serve a Pacific war theater was being transported slowly and expensively by rail across the country or by ships through the Panama Canal from East Coast plants. The U.S. Defense Plant Corporation decided to construct a huge steel production facility at Geneva just north of Provo, Utah, for the same reason Columbia Steel had built a plant in the area 20 years earlier: iron ore from southern Utah could meet up there with coal from eastern Utah. Ore was also sent to steel plants at Pueblo, Colorado, and Fontana, California.

The war time demand for steel resulted in a quadrupling of iron ore shipments by rail through Lund from the mines west of Cedar City, reaching two million tons in 1945. Iron industry workers in the area increased from 21 in 1940 to 300 in 1944.

After the war, the government sold the Geneva facility to the U.S. Steel Company which had absorbed Columbia Steel in 1953. For all practical purposes, iron mining in the area was dying. By the end of the 1970s, American steelmakers, beset by high labor costs, pollution controls, and foreign competition, began shutting down, which slowly killed southern Utah's iron ore industry.

With the wartime business, the role of the station master/agent as the Union Pacific railroad's key employee in Lund was enhanced. His primary duty was taking orders from the rail system's dispatchers in Milford or Salt Lake City and delivering them to train crews. He sold passenger tickets, kept track of freight and baggage business and the number and kind of cars on side tracks, served as paymaster for UP workers, and, more importantly for the community, sent and received Western Union telegrams.

During the war years, the Lund depot was staffed twenty-four hours a day with telegraphers trained to take dispatcher orders and give them to train engineers and conductors. If a train did not need to stop to take on water, the paper orders were clipped to a two-foot diameter bamboo hoop that was held up so an engineer leaning out of his still-moving locomotive cab could hook the hoop on his arm, quickly detach the message, and then toss the hoop out onto the platform or adjacent tracks to be recovered by depot workers.

Because of the draft, keeping men on the section gangs became difficult so the Union Pacific recruited Navajo Indians from northern Arizona. They were usually smaller in stature than "white" men and Mexicans but they were strong and tireless.

The UP also put together special gangs, such as for bridge repairs, composed of men with 4F draft classifications, old men, alcoholics, and 18-year-olds, such as Dick Johnston, awaiting a draft call-up. The gangs lived in bunk cars and had meals in a dining car. Dick spent a month in the summer of 1944 on a gang working mainly out of Milford where he could visit honky-tonk bars to listen to Hank Williams' music and then watch the alcoholics fall off the wagon and fall out of their bunks at night.

The itinerant gangs and the increased activity at the depot were a boon for the Lund Store business, particularly the highly profitable beer sales.

At the store, the Johnstons struggled to cope with the wartime federal regulations for rationing such items as meat, sugar, and gasoline. Customers had ration books and stamps. Gasoline was limited to ten gallons per week per family so theft of gas by siphoning became common. One Saturday evening, Dick and two friends drove to a dance in Milford. At midnight, Dick used a small rubber hose to steal a few gallons of gas from a car in a dark parking lot to make sure the troupe could get home.

Harlan, at age twenty-five, joined the Army Air Force in 1942 and early in 1943 was assigned as a sergeant to a Quartermaster Corps post in Hobbs, New Mexico, staying with his wife in an old hotel. The hotel caught fire the night of February 2, 1943, and was evacuated but Harlan dashed back inside in an attempt to recover clothing and personal belongings. While in an ambulance on the way to a hospital, he died of smoke inhalation.

Harlan, Army Air Force, 1942.

Dick, a junior at Wasatch, was presiding over an International Relations Club meeting when the school principal called him out of the meeting and told him about Harlan.

Dick's roommate was given a school car to take Dick to Nephi thirty miles away where he could catch a bus to Cedar City and home. Typical of the super-patriotic feelings of young men at the time, Dick regretted the fact that his older brother had died "without seeing action" in the war.

Harlan's body, in a flag-draped coffin flanked by two uniformed Air Force officers, was unloaded from a train at the Lund depot platform. Harley, watching through the big front windows at the store, waved a hand at the scene and tried to say something before he choked and began to cry, the first time anyone in the family had ever seen him cry. Mary had already cried herself out and watched with quiet stoicism as the officers put the coffin in a hearse for the trip to a Cedar City mortuary.

Millie, who was in a nurse training program in Salt Lake City, and Dick had come home and they accompanied their parents on the drive behind the hearse to make arrangements for a funeral at the Presbyterian Church and burial in the Cedar City Cemetery where Harley, with somewhat unusual thoughts about the future, had purchased six lots. Kent left the sheep herd two days later to join the family and a small audience of friends at the funeral and interment.

The most heart-breaking moment of the funeral proceedings was when Lucia, Harlan's wife of less than five years, asked to be left alone with his body "for a few minutes" in the mortuary's viewing room. The Johnston family had come to love her as a sister and daughter and kept in touch with her for many years afterward until she remarried and became a resident of Butte, Montana.

As the family drove home from the funeral, Mary thought to herself, *"One down and two to go."* At the family home a few weeks later she put the first of two gold stars in the front window signifying she had lost a son in the service of his country. The second star would be placed in the window in June 1945 and only remain there for a few months.

Chapter 17

Kent in the Air Force

Throughout 1942, Kent wavered between two choices: enlist in some branch of the military service as millions of young men had rushed to do or continue to accept deferments from the draft as granted by the Iron County Draft Board which considered the Johnston sheep herd as necessary for the war effort. His desire to enlist was offset by the need of his aging parents to have a dependable sheep herder.

In the summer of 1943, the Iron County Draft Board ended Kent's deferment as an essential producer of meat and wool so he soon received one of the millions of notorious letters to draftees that began "Greetings from the President." He immediately enlisted in the Army Air Force and was inducted August 3 at Fort Douglas near Salt Lake City.

It was clear that Harley should not be a sheep herder again, so he and Mary contacted Lyle Applegate who was exempt from the draft and was available for hire on short notice. He had liked working in 1938–1939 for Harley, who offered him a bit more pay for a second round as the Johnstons' herder.

Kent was sent to Buckley Air Base near Denver, Colorado, for basic training as a private followed by several months in the 766th Technical School Squadron to become a gunner on a bomber. His rare letters home were perfunctory and mostly about the training. He had no close friends there and went on passes alone to the city, occasionally visiting USOs and Denver's then notorious Larimer Street collection of bars, dance halls, and flophouses which was the target of most servicemen in the area. Since he was over 21 years of age, Kent could buy liquor quicker and easier than many of his younger colleagues but he would usually drink only a few beers and return to the base.

Early in 1944, Kent was sent to the Second Gunnery Squadron at the Laredo Air Field in Texas where he graduated May 22 with better than average scores in operation of machine guns. After Laredo, he polished his bomber turret gunnery skills at the Clovis Air Base in New Mexico, was promoted to sergeant, and was sent in July to the huge two-year-old Fairmont-Geneva Air Force Base near Lincoln, Nebraska. There he became part of a B-29 bomber crew of eleven men who would be his constant companions for a year and who would learn how to survive brutal treatment.

The huge, four-engine, long distance B-29s were designed to be the bombers that would end the war with Japan, and crews for them represented the best of Air Force trainees from schools around the nation.

The B-29 Superfortress was almost twice as big as the B-17 Flying Fortress used in the European war theater. The B-29 had a wing span of 140 feet and a fuselage length of over 100 feet. It weighed 70 tons. The four turbocharged radial piston engines with blade propellers generated 2,200 horsepower each with up to 1,000 revolutions per minute that continued on missions of up to 18 hours. In addition to the tail gunnery, there were 50 caliber machine guns in "blisters," one on the top of the plane and one on each side. A central fire control system could coordinate shooting from all guns. For a typical mission over Japan, the bomber carried 22 tons of fuel, 7,000 rounds of ammunition, and ten tons of bombs in two bomb bays. The B-29's maximum speed was 358 miles per hour, and it could fly as high as 33,000 feet above sea level. The cost of three years of development and mass production of the most complex machine of its time was $3 billion compared with $2 billion for development of the atomic bomb.

Sergeant William Kent Johnston of Lund, Utah, known as Bill to his crew, became a B-29 tail gunner squeezing his lanky frame into a Plexiglas capsule that sprouted a twenty millimeter cannon and two machine guns. Members of his crew were:

Airplane Commander, Capt. Marcus H. Worde of Erick, Oklahoma
Pilot, Lt. Arthur P. O'Hara of Teaneck, New Jersey
Navigator, Lt. Wallace Moritz of Brooklyn, New York
Bombardier, Lt. James Martin of Mayodan, North Carolina
Flight Engineer, Master Sgt. Oliver C. Thomas of Lubbock, Texas
Radio Operator, Sgt. Alan G. Kenniston of Vineyard Haven, Massachusetts
Radar Operator, Sgt. Bruce A. Yungclas of Webster City, Iowa
Central Gun Control, Sgt. John F. Ryan of New Haven, Connecticut
Side Gunners, Sgt. Abraham (Abe) Ginsberg of Boston, Massachusetts, and Sgt. Ward B. Lyons of Roy, Washington

Left to Right: Wm. Kent Johnston, Oliver Thomas, Abe Ginsberg, John Ryan, Bruce Yungclas, Jim Martin, Wally Moritz, Ward Lyons, Alan Keniston, Art O'Hara. Not shown: Marcus Worde

Fairmont was the initial home of seven B-29 bombardment groups including the 504th, activated on March 11, 1944, to which Kent's crew was assigned. At Fairmont in September, Lt. Col. Paul Tibbetts assembled his crew that would drop the first atomic bomb on Japan eleven months later.

In early December, Kent and his crew got their brand-new B-29 bomber which was produced in the Boeing Company plant, Wichita, Kansas, and flew to Mather Air Force Base near Sacramento, California. The crew was allowed to leave the base for Christmas Eve in the city and was photographed around a table in a bar. It was the guys' last night out before they headed for the Mariana Islands far away in the Pacific Ocean.

Radar Operator Bruce Yungclas, a teetotaler non-smoker from a beloved Iowa farm, was somewhat of a mother hen for the B-29 crew, making sure on several occasions that the enlisted men got back on time to their base or hotel after drinking and gambling parties. He was probably Kent's best friend since they had some common interests. They came from backgrounds that included lonely but pleasant days in a sheep camp and lonely but memorable dawn-to-dusk work in corn fields.

At the start of Christmas week 1944, while Kent was waiting to fly out to a Pacific Ocean island, Dick was settling in at the Lake Union

Naval Training Station, Seattle, Washington for four months of school to become an electrician's mate. He had graduated from Wasatch Academy as the third honor student in his class of fifty and enlisted in the Navy when he turned 18 years of age on August 12. He regarded four months in boot camp at the San Diego, California, Naval Training Station as a pleasant adventure. With him in boot camp were David Urie and Lewis Bergstrom, Cedar City high school basketball stars.

Also from the tiny town of Lund, Eddie Frahske enlisted in the Army, Verle Couch joined the Navy SeaBees, and Jimmy Holyoak enlisted in the Air Force.

With Dick's departure for the Navy, Kent ready to start on bombing missions, and the end of the war still more than a year away under the best of circumstances, Mary looked at the one gold star in her front window and desperately hoped there would be no more.

Kent's B-29 took off from Mather Field in California at 12:01 a.m., January 1, 1945, for Hickham Air Field near Honolulu, Hawaii, on the first leg of the 7,000 mile trip to the Mariana Islands. The next day, the plane flew to Kwajalein in the Marshall Islands followed by a flight to the huge and brand new bomber base on Tinian Island. From there B-29s were starting to fly 17-hour, 2,500-mile round trip bombing missions over Japan.

Under a League of Nations mandate after World War I, Japan had control of the Marianas and covered them with sugar cane fields. In World War II, U.S. military planners had targeted capture of Guam, Saipan, and Tinian as being within B-29 bombing range of the Japanese homeland, and by early 1944 the Japanese were aware of the plan.

On June 15, 1944, a week after the Allies' successful D-day landings on the Nazi-controlled coast of France, a U.S. fleet attacked Saipan. After two days of naval shelling, 40,000 Marines swept ashore, followed by 20,000 Army soldiers. They engaged in some of the fiercest fighting in the Pacific theater against 30,000 troops of the Japanese Imperial Army. All of those troops died, and most of the 16,000 Japanese civilians were killed or committed suicide in the belief they would be killed anyway. Some 3,000 Japanese soldiers were killed in one day in the worst banzai (suicide) attack OF World War II. By July 10, Saipan was securely in control of U.S. forces which had suffered 16,500 casualties, dead and wounded.

On July 23, about 18,000 Marines attacked Tinian which at 12 miles long and 6 miles wide is the size of Manhattan Island in New York City. Compared with Saipan, there was much less opposition, the fight ended August 7, and work started immediately to turn the sea of sugar cane fields there into the world's largest air base by early 1945. Guam was also invaded and secured by mid-August.

The North Field on Tinian was a huge rectangle with four runways 8,500 feet long built by 12,000 members of the Navy Seabees (Construction Battalions) using a layer of crushed coral followed by a layer of asphalt. There were hundreds of pits with winches for loading big bombs into the bellies of the planes. The aviation fuel storage facility had capacity for 165,000 barrels.

The West Field was half the size of the North Field. Together they were the base for 375 B-29s which formed nine bombardment groups.

Kent's crew and plane had the official designation of Crew 25, Aircraft #42-24814, 421st Squadron, 504th Bombardment Group, 313th Wing, Twentieth Air Force. The plane was assigned a maintenance crew of seven to nine members.

Soon after the arrival of Kent's plane, the crew learned it was customary for a name, a cartoon, or a symbol to be placed on the front of each Superfortress. Crew members chipped in $5 each and hired a sign painter from among the SeaBees to paint an almost-naked young woman with legs jauntily extended over the words *Sitting Pretty.* Styled after the many drawings of wartime "pinup girls" by artist Alberto Vargas in *Esquire* magazine, she became one of the most photographed examples of B-29 "nose art" on Tinian. The *Sitting Pretty* plane and art were the subject of an article in the *Houston Chronicle*, July 30, 1994, but the editor allegedly vetoed a photograph of the original painting "in the interest of good taste."

For plane crews, life on the Tinian air base was a mixture of boredom and "just lying around" between missions and the fear and adrenalin rush during the bombing runs. There were endless card games with poker being preferred over hearts, gin rummy, and bridge. The poker "professional" in Squadron 421 was gunner Abe Ginsberg followed in amount of winnings by Kent who sent the money home with his infrequent letters.

By early 1945 there was little danger of Japanese airplane attacks and movies were shown nearly every night including *Meet Me in St. Louis* starring Judy Garland, and the Academy Award-winner *Going*

The *Sitting Pretty* B-29 Superfortress and crew, early 1945.
Kent Johnston far left front row.

My Way with Bing Crosby. A large well-equipped stage was built for touring USO shows. There were radio broadcasts by English-speaking Tokyo Rose who told Allied forces that they would all die, but she played popular Big Band songs such as *Don't Get Around Much Anymore*, *Chattanooga Choo-Choo*, *I Don't Want to Walk Without You*, *Moonlight Serenade*, and *Amor.*

Meals, which were barely better than K-rations, featured Spam, powdered eggs, dried potatoes, peanut butter, and beans were served to enlisted men in one section of the mess hall and to officers in the other section. Occasionally there was fresh meat, but it was usually mutton from New Zealand which Kent liked but nobody else did. The rations of beer were warm

There were dozens of eight-holer outhouse toilets that were periodically "sanitized" by dousing the pits with gasoline and setting them afire for a few minutes.

Bruce Yungclas was one of the *Sitting Pretty*'s crew members who wrote long memoirs and letters about their wartime experiences. In letters to his sister Ginnie, he often mentioned Kent whom he called Bill. In one letter, he said "Bill thinks he should come home with me when we get a three-day pass [back home]." As events turned out, visiting Ginnie was the very last thing Kent had on his mind when the war ended.

The *Sitting Pretty* B-29 Bomber crew in Nebraska,1944. Officers in rear, enlisted men on front row. Kent Johnston front row far right.

The *Sitting Pretty*'s first mission was late in January when daylight bombings preceded the U.S. Marines' attack on the Japanese-held island of Iwo Jima, an ugly dark volcanic mole on the face of the shimmering ocean 660 miles south of Tokyo. It had to be captured because it had radar stations and two airfields from which Nipponese bombers could reach the Marianas, and fighter planes could harass B-29 missions. From the airfields, when captured, the United States' long-range P-51 fighters could protect Superfortresses over Japan. Also the airfields would be safe haven for big birds that had been damaged in raids or were low on fuel in returning to their Marianas base.

Covered with black sand, Iwo Jima was only about ten square miles in size, had no natural water supply, and had no value except as a military base. The top of Mount Suribachi was the site of perhaps the most famous photograph of the war, showing Marines raising the Stars and Stripes.

B-29s dropped 600 tons of bombs on Iwo, and naval ships shelled it for three days, but the 22,000 Japanese troops, protected in caves and tunnels, poured withering fire on 60,000 Marines whose landings began February 19. Imperial Army soldiers were told they would not be rescued and they must fight to the death, which they all did. A month of non-stop combat finally ended March 26. More than 6,000

Marines died and left a message to the rest of the world, "For your tomorrow, we gave you our today."

Kent and his B-29 crew came to appreciate Iwo Jima on two occasions, making a landing there once when the fuel gauges edged toward empty and once when an engine conked out at dawn on the way "home." In a 1994 memoir, Captain Marcus Worde noted that if Iwo had not been captured he and his crew probably would have crashed into the ocean twice. "To all those who fought and died there, I want to say thank you," he wrote. By the end of the war, B-29s had found refuge 2,400 times on Iwo Jima.

On one of the visits to Iwo Jima, Kent's crew learned about the death of President Franklin D. Roosevelt on April 12 and about Harry S. Truman becoming president.

The fatalism and fanaticism of the Japanese soldiers on Saipan, Iwo Jima, and later in the larger and longer fight for the island of Okinawa, convinced U.S. military strategists that Japan would not surrender under any "normal" war conditions. It was estimated that an invasion of Japan would cost hundreds of thousands of U.S. servicemen deaths and millions of Japanese civilian deaths. The calculations led to the decision to use atomic bombs.

A mission for Kent's crew on February 10 was when the men got their first terrifying experience of bombing the Japanese homeland in the midst of anti-aircraft flak and attacks from enemy fighter planes. The target of the daylight raid at 30,000 feet altitude was an aircraft factory near Tokyo. The flak could not reach the high altitude, but the crew could see layers of bursting shells just below them and got an idea of what later low altitude flights would be like.

In between bomb runs, the 421st Squadron participated in dropping large mines in Japan's inland waterways, which resulted in many Japanese naval and transport ships being blown up.

Few enemy fighter planes penetrated the B-29 formations which had massed firepower, but, when one did, the *Sitting Pretty* gunners felt adrenalin rushes as they swung their weapons toward a Zero flashing by at 400 miles per hour with all its guns firing and spewing tracer bullets. From that time onward, the crew knew what it was like, in the words of famed World War II writer Ernie Pyle, to be "flying against fate."

The day of a typical seventeen-hour overnight mission to Japan in the early spring of 1945 began with the flight and maintenance crews for each B-29 checking over engines and all equipment and communications systems, loading up on ammunition, and taking on the bombs. Negligence or a mistake by a maintenance crew member could mean the loss of a $1 million B-29 and all its men. After a series of briefings, lunch, nap time, and dinner, the takeoffs began. The *Sitting Pretty* and dozens of other B-29s would roar off the multiple runways at one-minute intervals, creating a steady sound of thunder. Out over the sea, gunners would test-fire their machine guns and cannon, and navigators would guide the planes proceeding at a set speed to the mission's "initial point."

The dormant volcanic cone of snow-capped Mount Fujiyama sometimes provided a visual initial point. There, a squadron would rendezvous, get into formation behind a lead plane and deputy leader, and start the bomb run over the designated target. Bombardiers using sophisticated equipment and in coordination with the plane commander and pilot would choose the moment to open the bomb bay doors. Amid shouts of "bombs away!" the planes would immediately swerve homeward.

On nearly every mission there were glorious tropical sunsets and sunrises, hours of rain, and hours of moonlight and puffy clouds. Lulled by the steady drone of the engines, crew members were mostly silent during the long hours to and from the target that bracketed the extreme tension of the bomb run. The crew ate a lunch of sandwiches, candy, and fruit juice before approaching the target.

At each landing as a squadron returned to Tinian, ground crews and base officials gathered near the runways to wave a welcome and wait anxiously to see if a plane was missing. Badly damaged planes trying to land were a hazard to everything. On one occasion, a plane crashed into a row of parked B-29s.

On some of the thousands of raids, a B-29 would be shot down usually in flames, watched by other crews who hoped the guys on the dying plane could bail out. Back on Tinian, Saipan, and Guam, there would be empty bunks, and plane captains would collect personal belongings to be sent to the homes of the missing men.

In war zones around the world, as well as in the Marianas, servicemen uttered this wartime prayer to God, "You come here yourself. Don't send Jesus. This is no place for children."

The high-altitude bombing of pinpointed targets in February and early March had sometimes been adversely affected by clouds and jet streams and was deemed ineffective by the Air Force brass. Major General Curtis LeMay took charge of the Twentieth Air Force, headquartered on Guam, and ordered a change to low level night time raids on Japan's principal cities using powerful incendiary bombs. The tactic was intended to destroy enemy morale by fire storms, civilian deaths, and the destruction of non-military targets.

B-29 crews were horrified at the prospect of heavy flak on raids at 8,000 feet or less, but losses on the first few missions were less than expected.

The stocky, cigar-chewing LeMay, 38 years old, was quoted as saying, "You've got to kill people, and when you've killed enough the enemy will stop fighting."

On March 9–10, he sent 325 B-29s loaded with 1,858 tons of jellied gasoline incendiary bombs over Tokyo which had a population then of eight million people. It was estimated that twenty-five percent of the city was destroyed, 267,000 buildings burned, 83,000 people died, 41,000 were wounded, and 1,000,000 people were left homeless. Similar raids followed, but regardless of the terrible devastation, the Japanese prime minister declared there would be no surrender.

The *Sitting Pretty* joined in the fire-bombing raids on the Tokyo region in mid-March and early April. In his 1994 memoir, Captain Worde described an example mission:

> For our 5:30 p.m. take-off, we will be loaded with 22 tons of high octane aviation fuel, 7,000 rounds of 50 caliber cannon ammunition, 600 rounds for each of the 12 machine guns, 10 tons of fire bombs.
>
> Planes will take off simultaneously from Tinian, Saipan, and Guam, all timed to fly over the target area at one-minute intervals. About 300 B-29s will have already gone over the target by the time we arrive. Tonight we may never see another B-29 until we land back here at Tinian some 17 hours after take off. In the darkness and in all the weather we will be flying through we hope we do not run into another B-29 and that another B-29 does not run into us.
>
> The weather over the target is briefed to be overcast with low clouds and heavy fog. We will be flying through severe weather with heavy turbulence and severe icing between Iwo Jima and Japan, but the bad weather is pretty tame compared to what is ahead.
>
> Taking off in a combat-loaded B-29 is a most dangerous part of every mission. We are surrounded by tons of fire-enhancing and explosive materials as we pass through the "Valley of Death." It refers to the small period of time when, if you lose an engine, you

> will crash near the end of a runway that is already marked by the ashes and twisted metal of planes that did not make it.

Fifty miles off the coast of Japan, Worde told his crew to prepare for the bomb run. He said everything in the aircraft must be securely strapped down, parachutes and survival equipment must be checked, flak vests and flak helmets must be put on, oxygen marks should be turned to one-hundred percent flow. Worde's memoir continued:

> At 5,000 feet altitude, it is pitch dark, and there are dense clouds. The navigator and radar operator confirm we pass our "initial point" for the bomb run.
>
> When we reach the target area, it will appear that we are inside a dome of fire . . . The red glow in the clouds up ahead continues to get brighter and then we are in the middle of total hell. It is bright enough that you could read a newspaper in the cockpit. There is fire and black smoke as far as you can see in all directions. Giant flames leap into the air to the point where it almost seems they are reaching your altitude, carrying with them great masses of burning materials that break up and fall back to the ground in raining sheets of fire. You can feel the heat; the smoke burns your eyes. It must be something like being inside the fireball of an atomic bomb except you do not melt.
>
> The air turbulence is vicious and continuous with violent updrafts and downdrafts created in the raging inferno . . . You wonder if the downdraft is going to pull you right down into the flames.

On this mission, the *Sitting Pretty* dropped its bombs and emerged without damage back into dark clouds, heading into, hopefully, a beautiful sunrise three hours later halfway home to Tinian. "Mission accomplished—one more time!" Worde's memoir concluded.

B-29 crews apparently seldom, if ever, discussed whatever feelings they may have had about the death and destruction that they had to know was caused by the fire bombings on cities and villages. As a matter of self-protection, the human mind draws a curtain over conscience in such situations. In an effort to offset whatever horror some airmen may have felt, the Air Force distributed pamphlets saying that the fire storms were necessary because the Japanese government had told all its people "to fight to the death." The pamphlets declared, "There are no civilians."

Kent may have wondered silently whether his childhood classmate, Moriko Azuma, and other members of the Azuma family, formerly of Lund, were somewhere down there in the fires.

Dick Johnston (left) and friend on Philippine Islands Navy Base, 1945

Dick finished the naval electricians' school in Seattle as a Seaman First Class at the end of April 1945 and early in May shipped out of San Francisco on a troop ship to a Seventh Fleet recreation base at Osmena Beach on Samar in Leyte Gulf, Philippine Islands. General Douglas MacArthur had returned in force to Leyte Gulf, and the region had been declared secure a few weeks prior to Dick's arrival.

In Europe, Nazi Germany surrendered May 7, and the world's attention turned to "America's war" in the Pacific theater and the prospect of a Japanese surrender.

Dick was one of the electricians on the recreation base crew that took care of newly-constructed walk-in coolers for the two bottles of beer that were served to each man of the Seventh Fleet crews that came ashore for a day of recreation. There were several softball diamonds made of packed coral sand and two asphalt-paved tennis courts, but very few guys from the fleet parties played tennis so Dick and a buddy from North Hollywood, California, had the courts to themselves nearly every day.

The base crew lived in wood-floored tents while waiting for SeaBees to finish Quonset huts later in the summer, ate three square meals a day in a tin-roof mess hall, and got two bottles of beer per week. Dick ended his Wasatch Academy habit of being a teetotaler and started drinking his ration. A large generator supplied bare-bulb electrical lighting. A well, pump and elevated water tank provided outdoor showers.

The electricians stood revolving eight-hour watches at the main bank of beer coolers and a small bank at the officers' club a quarter mile away. Dick learned to play the harmonica by ear on his all-night watches. Life was sweet, better than living in Lund.

After flying the *Sitting Pretty* a third of the way around the world from Kansas to Tinian and on two dozen combat and non-combat missions, Kent's crew had to give her up on May 14 and be assigned to a new B-29 delivered from the States. The "old" plane had never been seriously damaged, and the crew felt she was charmed. The new plane "never felt good" even after being used for two weeks while the guys trained to become a squadron leader for upcoming missions. The new plane lasted two weeks and one day.

On May 29, 1945, the *Sitting Pretty* crew was assigned to be the deputy leader for a daylight mission over Yokohama at an altitude of around 18,000 feet. The crew would be in a plane on its first combat mission—a plane that somehow made the men feel uncomfortable.

Chapter 18

P.O.W.

As April gave way to May 1945, Army Air Force General Curtis LeMay ordered a new strategy for B-29 attacks on Japan with emphasis on daylight pinpoint bombing to destroy military/industrial targets. He showed seemingly little regard for the danger to his planes and the men in them.

So, on May 29, up to one-hundred Superfortresses were ordered to hit industrial areas and docks at Yokohama on the west side of Tokyo Bay and south of Tokyo. The bombing altitude at about 18,000 feet would be well within the range of the enemy anti-aircraft guns. Bomb runs at that altitude and in broad daylight made the crews even more nervous than usual.

This would be the sixteenth full scale combat mission for Kent and his crew who were scheduled for a ten-day rest and relaxation visit to Honolulu the first week in June. For the May 29 raid they would fly a new plane. Their cherished "old" *Sitting Pretty* plane was reassigned to a replacement crew. It would survive the war and probably ended up in a bomber graveyard in the United States. The new plane would never leave Japan.

The crew in *Sitting Pretty #2* was assigned for the first time to a deputy lead position at the right rear of the lead plane. It was a promotion and an honor to be chosen for deputy leader which would take over the leading position if the Number 1 plane got into trouble. The success of a bombing mission depended heavily on the leaders of a formation getting good and accurate bomb runs, followed by the other planes.

The enemy anti-aircraft gunners sensed that if they could pick-off the leading B-29s they might disrupt a squadron bomb run. On May 29, their efforts to hit the leaders succeeded.

Shortly after midnight, Kent and this crew were routed out of their sacks, ate breakfast, and attended briefings. They checked out all the plane's equipment and all the survival kits to be used in case of a bailout. After an inspection by Captain Worde, the men assembled in front of the plane while the four engines were revved up for a test.

Finally, at 5 a.m., squadrons of B-29s began roaring off the Tinian runways into the dawn's pink and blue sky, flying "on the deck" just over the waves to conserve fuel. When *Sitting Pretty #2* was past Iwo Jima, the pilot began a slow ascent to 18,000 feet, and the crew put on oxygen masks in case of sudden decompression inside the plane.

The gunners in blisters on each side of the plane were "scanners," responsible for watching the engines for signs of oil leaks or smoke, watching the wings and positions of the flaps there, and reporting any signs of problems to the pilot and captain.

For Kent, in the tail end gunnery bubble, the flight was just another mission although he was rather glad to be working in daylight so he could see the other B-29s and enemy fighter planes if any appeared. He had not liked the night time incendiary bombings, the sight of the flames and smoke stretching beyond the horizons, and the darkness that hid other planes in collision proximity. As the flight reached the island of Honshu, the weather was clear. Kent looked down and saw blue waves lapping against the brown shore of Tokyo Bay. Snow-capped Mount Fujiyama loomed beautiful in the distance.

At the rendezvous point, the squadron planes did a slow circle to get into formation behind the lead planes which were identified by having their nose wheels down. Captain Worde assumed a deputy lead position behind the formation leader, Major Sid Hale.

The anti-aircraft flak was so thick it seemed to form a black cloud rising up into the planes and appeared to Pilot Art O'Hara to be the worst he had ever seen.

Just seconds before Bombardier Jim Martin was to release bombs from *Sitting Pretty #2*, members of the crew felt a shuddering thump, and the plane seemed to lurch sideways. Central Gun Controller John Ryan yelled, "We've been hit by flak!" and recalled later, "It felt like a giant hand giving our left wing a resounding slap upwards." The left side gunner shouted that engine number 3 was on fire. As the plane veered away from the target run, Martin dumped the bombs.

Worde and Radio Operator Alan Kenniston started sending out the distress signal of "May Day! May Day!" over the radio and asking if there were any U.S. submarines in the ocean patrolling the coast that could pick up survivors from a fallen plane.

There was considerable confusion in the plane for the next few minutes. Some crew members believed the captain had given an order to bailout so Ryan and the two side gunners, Abe Ginsberg and Ward Lyons, ripped off their flak suits and jumped with their survival kits strapped to their parachute harnesses. The nose wheel in its lowered position left an opening on the underside of the plane as the best place from which to bailout. After a moment of free fall, the trio's parachutes opened, and they drifted out of sight.

Kent had not heard a bailout order and was working his way forward from the tail to find out what was happening.

Flight Engineer Oliver Thomas had triggered a built-in fire extinguisher filled with carbon dioxide to quench the fire in engine number 3, but flak had torn a huge ragged hole in the left wing and there was other damage around the tail. The plane was sliding sideways and downward and was in some danger of being hit by bombs falling from other planes.

Thomas and Bruce Yungclas saw Kent emerge from the plane's central passageway, and Thomas shouted, "The number 3 engine is gone, and we're going down so get the f--- out of here!" but Yungclas said the Captain was expecting to get the plane out to the ocean to a submarine. Kent started swearing but his church-oriented friend ignored the stream of four-letter words.

At this point, Pilot O'Hara was losing control of the plane on its downward slide away from the bombing formation and toward the hilly, sparsely-populated, Chiba Peninsula on the east side of Tokyo Bay. The Captain had hoped to get past the peninsula and ditch into the ocean. However, as the plane descent reached 4,500 feet altitude, and the Chiba hills loomed ahead, Captain Worde ordered, "Everybody out, now!" O'Hara had been struggling to keep the plane from rolling over which would have prevented safe bailouts. He now applied full power to the remaining operable engines and managed to level out the plane long enough for the rest of the crew to bailout.

Yungclas and Kent stripped off their flak vests, checked survival gear attached to their parachutes, descended into the wheel well and jumped, followed very quickly by other members of the crew. Although Bruce and Kent both survived, they never saw each other again.

Worde and O'Hara were the last to leave, and their parachutes barely had time to open before the men hit the ground. In less than a minute, the brand new Superfortress cartwheeled along a hillside and exploded in a ball of flame and smoke.

Major Sid Hale's lead plane had been hit at the start of the bomb run, and one engine was spraying out fuel endangering the following planes. However, Hale stayed on course, dropped bombs, and ordered the rest of the squadron by radio to follow suit. The B-29s had a fuel system that was self-sealing in case of damage or leaks. It worked on Hale's damaged engine, and he managed to limp back to Tinian on three engines.

One of Hale's crew members later recounted watching the slow motion demise of Worde's plane and vowed the flak that day was the worst he had been through in 20 missions. A second deputy lead plane, commanded by Captain James W. Cornwell, was shot to pieces and went down with loss of the entire crew.

After clearing the plane and starting to fall at 100 miles per hour, Kent calmly pulled the D-ring on the rip cord to his parachute and was jerked to a vertical position as the 'chute billowed out above him. The first thing he noticed was how quiet it was compared with the noise in the plane and around the bomb run now 30 miles to the west over Yokohama hidden in clouds of smoke. He marveled for a moment at the early afternoon view of the bay below and a glimpse of the other parachutists, then realized he would be hitting a hillside in half a minute.

Like all the crew members, he had paid close attention in classes and briefings on what to do in case of bailout. They all knew very well that survival meant following all the rules. Most of them expected that as soon as they hit land they would be killed by Japanese furious over the terrible destruction of the bombings. B-29 crews were warned that if they were shot down over land in Japan they would have no chance of escape, and, rather than try to hide out, they might as well surrender.

Kent saw that he would hit on a fairly steep hillside so he turned to face downhill and landed with his heels digging into the ground and his rump sliding over gravel and some low bushes. He hurriedly unhooked the parachute harness and hid the chute and his orange "Mae West" vest in some bushes so he would not be spotted quickly and possibly be shot before he had time to reconnoiter his situation. He was dressed in khaki shirt, pants, and cap which was adequate for the warm but damp late springtime weather. He fished a half pack of cigarettes from his shirt pocket and lit one, wishing he had brought more with him, knowing it would be a long long time before he might get another pack. He took the survival kit apart but found that most of the items in it were not very relevant for his present predicament.

Kent realized he would soon be found by local residents or police or Japanese soldiers who would have seen the parachutes coming down onto the peninsula. He wanted to make sure he could surrender before he got shot, so he used a pocket knife to cut out a piece of the white parachute and attached it to a stick. As he walked slowly down the hill expecting to find a creek or a road, he passed terraced rice fields where green shoots poked up from the glassy water surface of the paddies.

He knew he would be captured, probably be beaten, maybe even be injured, and he began to steel his mind against cursing or striking back at captors. Striking back would mean death. He didn't realize it at the time but the self-discipline he had learned at Wasatch Academy would help him survive the next few months.

Off to the left, he saw the thatched roofs of a small village, and several farmers armed with hoe-like instruments began cautiously approaching him, chattering as if to encourage each other. Kent was a foot taller than his captors. He shouted the only Japanese word he knew, sounding like "ohio" and meaning "good morning." He put up his hands and waved the white flag, desperately hoping they knew what it meant. The farmers, seemingly pleased at the one word, motioned him to follow them into the scruffy little village where residents obviously lived a bare survival existence.

The biggest house was that of the major local government official, probably the equivalent of a U.S. mayor. He was an old man with white hair and slow movements. He and the farmers were joined by an interpreter who had lived in San Francisco for a few years and knew a smattering of English.

Kent reluctantly but wisely got out the half pack of cigarettes and watched it disappear around the group. Nearly everyone smoked quietly for a minute, then the mayor and interpreter laboriously managed to tell Kent that he would be taken to a military base. In the Japanese tradition of courtesy to all guests, the major's wife brought Kent a bowl of warm rice topped with fragments of green vegetables he did not recognize. He wolfed it down. The interpreter lectured Kent to "always tell the truth and you will be okay."

Kent followed two men to a somewhat larger town about a mile away where a young military officer in uniform with a sword swinging at his side took charge. They went to a narrow gauge railway station and boarded one of two cars. News of the parachutists and the capture had spread quickly, and crowds gathered at railway stations. The people shouted what were probably curses, shook their fists, and threw rocks at the tall American they now knew came from one of the bombers that had been blasting and burning the Tokyo region for four months. One man tried to jump into the rail car but the officer stopped him at sword point, probably saving Kent from a Japanese-style lynching.

Kent kept his hands clenched behind his back, kept his mouth grimly shut, and always looked straight ahead so as to give no sign of provocation. As evening darkness descended, the train stopped at a station where there was no crowd, and the officer led Kent up a rocky path to what appeared to be a military post. Kent was pushed into a small cell with wooden bars and a thin straw mat on the wood floor. He was cold and famished but was so tired he laid down on the mat and promptly went to sleep. Early in the morning a man was thrown into an adjacent cell. Kent sat up, and, through the bars between the cells, he saw Flight Engineer Oliver Thomas. They both quickly sensed it would not be a good idea to recognize each other or to say anything.

At sunrise, Kent and Thomas were marched down to the railway station and were given a bowl of cooked but sticky cold rice. They were blindfolded, their hands were tied behind their backs, and they were pushed into a regular-size railroad car. By careful nudging of his blindfold, Kent could see two of his crew's officers in the car—Captain Worde and Navigator Wally Moritz.

After a brief ride, Kent, Thomas, the two officers, and a few other Americans who had been captured recently were taken off the train in what they learned later was the town of Chiba near the top of Tokyo bay. They were marched to an old stable and were beaten with rifles and bamboo poles. It seemed as if the local officials wanted to get in a revenge beating before the airmen were shipped to Tokyo on a fast train.

The group got off in the big city and was marched for what seemed to be a mile or so through streets. From under the edges of their blindfolds, the men could see a few buildings standing amid vast piles of rubble. There was a strong smell of smoke, ashes, and garbage.

The entourage finally arrived at a five-story building that the crew members learned later was the headquarters of the Kempei Tai, Japan's elite military police. There they were joined by two more officers, Bombardier Jim Martin and Pilot Art O'Hara, who had been captured together. At this point, Kent and five members of his crew were together and by now, captors had stripped off every man's wrist watches and rings.

In a small auditorium, about twenty sword-bearing Japanese officers began hours of laborious interrogation of the Americans with interpreters relaying officers' questions and prisoners' answers. After each man was questioned, he was beaten for several minutes with bamboo poles. The higher the rank of a prisoner, the longer the beating. Captain Worde was barely able to walk after his extended session, and his face became so swollen from being hit that he was hardly recognizable.

After the interrogations, the prisoner group was marched to a wood-frame building that was probably a large stable for police horses in the past. The men had to take off their shoes and leave them outside a row of six prison-type cells. Each cell was about 9 feet by 12 feet with wood bars or thick bamboo poles on three sides and an outside wall of rough-sawn boards. A small window up high in the outside wall provided the only daylight. Each unit had a single electrical cord hanging from the ceiling with a bare bulb that burned night and day.

Each man was given a thin tattered army-style blanket which had to be folded every morning and stacked in such a way that guards could count them and make sure a prisoner did not run away with one!

In a corner of each cell was a three-foot-square concrete slab with a hole in it that served as a toilet. The droppings and drizzlings collected in a box underneath that had to be emptied each morning by one of the prisoners. Although each cell eventually was crowded with up to a dozen prisoners, they had so little to eat and drink each day that there was no waiting in line to use the "restroom."

Three times a day, each prisoner was given a ball of rice the size of a tennis ball and a drink of water from a cup hung from a pail. Some of the men ate their rice ball a few grains at a time to make it seem like more and to help kill time.

The initial six members of Worde's crew who arrived at Kempei Tai were soon joined by Alan Kenniston, Ward Lyons, and John Ryan. Kent, Moritz, and Thomas were placed in cell number 5. Abe Ginsberg and Bruce Yungclas had been sent to other prisons.

There was room for the new batch of airmen at the Kempei Tai building because sixty-five American and British captives had been transferred a week earlier to another prisoner of war camp in Tokyo where they all perished on May 25 in a fire caused by B-29 bombs. Five guards at that camp who refused to let the prisoners flee the fire and who shot those who tried to run were convicted of murder after the war and hanged.

In view of the extreme brutality and massacres by the Japanese army in conquering Manchuria and much of China in the 1930s and in view of the rage that must have prevailed throughout mainland Japan over the massive destruction and civilian deaths caused by the B-29 raids, it is puzzling that Americans, especially B-29 airmen, taken prisoner in the spring of 1945 were not summarily executed. One possible explanation is that lower level Japanese officers and guards, knowing without admitting it that their war was lost, began to worry about what would happen to themselves later as war criminals if most prisoners were killed or starved to death.

In any event, life in the Kempei Tai prison was a severe test of will to survive.

For several of the crew members, especially Kent, the lack of tobacco was agonizing for the first week but then hunger replaced the desire for nicotine.

Talking was forbidden, and guards would beat anyone saying more than a few words to anybody although the enforcement was gradually relaxed as the summer wore on. For weeks on end, the men merely sat and tried to think of something to keep from going crazy. Some thought in detail about farming, some about building things, some about high school days. There was no energy to think about sex.

In the crowded cells, the prisoners tried to sleep in tightly packed rows, and every time someone moved there was a ripple effect down a row that was especially hurtful to some men who had broken bones. The snoring was like a symphony of tubas.

There were, of course, no toothbrushes, no change of clothes, no opportunity to wash so the men soon became accustomed to the smell of unwashed bodies. And there were flies—big black buzzing flies.

One of the worst aspects of the confinement was the constant presence of fleas and lice that hid in the floor cracks and in the blankets. Many of the men used strips of rags to tie up their pant legs and shirt cuffs to help prevent invasions of the pests at night. Scruffy beards itched and were an additional home for lice and fleas. Everyone lost weight rapidly in the first two months—probably an average of 50 pounds per man—until they got down to prisoner minimum weight. The ragged uniforms hung on gaunt frames like shrouds.

About noon on June 19, Mary was in the Lund Store post office casually sorting mail. She paused over a letter addressed to "Mr. Johnson," then saw the return address, and yelled for Harley. He rushed into the office, saw her white face, took the letter from her trembling hand, and ripped it open. The letter, dated June 15, 1945, was from the Office of the Chaplain, 504th Bomb Group, APO 247 c/o Postmaster, San Francisco, California. (APO numbers were used to conceal the locations of military operations in the Pacific war theater.)

> Dear Mr. Johnson *[sic]*:
>
> As Chaplain of the 504th Bomb Group to which your son, Sgt. William Johnson [sic], 39919042, was assigned, I wish to extend to you and other members of the family my word of comfort, and of encouragement and hope, in regard to your son who has been listed as "Missing in Action."
>
> He and his crew were listed as missing after the mission to Yokohama on the 29th of May. Apparently the ship (plane) was damaged by enemy action over the target but it did not go down immediately. The pilot kept control until they had nearly reached the coast. Then, the men bailed out. It is believed that all of them were able to bail out.
>
> It is reasonable to hope and believe that they are prisoners of war. That is bad enough but prisoners of war do come back. Further, we are led to believe, through our intelligence reports, that prisoners in Japan are treated better now than they were in the past. I feel that you have definite reason to be hopeful.
>
> Naturally you will be anxious, and the uncertainty will be difficult to bear, and it may be many months yet before you are able to know the final answer. We pray that God may give you the strength and the courage to face bravely and patiently these months of waiting. It could have been so much worse. Let us thank God there is still strong hope.
>
> William and his crew were a fine group of men. They were very well liked in the group. They had flown quite a number of mission—16, I believe—and were counting the missions off, one by one, until they reached the number which would allow them to return home. They will be delayed a little now but we still believe they will get home

someday.

> You may rest assured that if any further word about William comes to us, we shall let you know. If in any further way we can be of service to you, please feel free to write.
>
> May God bless you.
>
> Earl Raitt
> Chaplain (Captain) U.S.A.

"Oh, dear Lord, I knew something like this had happened since we haven't heard from Kent for over three weeks," Mary whispered.

Harley stared at the letter for a minute, then patted Mary's shoulder. "Well, like the chaplain said, it's better than a notice that Kent was killed. At least we have hope about him being in prison, and the war can't last much longer so it won't be like he's in prison for years."

Mary nodded numbly. "But you know what a temper he has, and you know the Japs are going to beat him so pray God that he doesn't fight back or he will be dead."

On the morning of June 24, the Union Pacific station master at Lund hurried into the store and handed Mary a Western Union telegram. She glanced at it, slumped down on a chair, and handed the message to Harley. He scanned it silently for a moment, then sat down and took Mary's hand. "Kent's not dead. This is just another notice that he is missing in action." The telegram said:

> To Mr. John H. Johnston, Lund, Utah
>
> From J. A. Ulio, U. S. Adjutant General's Office, Washington, D. C.
>
> The Secretary of War desires me to express his deep regret that your son, Sgt. Johnston, William K., has been missing in action over Tinian since 29 May 1945. If further detils *[sic]* or other informations *[sic]* are received you will be promptly notified. Confirming letter follows.

The telegram was undoubtedly just one of dozens being hastily sent out every day to parents, wives, and other relatives of servicemen.

Mary went home and put the second gold star in the window in the living room.

A month later, Mary and Harley got a letter from Leon W. Johnson, Brigadier General, U.S.A., Director of Personnel Services for the Army Air Force. It summarized the shooting down of Kent's plane and reported that the crew had bailed out over land and were missing in action. The letter concluded, "Believing you may wish to communicate with the families of the others who were in the plane with your son, I am enclosing a list of these men and the names and addresses of their next of kin."

Mary and Harley read the letter several times and studied the list of the other crew members and families. "Since the guys in other planes said nine to ten parachutes came out of Kent's plane over land, I'm sure Kent ended up in a Japanese prison camp," Harley emphasized. "He's pretty damn smart, and I think he knows enough that when he's a prisoner he shouldn't lose his temper, hit anybody or say anything. He won't give up, he will be found, he will come home."

"Well, yes, we have to think that," Mary replied. "And we have to pray for him every day. What do you think about contacting some of those other people on the list?"

"Well, none of them live around this part of the country, and we don't have an easy way to talk to them by telephone, and they won't know any more than we ever do."

"I suppose I could write letters to them but Kent never seemed to be good friends with any one in his crew, at least he never wrote about any of them, so I don't know which ones I should write to. Most of the other men are from back East or down South, and they probably don't have much in common with a sheep herder from the Utah desert."

Mary never wrote any letters, but she received one from the mother of Bombardier Jim Martin of Mayoden, North Carolina, who expressed "sincere sympathy and love" for all the parents and added, "May we bear it proudly and bravely because of the courage they (the sons) have exemplified."

While waiting day by day for more details about Kent's status, Mary received a telegram from her brother Quil in Santa Barbara that their mother had died quietly at home of "causes incident to old age." She was 85. With the wartime restrictions on travel by civilians and with the concern about Kent, Mary reluctantly decided not to attend the funeral. She wired money to the mortuary for a flower wreath.

One July afternoon at the Seventh Fleet's Osmena Beach naval recreation base, Dick got a message to report immediately to the base commander's office in the one building that remained of the original Filipino village.

The commander, a middle-aged Navy captain, asked Dick to sit down and said there was some bad news about his brother Kent. He read from a report similar to the letters received by Mary and Harley and expressed deep regret at Kent being missing in action. He then cited the Sullivan rule that had been adopted in the military services after three Sullivan brothers had died in a naval battle in 1943. Under the rule, Dick was eligible to leave a war theater and return to the United States because one member of his family had already died in the military and a second member was either killed or missing in action.

"You don't have to go back to the States now, and you can decide at any time in the future to go back as long as this situation continues—your brother Kent is missing in action or, Heaven forbid, if he is reported to be dead," the commander said. "Your parents in Lund, Utah, have been notified, and I expect that they would be happy to know that you will return to the States."

Dick sat in silence for a minute, remembering how Harlan had come home in a flag-draped coffin and trying to cope with the idea that Kent was possibly dead or likely to die in a Japanese prison camp. He imagined the look on his mother's face when she read the first "missing in action" report. He got up and started walking back and forth.

"It seems that if most of the crew of the B-29 bailed out over land, there's a good chance Kent got down okay and is in a prison camp, right?" Dick said to the captain. "I guess you don't know any more than I do about when the war will end and how long my brother might be in a prison camp. I imagine the Japs don't much care about keeping their prisoners alive. But, who knows? I'm going to believe that he survives and gets home before I do.

"This may sound pretty dumb and maybe like I don't care about my mother's feelings but frankly I like it here. This base should keep going as long as the Seventh Fleet is in action from here to Japan, and I don't think I'll be sent into battle where I might get killed. So, I want to stay here, and I request that you report that to headquarters."

The captain cocked his head to one side, made a tent with this fingers, and studied Dick for a moment. "You sure this is what you want to do? Most guys would jump at the chance to go home."

"Yeah, I'm sure. Besides, I'm doing something useful here, and if I got sent to some Navy base in the States, I'd probably end up changing light bulbs in some barracks."

"Okay, but I'll wait a few days before sending in the report in case you change your mind. Some of your buddies will tell you that you've got rocks in your head."

"I know that but I'll just say I like to play tennis here."

Back at the Kempei Tai prison camp, Kent and his crew struggled every day to keep from going crazy. The most frequent topic of conversation was food, and everyone had a different favorite meal which was described in great detail and which would be the Number One priority upon return to the States. For Kent, it was a fried mutton chop with mashed potatoes and lots of brown gravy or springtime fried chicken with strawberry shortcake.

The crew members, both officers and enlisted men, got to know each other better than they ever would have on an air base. As rules against prisoners talking were relaxed, the men took turns telling each other about their lives, hometowns, wives and girlfriends, what they did before joining the Army Air Force, and what they wanted to do after discharge.

Kent usually just listened but, as time went by and the others' discourses became repetitious, some of the guys, especially those from big East Coast cities, would probe beyond Kent's drawl and self-effacing manner. They slowly learned about what to them was totally unique, such as the life of a sheep herder in a coyote-ridden Utah desert. They marveled about life in a strict Presbyterian boarding school where Kent never kissed a girl, church attendance was mandatory, tobacco was forbidden, and students had to study two hours every weekday night.

Another topic of conversation became more prevalent as the summer dragged on with the sounds of B-29 bombings every few days and frequent glimpses of flames and smoke sometimes nearby. The topic was, "When will the war end?"

There was an undercurrent of optimism that Japan could not long continue to endure the bombings and would surrender within months, and all prisoners would be rescued and would be treated to huge meals.

The optimism was dented when several prisoners succumbed to injuries or infections. One simply went stark raving mad and was taken away for execution. One who had been injured by flak died slowly of gangrene, and his body was left in a cell for two days. Another died of infection in wounds from beatings. A Navy fighter plane pilot was so badly injured in his bailout jump close to the ground that he died within a few days.

There was no medical care whatsoever, and the airmen did their best to help men who came to the prison with injuries. One had a broken ankle, and his cellmates put him in a splint made from sticks and rags. Severe dehydration was as much a threat as starvation.[1]

Kent, a sergeant, and Wally Moritz, a lieutenant, were in the same cell and for the first time could talk as equals. Moritz, who was reared as a typical street-smart kid in Brooklyn, New York, commented many years later that he may have survived the prison life because of long talks with the lanky and laconic rancher from Utah who looked and acted a bit like movi~~e star Gary Cooper.~~

1. A U. S. report November 1, 1948, on war crimes trials covered an investigation of mistreatment of American prisoners of war at Kempei Tai. It said 22 wounded airmen died, some from lethal injection. Of the Japanese guards and officers responsible, some committed suicide, some were acquitted in trials, and many were sentenced to prison terms for various lengths of time.

Chapter 19

Rescue

The evening of August 15, 1945, at the Kempei Tai prisoner compound in Tokyo, a guard on duty got drunk and tried to talk to the B-29 airmen, seeming to say that Japanese and Americans were shaking hands. The guys didn't realize until a few days later that he was telling them the war was over.

The next morning the prisoners were told to get shoes from the pile at the gate where everyone had left their shoes months earlier. No one could find a pair of matching shoes that fit. The men, despite their condition, laughed and joked about the situation and had a strong feeling of excitement that a major change was coming.

The prisoners were blindfolded and taken in trucks south through the bombed-out city across a causeway to an island on the edge of Tokyo Bay. The blindfolds were removed, and the airmen could see a high wooden fence surrounding a huge compound they soon learned was the Omori prison camp. They were allowed to go into the waves of the bay for what amounted to their first bath in three or four months although they had to keep their ragged clothes on.

After the salty water rinse-off, the Kempei Tai troop was marched into Omori and assigned to barracks with many other American airmen plus prisoners from Allied countries such as Britain, Australia, and New Zealand. Some of them had managed to survive for one or two years.

The next welcome event for Kent and his crewmates was a change of clothes. The rags they had worn for months were exchanged for ragged but clean clothes. Like sorting through the pile of shoes earlier, the guys scrambled to find something that would fit.

Next came shaves and haircuts! A pair of rusty scissors and a couple of dull safety razors were borrowed from long term Omori inmates, and the guys from Kempei Tai took turns laboriously cutting each other's hair and hacking off two-inch long beards.

Then came a big surprise; better food. Although nothing to write home about, it was a banquet compared with rice balls. In addition to large helpings of the inevitable rice, there were snippets of vegetables and small loaves of bread that probably included sawdust and tasted like it, but the men wolfed them down.

Undoubtedly the best thing of all about the new location and the change was the increasing realization that the war had ended and rescue was eminent. For all practical purposes, the prisoners started running the camp. Some of them painted "Omori" in huge white-wash letters on top of one of the barracks to guide planes seeking prison camps to provide food by parachute.

Within a few days, B-29s were dropping fifto-gallon drums of food out of bomb bays over Omori. The drums came down attached to parachutes but hit the ground hard. Several Japanese, who were as eager as the prisoners to get the provisions, did not realize the force involved, tried to catch the very heavy drums, and were killed. The food, which was carefully rationed, consisted mainly of canned goods, especially Spam, some ham and bologna, dried fruit, and cookies.

Late in the afternoon of August 23, all the prisoners were herded to the center of the compound for an "important announcement." An elderly Japanese officer accompanied by an interpreter climbed up on some scaffolding and announced that the Empire of the Rising Sun had surrendered on August 15. He was silhouetted against the orange sky of a setting sun.

On Saturday evening, a few days later, some British and Australian long-termers put on a celebratory stage show akin to the ribald song-and-dance episode in the wartime movie, *South Pacific.* The lads had a beat up guitar and a trumpet and used pans for drums. The next morning, a British naval officer conducted the camp's first church service, and every prisoner attended, joining in time-honored prayers and hymns such as *Abide With Me.* For many airmen, that religious service was the most memorable one of their lives.

Quite a few of the long term prisoners at Omori had been on work crews in the region and had many stories about their experiences.

One story was about an American crew that was mixing and pouring concrete for a small dam. A Japanese sergeant who was in charge of the project would visit the site on his motorcycle and would harass the workers. One afternoon, when he went behind some trees to urinate, the Americans pushed his motorcycle into the forms for the dam and hurriedly poured concrete over it. When the sergeant returned he couldn't find his machine and was too embarrassed to file a report. Another story involved prisoners having experience with machinery who were assigned to help repair a Japanese ship. They dumped a bucket of nuts and bolts into the huge cylinders of the ship's engine. A few days later when the engine was started it exploded.

Eventually the Americans learned how the war was ended. After increasingly heavy B-29 bombing raids on the Japanese home islands and after the conquest of Okinawa ended June 21, U.S. military strategists expected the Japanese government to surrender. However, Prime Minister Kantaro Suzuki, who had recently replaced Hideki Tojo, merely urged his people to keep preparing to repel an invasion of the homeland. So the decision to drop the first atomic bomb at Hiroshima on August 6 was made by President Harry S. Truman. When Suzuki continued to reject any prospect of surrender, Truman ordered the second A-bomb drop August 9 on Nagasaki. After that, Emperor Hirohito, revered as a god, over-ruled his militarists and in a radio broadcast announced surrender on August 15.

On the afternoon of August 29, exactly three months after *Sitting Pretty #2* was shot down, U.S. Navy landing craft from the Seventh Fleet crowded the bay beach near the Omori camp, and amid whistles and shouts of "Hurray" and "Hallelujah," the prisoners were hauled aboard the boats. Commander Harold Stassen, later a U.S. senator and candidate for President, took charge of the camp and emptied it with no opposition from the few remaining guards.

General Douglas MacArthur, commander of the Pacific Theater, wanted most of the fleet to stay out of Tokyo Bay until September 2 when he would be the center of world-wide attention at the formal surrender of the Japanese aboard the U.S.S. *Missouri* battleship. However, Admiral "Bull" Halsey, commander of the Seventh Fleet, entered the bay and insisted on evacuating the prison camps as soon as possible.

The Omori POWs were ferried out to a new hospital ship, the U.S.S. *Benevolence*. Everyone underwent a fast physical examination to see if any one needed an emergency operation. Then, the first priority for every man was a steaming hot shower. The guys were issued Navy "fatigues" and were assigned to beds in air-conditioned ward rooms with thick mattresses and blankets that smelled of laundry soap.

Then the eating began—"real" scrambled eggs, hot buttered toast, milk and coffee, and heaping bowls of ice cream. But the ex-prisoners' shrunken stomachs could not cope with the onslaught, and many of the men got sick and vomited. The Navy medical corpsmen knew that would happen, but did not have the heart to try to stop the gorging. The next day, the eating was more restrained.

On the afternoon of September 4, 1945, the station master from the depot in Lund rushed into the store waving a piece of yellow paper and shouting, "Good news!" The two-sentence telegram, dated that day, from the U.S. War Department, was headlined "Battle Casualty Report." It notified Mr. and Mrs. John H. Johnston that that their son, Sgt. William K. Johnston, "had been recovered from Japanese territory and returned to military control as of August 29."

Harley, hearing the hullabaloo, came in from the back room and was engulfed by Mary shouting, "He's OK! He's safe! He's been rescued!"

A second telegram, dated September 8, said Sgt. Johnston "is being returned to the United States in the near future and will be given an opportunity to communicate with you upon arrival." For Mary and Harley, two months of agonized waiting were over, and now they could relax and wait for Kent's telephone call, knowing it would probably be a few weeks until he could get back to the States.

In Tokyo Bay, Army Air Force officers from Omori prison were transferred from the hospital ship to air bases and flown to the Philippine Islands where they waited for their records to catch up with them. After two weeks on a troop ship to San Francisco and up to a week at Letterman Hospital there, most of the officers were on the way to their hometowns. For enlisted men, the return home would take twice as long.

The hospital ship *Benevolence* remained anchored in Tokyo Bay for a week, and the remaining airmen watched the arrival of the battleship, the Missouri, and the surrender ceremonies on its deck.

On September 17, enlisted men including Kent, Oliver Thomas and Alan Kenniston were transferred to a vehicle carrier-type ship along with about 1,500 other ex-POWs. Rows of army cots had been arranged in a huge space below the main deck. The guys were disappointed that they were not flown back to the States, but they all put on weight rapidly and even got suntans on their transport ship.

After 27 days, including stops at Guam and Pearl Harbor, the ship bearing Kent sailed under the Golden Gate Bridge into San Francisco Bay the morning of October 3 with all hands on deck. A multi-level excursion boat carrying a huge banner saying "Welcome Home!!" pulled alongside and escorted the ship to a dock where a crowd was cheering. On the excursion boat top deck was a bevy of lady Marines, all in uniform, all red-haired and all very pretty, at least in the eyes of the former prisoners of war. The women were accompanied by a band playing songs about states such as *California, Here I Come*, *Carry Me Back to Old Virginy*, and *The Eyes of Texas Are Upon You.*

Wendell Hickman McGarry, a Salt Lake City native, was an Army medic at the Philippine Islands/Manila Bay fortress of Corregidor when it was captured by the Janpanese early in 1941. He miraculously survived three years as a prisoner and was one of the 3,785 prisoners rescued by an Army unit in Manila February 5, 1945. In that Army unit was Norman Laub of Beryl, Utah, whose brother, Merrill, had been killed in a Leyte Island battle in October 1944. A ship bearing McGarry and other ex-prisoners from Manila arrived in San Francisco March 8 amid a tumultuous welcome as the first POWs to return from the Pacific war theater. McGarry had screaming nightmares and a drinking problem for five months after his return but he recovered, got married, and became a dentist in Manti, Utah.

Sergeants Bruce Yungclas and Abe Ginsberg had a prisoner experience very different from the group at Tempei Kai. They were captured separately on the Chiba Peninsula, were beaten several times, and then transported past rock-throwing crowds through Tokyo to a prison camp named Ofuna where the guards were almost friendly. After the first month, Yungclas and Ginsberg got baths, clean clothes, exercise privileges, and bits of fish and seaweed in their rice bowls. On September 1, rescue teams from the Eleventh Airborne Division arrived at Ofuna, and the prisoners were flown to Okinawa. There, Yungclas ran across Captain Worde and learned that the rest of their crew had survived. The Ofuna crowd was flown to Manila and on September 19 caught a troop transport ship to San Francisco.

Letterman Hospital in San Francisco was the main medical clearinghouse for POWs from the Pacific Theater. As various members of the *Sitting Pretty #2* crew checked in there, everyone was amazed to learn that the entire crew had survived.

Kent and several members of his crew disembarked at Treasure Island in San Francisco Bay and were allowed to make long distance calls home courtesy of the Red Cross. He called home and had to wait for the call to get through the four-party telephone line to the Lund Store.

"Hello, Mom. This is Kent. I'm back, and I'm okay. I'm going to a hospital in San Francisco. I'll probably be here for a few weeks for a checkup."

"Oh, thank God! Thank God!" Mary shouted. "We got letters and telegrams saying you had been rescued, and we've waited every day for you to call. It's so wonderful to hear your voice. Are you all right? Did you get hurt? When will you be home?"

Kent patiently assured her he was okay, adding that he had lost a lot of weight and needed to get back to home-cooking. He was not sure how long he would be at Letterman Hospital.

He was admitted to the hospital October 7 for a thorough health screening and treatment of any ailments. A hospital ship report said he was very thin and had dysentery, scabies, and a rash on one leg but all his vital signs of temperature, blood pressure, and pulse were close to normal.

After a few days at Letterman, Kent was allowed to go home for a few days with orders to then report to the Army's Fitzsimons General Hospital in Aurora, Colorado, near Denver.

In Lund, Kent found his grade school classmates, Eddie Frahske and Verle Couch, home on leave at the same time. Mary's favorite photograph of the war years was titled "Three Sons of the Desert" and showed the trio together, Kent in his Air Force uniform, Eddie in his Army uniform, and Verle in his Navy SeaBees dress blues. Mary's title for the photo reflected a subtle change from

"Three Sons of the Desert"
Kent Johnston, Eddie Frahske, and Verle Couch

her dislike of the desert to her acceptance of it, even pride in it, as her home.

At Fitzsimons Hospital, Kent underwent a final medical screening including a thorough dental examination. One report said he had weighed 165 pounds when he was shot down, 120 pounds when rescued, and 171 pounds after two months of hospital care. A hospital report on October 24 said he had returned to good health, and a Board of Medical Officers recommended that he "be returned to full military duty."

Kent left Fitzsimons in mid-November and was given leave to go home over Thanksgiving Day. He caught a train from Denver arriving in Lund late in the evening so there was no fanfare about a POW coming home. That would await his return to stay after discharge. He spent the days of leave sleeping, eating, reading, and steadfastly avoiding questions about being shot down and being a prisoner. He visited Lyle Applegate at the sheep camp several times and went off on horseback around the range for several hours.

The day after Thanksgiving, Kent caught a train to the Army Air Force Redistribution Center No. 4 at Santa Ana, California. The U.S. military establishment was overwhelmed by the millions of discharges needed in the last half of 1945 and the first half of 1946, and Kent had to simply hangout for ten weeks at the Santa Ana base. On February 13, he received his discharge with "mustering out" pay of $400 plus $32.07 for travel expense home. His length of service was two years, six months, and nine days. The next day he caught a Union Pacific train to Lund where he would spend the rest of his life.

His military service decorations included the Air Medal with Oak Leaf Cluster, Aerial Gunner Aviation Badge, Good Conduct Medal, World War II Victory Medal, and ribbons for service in the Asiatic-Pacific Theater of War and American Theater.

In the year after World War II ended, politicians at all levels rushed to thank veterans for their service and, incidentally, to seek their votes.

President Harry S. Truman wrote, "To you who answered the call of your country and served in its Armed Forces to bring about the total defeat of the enemy, I extend the heartfelt thanks of a grateful nation . . . We now look to you for leadership and example in exalting our country in peace." To those, including Kent, who had been repatriated from prisoner of war camps in the early fall of 1945,

Truman wrote, "It gives me special pleasure to welcome you back to your native shores, and to express, on behalf of the people of the United States, the joy we feel at your deliverance from the hands of the enemy . . .You have fought valiantly in foreign lands and have suffered greatly. As your Commander in Chief, I express the thanks of a grateful nation for your services in combat and your steadfastness while a prisoner of war. May God grant each of you happiness and an early return to health."

In an August 9, 1946, letter to William K. Johnston, Governor Herbert Maw, of Utah, wrote, "With sincere happiness I welcome you home on behalf of the people of Utah. You have brought great honor to our State . . . We are proud to have you back." He cited a Utah State government service for returning veterans.

Also in the year after their discharges and return to civilian lives, the crew of the *Sitting Pretty* had a chance to learn more about a restricted and secretive part of Tinian's North Field and about an isolated B-29 crew that was part of a "composite 509th Bomb Group," a very special sister to the 504th Bomb Group. The commander of the secret crew was Colonel Paul Tibbetts who named his plane after his mother, *Enola Gay*. That plane dropped the first atomic bomb on Hiroshima on August 6, 1945, at 8:15 a.m., an event that was instrumental in ending World War II, that ushered in the nuclear age, and that stirred a generation of controversy thereafter.

On September 1, 1945 the Twentieth Air Force awarded a "Distinguished Flying Cross" to the 421st Squadron of the 504th Bomb Group regarding the May 29 raid on Yokohama. The award cited successful bomb runs despite heavy flak and the tragic shooting down of the deputy lead planes of the squadron. The citation concluded, "The courage and determination the crews displayed in carrying out the attack against severe enemy opposition reflect great credit on themselves and the Army Air Force." A "Distinguished Unit Badge" was also awarded to all the officers and enlisted men of the 504th Bombardment Group.

The 504th lost 26 planes and 157 airmen in combat. It was deactivated June 15, 1946.

The *Sitting Pretty* bomber crew was the only one shot down in which all the members survived to return to the United States. That was especially amazing since the survival rate for airmen shot down was only about ten percent. Also, while their survival during three months in prison was largely due to their individual tenacity, they apparently suffered less than longer term prisoners, especially in regard to brutality by guards. Sergeant Alan Kenniston died in the polio epidemic that swept the U.S. in 1947–48. Nine other members of the *Sitting Pretty* crew returned to wives and to sweethearts who became wives, to college educations on the G.I. Bill, and to various successful careers in farming, business, and the Air Force. Most of them lived to be 80 years of age and older. Kent returned to a solitary life of eleven years in the Escalante desert, first as a sheep herder and then as a cattle rancher and creator of a farm for his father.

Chapter 20

Post-War

Kent had written to his parents that he was being discharged at Santa Ana, California, and would be home February 14 on a train arriving in Lund in mid-afternoon. Mary alerted the community that its most famous veteran, a B-29 bomber crew gunner and former prisoner of war, was coming home to stay.

When the train stopped at the depot nearly all the 60 residents of the area were on hand waving small U.S. flags. Mary was dressed up and wearing her usual brown felt hat at a jaunty angle. The railroad section foreman had decided to work on the sidings at Lund so his crew members in their oily overalls were near the depot when the train arrived.

The conductor hurried to plop down a stool at the steps of a passenger car where a tall and somewhat gaunt figure in full dress Air Corps uniform with rows of ribbons was waiting to get off. The crowd cheered, and Kent, in mock fear, pretended to re-enter the car. Then he stepped down, saluted, and in two long strides reached his mother who, with tears rimming her eyeglasses, whispered, "Welcome home, dear one."

Kent hugged her awkwardly since he was not used to hugging people. He shook Harley's hand and, patting his parents on their shoulders, turned to face the crowd. He looked around and declared, "The old town sure hasn't changed much!" Everyone laughed and gathered around to shake the veteran's hands.

As the crowd dispersed, Kent, eager for a beer and a cigarette, headed for the store with his proud parents. A few residents tagged along, asking the obvious questions about what it was like to be shot down and about life in the Japanese prison camp. Kent, as usual, gave short replies such as, "When you jump out of a plane in a situation like that, you really don't think much, you just do what you've been trained to do." or "The prison camps were bad but not really as bad as we had expected." and "I'm really ready for one of Mom's dinners. I hope she doesn't have rice. I had enough of that in Japan." Everyone laughed.

Kent finished his bottle of beer, and Mary tugged at his sleeve, "Come on, let's go home so I can start fixing dinner there rather than here at the store. Harley can close the store early."

As she and Kent walked along the weed-fringed dirt path to the now-tired-looking old Johnston house, Mary bubbled on about how glad she was that he was home, about Dick who was still in the Philippine Islands, but expected to be home in a few months, and about Millie and her new husband who was preparing to enter a university in Tulsa, Oklahoma.

At the house, Kent dropped his duffle bag on the sagging old bed in the very dusty boys' room, took off his tie, and sat for a moment looking around the room that was exactly as he had left it and as it had been as far back as he could remember. It seemed as if the past two and a half years had simply evaporated.

Mary hurried to fix a mutton chops dinner that included a pie made with Elberta peaches she had canned the previous August. Harley came home and lighted the gasoline lamp. At dinner, Kent wolfed down two chops and two helpings of everything else. The conversation was mostly about what was happening or not happening in Lund, how the railroad was cutting back on jobs, the gradual decline in business at the store, and Millie's marriage to a fast-talking "city boy."

Mary, Harley and Millie, 1946

Finally Harley cleared his throat and asked, "You have any idea what you want to do now?" It was a loaded question. Obviously Harley was hoping for an answer that Kent would stay in Lund and take over the sheep herd until they could all think about the future of the sheep business and maybe a farm on the old homestead.

"Good Lord, Harley, give the poor boy a chance to relax!" Mary interrupted.

"That's okay, Mom," Kent replied. "I had plenty of time to think about the future while I was waiting around for a discharge. I'm planning on just staying here. I don't much care about chasing a career in a big city like Harlan did. And right now, I don't see any need to go to college on the G.I. Bill, but I might eventually take some courses at the Branch Agricultural College in Cedar."

Harley had the answer he was hoping for. Not only would he have a wife younger than him to take care of him in his old age he would now have a reliable son as a backup—a son who might help him get back to farming. The other two kids certainly would not return.

Millie was heading for her own life with her Army Air Force veteran husband, Joseph W. Vittum, of Muskogee, Oklahoma. A handsome fast-talking extrovert, he had trained at the Wendover, Utah, Air Base, to be a bombardier, had dated Millie in Salt Lake City in 1943, and had vowed they would get married sooner or later. He completed 25 missions on B-17 bombers over Germany, returned to the States, and looked up Millie in Salt Lake. She finally agreed to marry him March 8, 1945, at Kirtland Air Base, Albuquerque, New Mexico. After his discharge in September 1945, Joe set out to get a degree in business administration at the University of Tulsa using the G.I. Bill. Millie helped support them as a registered nurse.

Dick was happily finishing up his second year in the Navy. He had made it clear that he would get a college education under the G.I. Bill and would pursue a career elsewhere.

As Kent finished his pie at dinner on his first evening home, Harley said, "Well, as you know, we've been hiring Lyle Applegate to take care of the sheep. He'll want to know if you plan to take over the sheep herding."

"Well, I hate to put him out of a job but, yeah, I'll take over the herd until we decide what to do in the future."

Kent started to light a cigarette, but quickly caught Mary's look of disapproval so he went outside. When he came back into the kitchen, he said, "I've been up most of two nights getting here on the trains so I'm going to bed." He closed the boys' room door as tightly as it would go in its unsquare frame and climbed into bed. The whisper of the eternal desert wind around the windows quickly lulled him into a deep sleep. At dawn in the dreams that come just before awakening, he saw again the flames of Tokyo down below and then the gaunt bearded faces of his crew in the Kempei Tai cells.

He got up in the winter-cold room and hurriedly put on one of his Air Force khaki shirts, an old pair of Levis that still fit him, his old work shoes, and the sweat-stained rancher-style hat he had worn for years. In keeping with the frugal life style of his parents, he would eventually wear out all his military uniforms and shoes as workday clothes. His Air Force cap was placed on the top shelf in the closet; he never wore it again, and it eventually disappeared. The military service badges were stored in a small box in the dresser. They were the only mementos of the war that he kept.

After breakfast, Kent and Harley drove the old pickup truck out to Homer Green's place where they met Lyle who had been expecting them. "Hey, Kent," he said, "It's sure good to see you back. You look pretty damn good considering what you've been through. Hi, Harley, how are you?" He shook their hands and then leaned against the truck to await the verdict on whether he still had a job, and, if so, for how long.

Harley asked how the sheep were doing and if there was anything Lyle needed. Finally, he got down to brass tacks.

"Lyle, as you might guess, Kent is going to stick around and can take over the sheep herd, so we'll have to let you go. With all the veterans coming home, the job market is getting tough so we'll keep paying you for maybe a couple of months until you can find some other work. You've been a darn good herder, and you sure helped us out of a jam when Kent had to leave, and we'll be real sorry to see you go. If we can help out in any way just let us know."

Kent interrupted, "I got spoiled in the Air Force, getting served three meals a day and sleeping in warm barracks or Quonset huts, so I'll have to learn again to be a herder."

Lyle smiled wanly, "I doubt it will take very long for you to remember what it's like. And, Harley, I understand the situation and thank you for giving me some extra time. Of course, Jewel and I have been expecting this, and I can probably find something to do. We have the house in Lund, the kids are in school, and we won't be in a hurry to move."

"Well, then, I might as well take over the camp tomorrow afternoon, and let you get started looking for work," Kent said. "We can take you home for lunch now so Jewell will know what's happening."

That evening over dinner, Mary, Harley and Kent talked sadly about letting Lyle go and about what he and his family were facing with a change in the middle of winter. "I'll see what I can do to help Jewell," Mary said. "She's run up a little bill at the store but we can let that go, can't we, Harley?"

"Yeah, sure," he replied.

While Kent prepared for sheep shearing time in April and the start of the lambing season in May, Lyle found springtime planting work in the Milford area. The family, including daughter Donna and son Elbert, eventually settled down near Milford.

In the summer of 1946 when Dick came home from the Navy, he gave his old red Schwinn bicycle to Elbert. Many years later, Elbert recalled that the bicycle gears kept slipping, and Donna remembered that, one day when she was a mischievous 10-year-old, she found Kent sitting on the edge of the stock water trough at the Johnston yard front gate. She pushed him so he fell into the water. He stood up laughing and said, "I probably won't get married but I might wait for you and marry you," she said with a giggle. He never married, and she married a very successful cattle rancher.

In mid-1946, with Kent home to stay and take care of the sheep, Harley and Mary started thinking about selling the store and retiring. Harley had been keeping the store open ten or more hours every day. At age 70 he was still in excellent health but, whether he was willing to admit it or not, he was beginning to slow down, and Mary was beginning to tire of the postmaster routine seven days a week.

They let it be known among their business associates in Cedar City that the store was for sale, and they put a brief advertisement in the weekly *Iron County Record* for a few weeks. Somewhat to their surprise, Otto Fife of Cedar, the county sheriff, bought it for $800 giving Harley a big profit over what he had paid a decade earlier. The sheriff installed three slot machines in the back room, promoted a pool hall and bar there, and a year later sold the business to Howard M. Carroll, son of D. M. Carroll, former Union Pacific station master in Lund. Howard's wife became the postmaster, and their son, Carroll W. Carroll, became Kent's deer hunting companion.

After a few years, Howard Carroll committed suicide with a pistol shot to his head, and Mrs. Carroll sold the store to James L. Holyoak, best known as Wally, and his wife, Alta. They had two sons, Paul and Bob, who attended school first in Lund and then in Cedar City. Wally and Alta operated the store until 1967 when the U.S. Post Office Department closed the post office. The loss of revenue meant they had to close the store and move to Salt Lake City. Wally was a brother to Del Holyoak, custodian for many years at the Lund depot and father of Jimmy Holyoak, Dick's grade school classmate and lifetime friend.

For 40 years, Paul, who retired from a successful career with the Boeing Company and settled in Cedar City, continued to own the store even after the roof started caving in. He maintained the separate building that housed bedrooms and a bath so he and his family could visit Lund on weekends, mostly in the summer. Many years later, when asked why, he replied, "Bob and I feel close to our parents out there."

A favorite story shared by young Carroll and Bob Holyoak was about Kent shooting a three-prong buck deer. It collapsed but struggled to its feet as Kent approached with pocket knife to cut its throat. Kent wrestled with the deer in some bushes, one arm around its horns as he slashed at its throat with the knife. When the deer finally gave up, Kent was bloody, his clothes were torn, and his legs were scratched.

For the Johnstons, selling the store meant giving up the flush toilet, bath tub, and kerosene-fired water heater. Mary had made it clear that, as a condition of her approving a sale, Harley would have to install a bathroom in the old home. Kent and Harley, with the help of a plumber from Cedar City, carved a narrow bathroom out of part of the screened porch and Millie's former bedroom and installed a hot water heater, toilet, and bathtub with piping connected to the old cold water faucet in the kitchen. When the project was finished, Mary, for the first time since she had moved to Utah in 1915, did not have to use an outhouse or a Combinet when she was home.

Kent continued to frequent the outhouse where he could smoke because Mary's lifetime rule against smoking in the home remained in effect.

The next step in "modernizing" the old house was installation of a small gasoline engine-operated electricity generator that allowed one light bulb per room and, more importantly, powered a small refrigerator.

Kent eased back into the routine of sheep herder and seemed perfectly content to be alone most of the time.

In the post-war period, the prices for wool and lamb rose slightly, but it was increasingly clear that the nation's tastes were changing and that beef was the meat preferred in place of lamb. Also, synthetic fibers were decreasing the market for wool. The Johnstons acknowledged that the time for a change had come.

Since Mary and Harley first arrived in the Escalante desert, the weather had slowly become drier, and the effects of over-grazing by sheep were increasingly apparent. The range that had barely supported the Johnstons' 600 to 700 head of sheep could support up to 150 head of beef cattle, and fulltime care would not be needed.

In one of their talks about switching from sheep to cattle, Harley casually mentioned that the old homestead could become a farm.

"The soil is not the best but the land has just enough slope without further grading to be good for irrigation. We could certainly grow corn and hay for feed for the cattle. The well that I dug by hand there had water at about twenty-five feet, and I bet we could put in an irrigation well at three or four times that deep."

"It would make sense," Kent agreed. "Cattle can survive out here in the winter, but they don't do as well as sheep. If we could feed them maybe in January and February it would keep their weight up and the calf crop would be better. From what we've seen around Cedar City and Beryl, we can certainly produce good alfalfa hay. We'll have to learn a lot more about turning corn into silage for winter feed but it can be done."

In the fall of 1946, Harley and Kent found a buyer for the sheep and a seller for a herd of cattle. The sheep herd was delivered to a buyer in Beaver, north of Parowan, in the same way that Harley and Mary had brought the sheep to Lund 18 years earlier. After that trip, Kent and Harley bought white-faced Hereford cattle in Pine Valley southwest of Cedar City, and Kent drove them to Homer Green's place. The Johnston herd would be a cow-and-calf operation with most of the calves sold each year for fattening and slaughter.

The prices for sale and purchase were a wash. Mary who had kept a close eye on the negotiations was quietly very happy to be rid of the sheep.

Kent introduced the cows to their new range and the watering places there. He got blocks of salt to be placed around Homer Green's for the cattle to lick. The saddle horse was kept in the barn and served as a cow pony.

The Johnston cattle herd at Homer Green's place, circa 1950.

Two Hereford bulls, one four years old and one two years old, were included in the cattle herd price. The bulls were fed well to build up their strength for the "work" of the breeding season so that calves would be born in April. In the second year, the young bull broke his tool somehow, perhaps by getting caught in a fence or by being too eager with a cow. Since he could no longer perform, he was sold to a slaughter house and replaced at a cost of $200.

With the switch from sheep to cattle, Kent could now eat and sleep at home. However, he went out to the range nearly every day to check on the herd, especially during the spring calving season. There was no frenzied shearing time, but there were the days of hard work in early summer when new calves had to be branded using a hot iron that burned a stylized "J" on the calves right rear hips. At the same time, a veterinarian from Cedar was hired to castrate the male calves so that they would become fat docile steers instead of rambunctious bulls.

Calves born in early spring were weaned by separating them from their mothers for a few weeks, then putting them out on the range to gain weight until fall sale time. The young steers were sold to feed lots for fattening for slaughter. The heifers were mostly sold for slaughter as "canners and cutters" along with "dry" cows that had not produced a calf for a year or two. Kent soon came to know all the cows and which ones were dry. Some heifers were kept to replace old unproductive females.

The Union Pacific railroad tracks that divided the range posed a threat to cattle getting hit by trains, so, starting in the fall of 1946, Kent worked hard to build fences for several miles along both sides of the railroad tracks. Cedar trees in the foothills provided fence posts three to four inches in diameter and seven feet tall. Posts were set about every fifty feet, and three strands of barbed wire were stapled to them. One of the main skills of fence building was getting the barbed wire strung tightly. Rusting barbed wire was salvaged from several fences around abandoned homesteads.

After World War II ended in August 1945, Dick, who had become an electrician's mate third class, remained at the Osmena Beach Naval Base for seven months helping to decommission it and other naval installations around Leyte Gulf. He was then sent to the bay at Manila, the Philippine Islands capitol, and was assigned for three months to an old submarine chaser, #769, which the Navy was about to donate to the Philippine government.

Duty on the sub chaser was very light, and the crew, like most of the Navy personnel in the small boat docks area, was allowed liberty every other night and weekends for party time in Manila. Many of the sailors were in greater danger on the streets of the city after midnight than they ever were during the shooting war.

Dick returned to San Francisco on a troop carrier, was discharged June 16, 1946, and caught trains to Lund. His mustering-out pay was $144. He enrolled that fall at the University of Colorado in Boulder where his 22 months in the Navy entitled him to almost four years of college under the education benefits of the G.I. Bill. It paid his tuition and books and most of the cost of room and board.

The G.I. Bill—Servicemen's Readjustment Act of 1944, Public Law 346—was one of the best assistance laws ever passed by Congress. A college-educated veteran would, on average, earn twice as much salary and pay twice as much in federal taxes in a lifetime as a high school graduate or dropout.

In summers until his university graduation in May 1950, Dick returned to Lund to keep Kent company and help him with the cattle and the then new farm on the old homestead. Harley paid him fifteen dollars a month plus room and board.

In the winter of 1947, in order to learn about irrigation farming, Kent used the G.I. Bill for evening courses at the Branch Agricultural

College in Cedar which was part of Utah State University in Logan. When spring came, Kent and Harley began the series of investments totaling about $2,500 that would result in an irrigation farm on the old homestead and fulfillment of Harley's dream. The money had been saved from the store business.

Harley and the brand new irrigation system on the old homestead.

Within two years, Kent and Harley acquired the machinery and equipment they needed on the farm. A drilling and equipment company was hired to put in a well about eighty feet deep to produce enough water for up to fifty acres of crops. A small shed was built to cover the wellhead and a diesel engine-powered pump. With a shovel, Kent prepared a catch basin and installed a wooden gate through which the well water would be released into main irrigation ditches, called laterals, which were dug across the top of the fields.

A small FarmAll tractor was used to clear the regrowth of brush from fields once worked over by Harley and his mules. Harley drove the tractor, and Kent followed with the equipment needed to prepare twenty acres for alfalfa. A five-foot-high fence was placed around the fields to keep out the cattle and voracious jack rabbits.

On the day the pump and well were officially tested, Mary and several friends came out to the homestead with a picnic lunch to celebrate the occasion. Kent started the engine, pulled a handle, and clear cold water burst from a short pipe into the catch basin. The water gurgled into a ditch and, guided by Kent and his shovel, began flowing in a thin layer over the alfalfa field. Everyone cheered.

By mid-summer 1947, the first of two cuttings of alfalfa were raked into windrows for drying and then hauled to a stack from which the cattle would be fed. Later, a baler was used to produce circular bales of hay. In the winter of 1947–48, the cattle got their first taste of Johnston hay.

Since the nearest machinery repair shops were 35 miles away in Cedar City, Kent, as is the case with most operators of small farms, became a mechanic and jack-of-all trades.

When Dick came home from college June 1, 1947, he replaced Harley as Kent's helper for the summer. He and Kent began preparing 20 acres for a corn crop to be undertaken the following spring and summer. Lateral ditches were expanded across the top of the fields area, and furrows were laid out to carry water from the laterals to the rows of corn.

In the next few summers, the brothers replaced the sagging wire fence around the largest corral at Homer Green's place with a six-foot high fence of old railroad ties. They also created a reservoir pond at Homer Green's and one that could catch thunderstorm runoff in the part of the range east of the railroad tracks.

In the spring of 1948, Kent and Harley planted the first crop of corn and began irrigating it along with the alfalfa field.

Irrigation of the crops required round-the-clock work for several days every few weeks. It involved a then-common technique of using pieces of canvas nailed to boards to create movable dams in the lateral ditches. Water built up against a dam and then flowed into the alfalfa field or into corn row furrows through shoveled cuts in the ditch's lower

Kent (left) and Dick (right) taking a break during the Spring of 1948.

bank. When a portion of a field was soaked, the operator prepared another canvas dam downstream on the lateral ditch, removed the first dam, and repeated the process.

In later years, curved pipes about three feet long were used to siphon water from the lateral over its lower bank into the corn row furrows or onto a hay field.

Instead of turning the pump on to irrigate just one part of the farm at a time, it was more efficient to irrigate all the fields in one continuous pumping and ditch-filling operation that required all-night shifts alternated between Kent and Dick throughout the summers.

Early in August 1948, Dick complained one afternoon that he was having increasing difficulty swallowing. The next morning Mary drove him to the family doctor in Cedar City who did a spinal tap on Dick as the customary test for poliomyelitis which had emerged as almost an epidemic in the nation that summer. The doctor said Dick should go as soon as possible to Salt Lake City's General Hospital which was the state's center for treatment of polio cases. Kent drove Dick on the five-hour trip to the hospital. Doctors there said Dick had a rather rare form of polio in which the virus paralyzes nerves that emanate directly from the brain to the face and throat, covering many voluntary and involuntary functions ranging from swallowing and laughing to the blinking of eyes. In the more common form of polio, the virus attacks the spinal column. It remained a mystery as to why Dick got polio when he had been so isolated for two months in Lund and on the farm. The mostly likely explanation was that flies spread the virus everywhere.

Dick's face and throat were totally paralyzed to the point that his eyelids had to be taped shut at night, and he had to have intravenous nourishment and hydration. He could see and hear but could not talk. The doctors noted that his excellent physical condition from the farm work may have saved his life and would speed his recovery.

Back home, Mary was distraught at the expectation that polio would paralyze her youngest son and asked God why her sons kept getting into serious dangers.

Against the advice of doctors, Dick left the hospital the first week in September and returned to the University at Colorado to meet a required sequence of courses. He had become a member of the Gamma

Kappa chapter of Sigma Nu Fraternity at Boulder the previous year, and the fraternity played the role of Good Samaritan, giving reduced rate room-and-board to Dick for the 1948–1949 school year. His face gradually returned to near normal so that in a few months he could ask girls for dates.

During the next summer of 1949, the brothers dug a large trench where harvested corn could be turned into silage. The homestead farm was now a complete operation for crops and wintertime feed for the cattle. Harley, approaching seventy-five years of age, visited the farm in good weather and walked around the fenced perimeter ostensibly to look for rabbit holes in the fence while actually just relishing the appearance and smell of crops on his land.

Dick graduated with a degree in newspaper journalism in May 1950, married Joan Ora Simon of Tampa, Florida, whom he had dated in Boulder, had a daughter, and began a career as a reporter and editor. Millie and husband Joe were in Dallas, Texas, raising a family and earning a living in the plumbing supply business.

In Lund, life for the remaining Johnstons settled down to a routine of farm and cattle work and fence repairs by Kent, housekeeping and book-reading by Mary, and a few chores and lots of naps by Harley. Mary began receiving a small pension from the Post Office Department. Her involvement in the Lund school had faded after Dick finished the eighth grade. The school closed in 1947 leaving the town with one less activity and a greater sense of loneliness.

Harley checking the corn crop on his homestead.

Kent seemed to be as happy as he had ever been although it was impossible to tell what he was thinking about his life and perhaps about his future. No one knew what memories ruled his nights. He had always been too quiet and shy to seek romance wherever he might be including saloons in Cedar City. There were no unmarried women in Lund.

The family's sagging old clapboard house had not been painted in 35 years, but no one seemed to mind. Mary was as relaxed and content as she had been since Harley worked for Conoco in the 1920s. She could do housework when she felt like it rather than on a schedule. The old linoleum floor looked no better clean or dirty. Men were home to start the balky old washing machine and to empty tubs of wash water. The only consistent exercise she got was walking to the store for the mail, and she began to gain weight.

Despite the time of tranquility, Mary continued to wish that she could move from the dying little town to Cedar City where there was a church, a piano, and friends different from those she knew in Lund. She could not help but look to the future and the question of whether she and Harley would stay in the creaking old house for the rest of their lives in a town that conceivably could cease to exist.

One day, Mary told Harley, "You know, dear, one of these days there might not be anyone around here but you and me and Kent. Last Sunday, I talked to one of the women at the church in Cedar, and she asked why we don't really retire and move to Cedar. She said it would be easy to find a small comfortable house there within walking distance of stores and the church."

"Yeah, we could do that," Harley replied and threw up his first line of resistance to the idea. "But we'd have to pay for sewer and water and electricity. And you can bet your life the property taxes would be a lot more than the few dollars a year we pay now."

"Well, that's true," Mary admitted, "but we have to drive to Cedar every few weeks for groceries and for gasoline now that Conoco has stopped delivering gas to the pump at the store. And we are paying a little bit now for the gasoline generator for electricity and kerosene for the bathroom water heater."

"Well, there's no need to do anything now," Harley declared with an edge to his voice that told Mary the conversation was ending.

A month later, Harley stumbled and fell, spraining his right wrist and scraping a knee.

Mary took the occasion to again carefully bring up the subject of moving. "You know, dear, we're not getting any younger, and it would be better if we were nearer a doctor and a hospital."

"We're only forty-five minutes from a doctor now," Harley retorted. "I don't think we'll be needing a doctor for quite a few years."

"Well, all of us seem to be healthy now but you've never had a physical examination, and it's been years since I've had one. We could have a heart attack any day."

"And we can be hit by lightning. Anyway, I don't think we can just move away and leave Kent here alone. He came home from the war when he could have gone off and done something else. I guess he likes it here. I like the farm, and after all we've gone through to get it going, I don't want to leave it."

Mary shrugged and went to the kitchen to fix dinner.

In 1951, Dick was hired by the *Salt Lake Tribune* and *Telegram*, and he wrote a series of articles about Utah's tourist attractions. He and his wife, Joan, and one-year-old daughter Kathleen, took a train to Lund, borrowed the family's old car, and visited tourist spots in southern Utah. Mary was delighted to meet her little blond granddaughter.

Dick took the occasion to get Kent alone and ask him about the old folks staying in Lund or moving some place. "Should we be doing something to maybe get them to move to Cedar?" he asked. Kent shrugged, "Mom has mentioned it a few times but Dad is not interested, and he's always concerned about expenses. Anyway, I stay out of it. They can do what they want."

He gave no clue as to his own views or what he might do if Mary and Harley left Lund.

In one of their rare telephone conversations, Dick talked with his sister about the future for their parents and Kent. However, he and Millie remained caught up in the demands of raising families and balancing household budgets. They took no action to try to get Mary and Harley to live in Cedar City.

The population of Lund continued to dwindle, leaving the Wally Holyoak family at the Lund Store and a few railroad families who were Mexicans or Navajo Indians. Mr. and Mrs. Oscar Frahske still lived on their old homestead north of Lund, but Mary had little social contact with them. Arlie and Ottie Fourman had sold their holdings near Beryl and moved to California so Mary and Harley lost them as long-time good friends. Although Arlie had migrated to the West as a sickly young man, he out-lived Ottie, his long-suffering wife, and died at the age of one-hundred. As things turned out, Harley would also outlive his long-suffering wife.

The Union Pacific railroad which had given birth to the town of Lund and others in the Escalante desert had also served as a lifeline linking them to the rest of the world. The UP nurtured those towns for decades with steady jobs and economic activity, but then began slowly draining away that life support. The end was forecast one summer morning in 1936 when the UP's brand new streamliner, the *City of Los Angeles*, with its yellow, bullet-nosed, diesel-powered locomotive blew through Lund without slowing down.

When the world war time economy ended in 1946, railroads everywhere were forced to become more efficient, developing new diesel engines and steadily phasing out the super-heavy and obsolete "Iron Horse" steam engines and all the facilities they had required from water tanks to roundhouses. The companies installed centralized dispatching that increased system capacity but wiped out station master and telegrapher jobs. The old system of using telegrams for orders to engineers was replaced by radios, on-board computers, and finally cell phones. For the Union Pacific, traffic control was ultimately totally centralized in the UP headquarters in Omaha, Nebraska.

Huge mechanized track maintenance equipment with itinerant crews began replacing mostly unskilled section gangs whose foremen knelt down and squinted along the rails to decide where raising or straightening was needed. Laser beams replaced the squint.

Union Pacific diesel-powered locomotive and freight train
on the desert south of Lund, circa 1950.

The use of large steam engines weighing 150 to 175 tons that needed water stops every fifty miles or so began fading rapidly in the early 1950s. Oil tanks gradually replaced heavy, space-consuming, dirty coal—and firemen—to provide fuel for generating steam. The "big boy" series of steam engines were visually stunning personifications of power but were like dinosaurs. The locomotives had twelve drive wheels six feet in diameter, boilers that were sixty feet long, fire boxes that were fifteen feet long, and water tanks that held 18,000 gallons. The last one was built in 1944. On October 24, 1951, a steam locomotive train from San Bernardino, California, passed through Lund to Salt Lake City and marked the end of regular use of steam on the LA/SLC line.

The advent of diesel meant two to three times fewer crew members. Charming red cabooses with windowed cupolas became relics of the past. The nostalgic smell of smoke, the sound of steam whistles, and the hissing of released steam became a memory in the little railroad towns.

One of the most exciting events in Lund's history occurred in 1946 when a string of iron ore-laden rail cars broke loose at the mines near Cedar City and rumbled down the gentle slope of the spur track toward Lund. There, the station master threw a rail siding switch to make sure the rogue cars did not get onto the Union Pacific main line. The runaway, by then traveling probably 20 miles an hour, derailed, and a half-dozen cars of ore tipped over in the middle of the town.

Wrecked iron ore cars, 1946

The Union Pacific's total transition from steam to diesel in two decades inspired forecasts of steady passenger traffic in the 1950s as railroads tried to hold onto the business with astrodome/vistadome streamliners through the scenic West. For most of the decade, Union Pacific passengers who held tickets for the Utah Parks Company tours continued to come to Lund where the UPC busses met the trains and carried the so-called "dudes" to Bryce and Zion canyons, as well as south to the North Rim of the Grand Canyon. However, production of automobiles and trucks, which had been halted during the war, exploded and the Americans' love affair with the versatility, convenience, speed and freedom of cars doomed the romantic era of passenger trains and eventually the Utah Parks Company as well.

Trucks capable of hauling a load almost equal to a railroad freight car to any destination on almost any road replaced the rigidity of railroad lines. Trucks, and eventually airplanes, replaced trains for transport of mail.

The bottom line cause of the demise of rail freight and passenger business was petroleum, which in its many product forms, especially gasoline, became plentiful and comparatively cheap after World War II. Diesel fuel helped railroads for a time but gave a rocket boost to competing forms of transportation.

The 1950s start of the interstate highway system, heavily subsidized by the federal government compared with the privately-owned railroad tracks, left railroads to depend on comparatively limited types of freight including coal and ore. For a decade, Congress and other government agencies retained rigid requirements for railroads to provide traditional services, especially for passengers, regardless of cost. The lifeline of the Union Pacific railroad through western Utah was largely replaced by the parallel Interstate Highway 15 forty miles to the east.

White jet trails began to criss-cross the deep blue desert skies as huge and ultra-fast airplanes competed for the passengers, mail and freight that were once the almost exclusive domain of trains.

The final run of the *City of Los Angeles* streamliner eastbound from L.A. was April 30, 1971. The electric lights at the Lund depot had already gone out when the last station manager left years earlier.

Chapter 21

Mary

In a letter to her son Dick and daughter Millie, dated April 30, 1955, Mary Johnston, then 62 years of age, chatted in gossipy detail about the Presbyterian Church pastor from Cedar City bringing several of the church ladies to Lund for lunch and then added her usual report on bad weather in Lund.

"We are still having wind storms. It is blowing a gale today. Twice, the dust storms here have made newspaper headlines. We haven't had any moisture for two months—just wind! Last week (late April) the temperature dropped to sixteen degrees for two mornings in succession. The trees haven't leafed out yet. The cattle are getting as poor as they can get and still keep going. We have been hoping and hoping for some rain."

It was Mary's last letter to her children.

On a balmy afternoon May 9, Mary smelled smoke, went out into the yard to investigate, and saw a small plume of smoke rising from the side of a shed. She screamed, rushed into the house to get a bucket of water, and was running toward the fire when she dropped the bucket, clutched at her breast, and collapsed.

A woman who lived in a railroad house a block away had noticed the smoke and was walking toward the Johnston home when she saw Mary fall. The neighbor knelt beside the motionless Mary and shouted, "Are you all right?" She felt no pulse in Mary's wrist, gasped, "My God, she's dead!" and ran to the store shouting to Wally and Alta Holyoak, "Mary Johnston has had a heart attack or a stroke or something, and I think she's dead!" Harley, who was at the store getting the mail, heard part of the nearly hysterical report and started running home.

Wally immediately telephoned the county sheriff who said he would send an ambulance out along with a deputy sheriff. Wally told his wife to drive to the homestead farm to try to find Kent, and he then hurried to the Johnston home. When he saw the still-thin column of smoke, Wally yelled to a couple of neighbors who had gathered in the yard, "Get some buckets or tubs in the house and start filling them with the hose from the faucet over there so we can put out the fire."

Harley had stopped at the front gate and stood as if paralyzed, his mouth working but no words came out. A neighbor took him by one arm and steadied him as he tottered to the inert form on the ground beside a spot of mud from the dropped bucket of water. Harley knelt down, "Mary, what's the matter? Come on, get up. I'll get you a drink and you can go lie down." He held one of her limp hands and tenderly brushed hair from her face. "Mary, for God's sake, get up. What happened?"

A neighbor said, "Harley, it looks like she's had a heart attack."

"What do you mean, a heart attack? She hasn't had any problem with her heart. She was perfectly fine when I left for the store a little while ago."

"Heart attacks are usually very sudden, and you can't tell when one will happen. Wally has called for an ambulance, but I think it probably won't help."

Harley struggled to his feet. "If she's dead, I'm going with her."

He brushed the women aside and dashed into the house. "Oh, my God, what is he going to do?" one woman gasped. They rushed into the house and found him in the closet in the boys' room, throwing boxes and clothes aside in a frenzy.

"What are you doing? What do you want?"

"There's a rifle in here somewhere, and I'm going to use it."

The women tried to restrain him, but he lunged into a corner of the closet and emerged with a .22 rifle that the Johnston boys had used for thirty years to hunt rabbits and gophers.

Harley used the rifle to ward off the two women and began searching frantically through the top drawer of the dresser. "There were some shells in here. Where the hell are they?"

Wally Holyoak burst into the room. "Harley, what the hell do you think you're doing? Give me that gun!"

"Get out of my way." Harley yelled. "I'm looking for bullets so I can use the gun."

Wally wrestled the rifle away, opened the bolt to make sure the gun was not loaded, and, with help from the women, pushed Harley into the living room and sat him down on the sofa. His face was chalk white, and he kept running his hands through his thinning ash-blond hair. "Mary! Mary! What am I going to do? You were supposed to stay with me. Remember, you promised."

Wally told the women, "Keep him there. Don't let him get near the kitchen and any knives. I'm going to go check on the fire." Outside, neighbors had formed a water bucket brigade from the end of the faucet hose to the shed and had the fire put out in a few minutes. Fortunately, there was no hay in the shed. It was not clear what started the fire, but there was speculation that kids had been hiding behind the shed trying to smoke cedar bark in place of tobacco.

Wally went back to the store to await the ambulance and deputy sheriff and guide them to the Johnston home. The sheriff assumed that Mary Johnston was dead or would be beyond saving by the time an ambulance could arrive in 45 minutes at best, so he suggested the county coroner accompany the deputy sheriff. The coroner and deputy could get the full picture immediately and decide whether an investigation and perhaps an autopsy would be necessary.

Kent and Mrs. Holyoak drove up to the front gate. Kent got out of his old truck and stood for a minute looking over the gate to where a half dozen neighbors where standing around the prostrate form of Mary. Kent took off his hat, twisted it in his hands, stared at the ground for a moment, and then looked around slowly as if in a daze. Everyone watched closely to see what he would do, expecting him to swear but knowing he would not cry.

He walked slowly through the gate without saying anything, knelt beside Mary, and felt for her pulse. Shaking his head, he stood up and asked, "Anybody call the sheriff and a doctor and an ambulance, just in case?"

Someone said Wally had called and added, "We thought we should wait for the sheriff before we did anything with her. Your father is like a crazy man. He wants to shoot himself. He's in the house now so that he can't keep seeing Mary. There was a little fire in the side of one of the sheds in the back yard, but we got it put out."

"Well, I'm not going to leave her lying there on the ground in the sun," Kent declared, his face showing no emotion except for some rapid blinking of his eyes. He picked up his mother, carried her into the house, and laid her on her bed. He asked the women, "Will you stay with her?"

"Of course, as long as necessary," one replied.

Harley had watched Kent carry the body through the living room. He started to get up, then sat back down and began to cry. Kent sat down beside him and gently patted his shoulder. "Dad, I'm afraid she's gone. There's nothing we can do. You just rest here while I go try to reach Dick and Millie."

Kent could have tried to telephone his brother and sister from the store, but he couldn't steel himself to describe the situation even once, let alone twice. He found Mary's address book in the front room table/desk, went to the depot, and sent a telegram to Millie in Dallas, Texas. "Mother died this afternoon." Signed: "Kent." He sent the same message to Dick who was working for a newspaper in Fremont, Nebraska, after losing his job in Salt Lake City due to a newspaper merger.

A deputy sheriff, the coroner, and the ambulance arrived about 5 p.m. The coroner examined Mary briefly, confirmed that she was dead, probably from a heart attack, and said there appeared to be no need for an autopsy. The two officials quizzed the Holyoaks and a few other neighbors and verified that Kent was at the farm and Harley was at the store when Mary collapsed and died. They tried to question Harley, but he was too distraught to give coherent answers. Mary's body was placed in the ambulance to be taken to the Jensen Mortuary in Cedar City. Kent said he would visit the mortuary to make funeral arrangements as soon as his brother and sister could accompany him.

The ambulance attendant talked briefly with Kent. "Did she show any previous signs of a heart problem?"

"No, not that I know of."

"We're sorry we couldn't get here sooner, but you know that road from Cedar is mostly rough gravel, and we didn't dare go much over fifty. Time, of course, can be very important in saving people with heart attacks. Ten minutes can make the difference. If she had lived in or near Cedar, we might have been able to save her."

"Yeah, I guess so but that's the way it is out here in the desert."

The mid-spring twilight lasted to 8 p.m., and a group of Lund residents gathered to talk in hushed tones about the day's events. The Holyoaks invited Kent and Harley to dinner at the store and awaited responses from the two other siblings.

In Fremont, Dick had just finished dinner when the telephone rang and an operator said, "I have a telegram from Kent Johnston for Dick Johnston."

"This is Dick."

"The telegram says 'Mother died this afternoon.'"

"What's that again?" Dick asked.

"Mother died this afternoon," the operator repeated.

"Where is it from?" Dick asked again.

"Lund, Utah." The operator replied. "It was dated 5 p.m. May 9, today."

"Okay. Thank you." Dick hung up, stared at the telephone, and muttered, "It must be true. Only Kent would send something that brief."

Dick called AT&T information and asked for the telephone number of the Lund Store in Utah. He had to argue briefly with the operator about the existence of Lund before she finally gave him the number. He called, and Wally gave him a short summary of what had happened. Dick asked, "Have you heard from my sister Millie yet?"

"No, not yet," Wally answered.

"Well," Dick continued, "if she calls, tell her I'll be trying to call her, and tell Kent that Joan and I will try to catch a train to Lund as soon as possible, probably tonight."

"Okay. Mrs. Holyoak and I are so sorry. We were very fond of your mother."

When Mille got home in Dallas from being out to dinner, she found a message from Western Union and had just finished listening to it when Dick called.

"Did you get a telegram saying Mom is dead?" she shouted.

"Yes, it is true. I talked to Wally Holyoak about an hour ago, and here's what he told me," Dick replied. As he recounted Wally's report, Millie began crying. "Oh, my God, this is terrible. Dad is probably losing his mind. What will they do with her gone? You remember how often he said he married her young so she could take care of him when he got old."

They talked for a few minutes until Dick commented, "This long distance call is on my nickel. How are you going to get home? The Union Pacific main line goes through Fremont so we'll be coming by train."

Millie replied, "We'll drive. We won't be able to leave until in the morning because Joe will have to make arrangements about his plumbing supply business schedule. I'll have to get our two kids ready and tell their school they'll be gone for a while. It will take us two days to get to Cedar City. I'll try to telephone Kent and tell him what we plan to do."

Dick called his newspaper editor and got permission to take a week off. He then called the Union Pacific station and learned he and Joan and their four-year-old daughter Kathy could get a train at 10 p.m. to Ogden, Utah, and transfer to a train south to Lund, arriving there the evening of May 10.

After dinner at the store, Kent walked home almost carrying Harley who kept wringing his hands and mumbling something over and over about Mary. He refused to lie down on their bed, so he stretched out on the sofa. Kent dug out a pint of whisky he kept hidden in his dresser, took a few big swallows with water chaser, and fell into a fitful sleep in his clothes.

The next morning Kent fixed breakfast, then asked Mrs. Holyoak to stay with Harley for a few hours. He went to check on the cattle and to make sure the saddle horse had enough water in a tub and enough hay for a few days. That evening he met Dick, Joan and Kathy as they got off the train and arranged to stay at the Lund Store hotel.

At the house, Dick hugged Harley, and whispered, "It's going to be all right. You know she's in the heaven she was so sure existed, and in a way she will still be taking care of you." Harley looked at Dick with vacant eyes and frozen face as if he didn't recognize his youngest son.

The next day, the Vittum family drove up to the house, and Millie, in tears, rushed in to embrace her trembling father. Joe and the kids, Jan, then eight years old, and J. H., four years old, stood by awkwardly, not sure what they should do or say.

After an hour of discussion about what to do, it was agreed that Dick and his family would continue to stay in one of the guest rooms at the Lund Store, and the Vittums would stay in a motel in Cedar City. Millie and Joan chose one of Mary's dresses to take to the mortician to replace the old house dress Mary was wearing when she collapsed. Then everybody piled into two cars and drove to the mortuary in Cedar. The coroner had left a death certificate there listing cause of death as a coronary thrombosis.

Kent told the mortician the Johnston family owned lots in the Cedar City cemetery which Harley had purchased in 1943 to have a place where Harlan could be buried. The families agreed to order a headstone to span two lots where Mary would be buried and where

Harley would eventually be placed beside her. It was assumed that a lot would be for Kent.

Arrangements were made for a casket and other details such as a hearse to lead a caravan to the cemetery, the choice and wording for the leaflets to be handed out at the funeral, and a viewing at the mortuary. The mortician gave recommendations about ordering floral displays and was given information about Mary for an obituary to appear the next day in the *Iron County Record.*

Then the families visited the part-time minister at the little Presbyterian Church where Mary had become well known. Arrangements were made for the funeral to be held three days later at 10:30 a.m. Mary's friends at the church insisted on providing a lunch reception at the church after the service.

After a brief visit to the cemetery and to the park across the street from the church where the children could play for a while, the families had dinner at a Cedar City restaurant. Dick's family returned to Lund with Kent and Harley for early bedtime after the mostly sleepless train trip the night before and the tension of the funeral arrangements. The Vittums, although also tired by the long drive from Dallas and the day's negotiations, toured the city briefly and then settled down at a motel.

The next day, the Vittums drove out to Lund for a more relaxed family reunion and homecoming for Dick and Millie, and a chance for their city-reared children to learn what life was like in a little railroad town in the middle of a desert. The families drove to the hills to see Homer Green's place, where the cattle were browsing and where the old sheep camp sites were.

The morning of the second day of waiting for the funeral was spent at the homestead farm where Kent turned on the well pump ostensibly to continue the irrigation but in reality to show the city folks how the farm worked. The children delighted in splashing barefooted in the cold water in the catch basin and in the mud of the irrigation ditches. Harley led the youngsters around the farm perimeter to show them where rabbits tried to get under or through the fence.

While Harley took a nap in the afternoon, the families visited the Holyoaks at the Lund Store and reminisced about the "old days." Then everybody drove to Cedar City for a fried chicken dinner at a restaurant and attended the viewing at 7 p.m. at the mortuary.

Mary looked very peaceful in a lace-collared dress, wearing the eyeglasses Kent had recovered from where she had fallen in the yard.

Her brown hair, barely tinged with gray, was arranged in soft waves. At the foot of the casket was a vase full of purple lilac buds from a bush Mary had nurtured for decades against the antagonism of the desert. In addition to the families, only a few of Mary's friends from the church attended the viewing.

On the day of the funeral, the Lund-based contingent was up early for a breakfast of scrambled eggs and toast and was on the way to Cedar City at 7:30 a.m.

At the funeral, the little church was almost full. The Holyoaks and the Frahskes came from Lund to join two former Lund teachers, Helen Stone and Metta Bastien Mortensen, two dozen friends from Cedar and Parowan and a few livestock men that Harley and Kent had dealt with over the years.

One of Mary's Cedar City friends read the 23rd Psalm and another read quotations from Jesus in the New Testament Book of Matthew, such as "Come to me ye who are burdened, and I will give you rest," and in the Book of John, "In my father's house there are many mansions . . . I go to prepare a place for you." Hymns included Mary's favorites, especially *The Old Rugged Cross*, which Harley also liked.

The pastor, Ray Wilson, reviewed Mary's life, noting she had come from a church-focused and very pleasant life in Santa Barbara to join her new husband on a new homestead in the Escalante desert.

"Mary Johnston was a perfect example of the hardy pioneer women who settled this nation. She endured the hardships of the last frontier and was a steadfast mate to her hard-working husband through 40 years of hungry times and happy times.

Mary and Harley on the back step of their home in Lund, 1954.

"She was a pillar of her desert hometown, organizing a Sunday school for years where few people owned Bibles, nurturing the one-room school and the itinerant teachers there, quietly imbuing her four children with love of learning, and serving as a very diligent postmistress.

"She and Harley gave three sons to the cause of freedom in World War II, one of whom came home in a casket.

"Mary Johnston was a Christian of deep but quiet faith through many years of adversity and made sure all her children attended Wasatch Academy, a Presbyterian mission school. She helped several desperately poor families through the Great Depression. She truly earned a place in one of the mansions in heaven.

"We are deeply saddened by her sudden and untimely death but God had his reasons to call her home. Those of us who were privileged to know her will keep her memory in our minds and hearts."

The Lord's Prayer ended the service.

The sad little cortege to the cemetery was led by a solitary Cedar City policeman. At the cemetery, Mary was lowered into a grave in a patch of dry grass a few feet from Harlan's headstone. Harley, dressed in a suit and tie for the first time in many years, stood silently looking down into the grave for five minutes while the small audience watched and wondered and whispered. No one was crying. Finally, he raised one hand, waved at the coffin, and turned away.

From the site, there was a clear view of barren Bald Hills to the west and of the top of a dust devil whirling above the Escalante desert.

When the reception lunch in the church basement ended, the Johnston tribe thanked everybody for their generosity and help, and then drove back to Lund. While Harley took a nap in the bedroom with the door closed, the children went out to play in the barns, and the adults gathered in the living room for a post-mortem.

After an evaluation of the funeral, Dick and Millie laid out the schedule for swift returns to their own homes because the men had to get back to work as soon as possible. The Vittums would return to a motel in Cedar City that night and early the next morning would start the 20-hour drive back to Dallas. Dick and family would catch a mid-morning train north to Ogden and transfer to a train to Fremont, getting there late the next day.

The group then turned to the subject everyone had been nervously thinking about for five days. Millie started, "Well, I guess we better talk about the future. What should we do about Dad? He could come to Dallas and stay with us but I doubt he would agree to that, and it would be a burden on us. Joe is on the road a lot on sales trips, and we've been planning to have another child before long. Joe knows that, of course, but I wanted to wait to tell the rest of you until after things had settled down here."

Joe remained silent but everyone suspected he was not enthused at the prospect of the old man joining his family in the near future. Joan also remained silent since the whole life style of ranching, farming, and living in the desert was totally foreign to her and her upbringing as a pampered only child in Florida.

Dick said, "If necessary, Dad could stay with us in Fremont but we are currently renting a one-bedroom basement apartment, and Kathy stays with a babysitter when Joan works part time. I'm lined up to attend the University of Illinois for a year, starting this fall, to get a master's degree, and I won't be settled in another job for about two years. And I agree, Dad will not leave here unless forced to. I know it seems selfish but, Kent, I suspect you have known all along that you would probably be the caretaker."

Kent, who had been sprawled in a chair and looking out the window with his usual stoic face, sat up and drawled, "Yes, I pretty well figured that out, and I have no problem with it. Dad will stay here. He wouldn't be happy anywhere but here near the farm and in this house where he and Mom seemed to be happy for thirty-five years. I'm not thinking about doing anything but staying here. Moving to a strange place, even to Cedar, and working for somebody doesn't make me a bit excited.

"We have the house here and everything we need. The fencing is all done for the cattle range, fixing up the farm is all done, and with a little help from Dad or from the Holyoak kids, I can run the ranch and the farm pretty much by myself. Dad can do most of the cooking since we don't need fancy food. I can do our little bit of laundry in the washing machine twice a month, and we don't need much housework to be done. And we don't need to have our clothes ironed. Remember, both of us spent a lot of years in a sheep camp. So we can just stay on here and see what happens."

"I trust you won't forget to wash the bed sheets now and then," Millie smirked.

"That will be a low priority. We'll wait until they start to smell," Kent shot back.

"Mom always prided herself on having balanced meals with meat, salad, vegetables, et cetera. She won't be here to can peaches to eat in the winter, and she won't be here to bake bread and cinnamon rolls," Dick commented.

"Yeah, sure, the meals won't be as good as they have been," Kent replied, "but we can buy about everything we need at the store or in Cedar, and we keep a locker in Cedar filled with frozen beef from when we butcher a steer now and then. So, we'll be all right."

"It will be awfully lonely," Millie interjected. "What will you do for entertainment? You can't get television here, can you?"

"Wally is trying to figure out how to get TV here, but we get whatever news we need by radio, and sometimes I listen to music on the radio," Kent replied. "Now, I suspect some of you are thinking—will he ever get married? Well, the answer is, probably not. You all know I've never been any good at getting to know women in school or in the Air Force, let alone in Lund, so for better or worse, I expect to be a bachelor all my life."

Finally, Millie asked the next biggest question. "Brother, dear, have you thought about what you will do when Dad dies?"

"Yes, I've thought about it for a minute but so what? Who knows how long he's going be around even if he is 80 or even how long I'll be around? I might even go before he does. So, we'll just go on day by day. And, anyway, you all know how much he has always wanted his own farm, and now he has one with tall corn and the smell of hay, and it makes him happy. And, now with Mom gone, the farm is about all he has to live for. So, we'll stay."

"There is one other thing maybe we should talk about," Dick said. "Remember, some years ago, we had conversations about whether Mom and Dad should move to Cedar where Mom, at least, would be more comfortable, and they would be close to medical care in their old age. Now, its seems there was at least a slight chance that Mom could have been saved if they had lived in Cedar near ambulances and a hospital. Should we think about Dad having a heart attack out here?"

"Well," Kent replied, "there's a big difference between Mom and Dad in this respect. He has always been skinny and healthy, no matter what, and he wouldn't get very excited or worried about anything compared to Mom who got upset a lot more and worried a lot more. I'd be surprised if Dad ever has a heart attack. He's likely to stay here until he dries up and blows away like a tumbleweed. Besides, at his age, an attack wouldn't cut short a good life too soon as happened to Mom."

Everyone nodded and sat silent for a minute thinking over Kent's astute observations.

Harley emerged from his nap in the bedroom, and it was time to have supper. Then the Vittums hugged everybody, said tearful goodbyes, and headed for the Cedar City motel and then back to Texas.

The next morning, Kent and Harley helped Dick and his family get on a passenger train, Harley returned to the lonely house and memories of his beloved Mary, and Kent went out to the farm.

An epitaph came in the mail a few days later. Quil King, of Santa Barbara, Mary's youngest brother and uncle to Kent, Millie and Dick, wrote to them:

> Your mother was indeed very near and dear to me as we were the youngest and closest together in our childhood . . . I know you have been fine children . . . Of course you had extra good parents . . . It was quite a shock to hear of your Mother passing on, but I am very glad she did not have to suffer. To Kent: I want to thank you for both of your telegrams with the very sad news. To Mildred: I wish the very best for you and your husband and children. To Richard: Thanks for the well-composed but heart-breaking letter. God bless you all.

Eleven years later, Eugene Aquila King, who had been the sole surviving member of Mary's family in Santa Barbara, died, and, in his will, he bequeathed $100 each to Dick and Millie as the sole surviving children of the sister he loved so much.

Chapter 22

Kent

In his best-selling book, *The Greatest Generation*, Tom Brokaw praised the generation that fought in World War II and rebuilt the United States with a sense of duty, responsibility and discipline. Like most newly-discharged veterans, Kent Johnston faced a watershed decision about what to do with the rest of his life. In a somewhat unusual example of his generation, he opted for a predictable ranch-style bachelor life that morphed into caretaker responsibility for his aging parents.

According to the vast amounts of literature published about the lives of old people, the elderly usually prefer to remain in a single family home rather than go to a rest home or nursing home. Also, in typical families, daughters usually bear the emotional and economic burdens of elder care, and the dependents are usually mothers. In the Johnston family, the son became the caretaker for his father at their home.

After Mary's death, Harley took over most of the cooking. He dismissed salad as rabbit food. Baking required a skill Harley was not inclined to learn. Some food got boiled, but greasy frying was the basis for most meals. The diet was one that would horrify latter-day doctors. Harley had followed it for ten years in the sheep camp, and his skinny frame and constant good health had shown no ill effects.

The fat and cholesterol didn't seem to bother Kent, at least not in the short run. His constant physical work seemed to offset the greasy diet. Compared with the typical life of hurrying in a city, his ranch life was mostly relaxed with only occasional worries about Harley or the extremes of the desert weather. However, his constant smoking may have hidden some unmentioned tensions. After coming home, he gradually gave up the expense of store-bought cigarettes and started using roll-your-own tobacco from little sacks of Bull Durham or from Prince Albert fliptop cans. It was the cheapest and strongest product of the tobacco industry, and there were no health affects warnings on the packages.

As Harley approached 80 years of age, he showed signs of a sharp slowdown in physical activity. Mary's death seemed to take the wind out of his sails. He still helped Kent on the farm, but was able to drive the tractor for only an hour a day and could barely lift feed for the cattle. He caught colds more frequently and began to complain about rheumatism. He became crankier as his hearing and eyesight grew dim.

Near the end of May 1955, the Jensen Mortuary notified Kent and Harley that Mary's tombstone had been delivered. They went to Cedar to oversee placement of the twenty-inch-high piece of granite.

Mary and Harlan's headstone.
Harlan's death date was added after he passed away.

Through the long hot summer after Mary's death, Kent patrolled the cattle range on horseback, made sure the windmill was working at Homer Green's place, and toiled alone at the farm including 24 hour shifts of irrigating. Occasionally he hired one of the Holyoak boys to help out especially with harvest work. Once in a while he went to Cedar City on Saturday evenings for a few solitary beers and a movie.

Dick left the Fremont, Nebraska *Guide and Tribune* on September 1 the same year to start work on a master's degree in political science at the University of Illinois in Champaign-Urbana. He and Joan and their daughter Kathy moved into barracks-style housing for graduate students.

In mid-1956, while Millie was pregnant with her third child, she and her family moved from Dallas to Denver where Joe founded Universal Plumbing Supply Company to sell Universal Rundle products wholesale (cash only) to plumbers. An astute and hardworking businessmen, he swiftly built up the company sales and profits. The Vittums settled in a modest bungalow in southwest Denver, and Millie gave birth to Jill on September 25, 1956. A few weeks before that, Harley showed up for a visit. Having a new baby, getting settled in a new house in a different city with a new business, and having Harley under foot in an already crowded house was too much for Millie. After a month, she sent him back home to Lund.

Due to the difficulty of telephone communications through the Lund Store, infrequent exchanges of letters kept the surviving members of the Johnston family in touch with each other in the mid-1950s. Millie wrote the longest letters. With Mary gone, Kent had to take over the letter-writing from Lund. His penciled letters during this period often revealed his dry sense of humor and laid-back view of his solitary life. He usually mailed them to his sister with a request for her to pass them on to Dick.

One letter, in early November 1955 said, "We shipped a (rail) carload of old poor cows last Saturday. Haven't heard yet about the price but hope to get enough to pay the freight bill for them." The letter continued:

> Young Carroll was here for deer hunting season. We got a couple of nice bucks. I gave most of the meat to some Navajo Indians (who worked on the railroad). Thought they were going to make me an honorary chief for a while.
>
> Old Fred Staats shipped a truck load of ore from his old fluorspar mine. He said it paid $170 but the men working for him went to Caliente on a (gambling) party and hiked the price up to $1,300. Whisky can sure make men rich in a hurry.
>
> Dad says he will come to Denver about the 15th of Dec. He wants you to send him a card with your name, address, and phone number on it for him to carry in his pocket. Don't know how he will come yet—train or plane. I'll let you know soon as he decides.
>
> I've either got to get glasses or quit reading and I am not going to wear glasses.
>
> Just forget about presents for Christmas.

In the summer of 1956, Dick received a master's degree and Joan a bachelor's degree at the University of Illinois. A son, Doug, their second child, was born July 2. Dick went to work as a reporter for the Rockford, Illinois *Register-Republic*.

Harley with grandson Doug

On July 4, 1956, Kent wrote separate but equally poignant letters to his sister and brother:

> Well, we are still here because we have not any place else to go to.
>
> Dad has not been feeling too well. He got a little too much sun about a month ago. He made it into the house before he passed out and was apparently pretty sick for a while. He has not been eating much. If he will just stay in out of the sun, he will be all right.
>
> Short rain storm last week cooled things off some and made the desert more liveable *[sic]*, but not enough to make the feed [grass] grow. Another dry year on the desert. It has been pretty rough here so far. Looks like a matter of selling the cattle and waiting until it does rain. Only consolation is that things can't get any worse so they have to get better.

To Millie, perhaps only half seriously, he said,

> When I get these cattle sold, I'll be looking for a job. Can that plumbing concern [Joe's business] use a strong back and a weak mind? Fact is, the back is getting kinda weak too.

To Dick, he wrote,

> Congratulations on your latest production [birth of son Doug] and may you have many more. Grandad Johnston says that may be the only grandson with the Johnston name he will ever have . . . Received the picture of Kathy. Write Dad a note more often. He gets pretty blue sometimes.

In a letter December 10 to Millie, Kent wrote,

> Received the candy and it was very good. Dad encloses some money orders for your Christmas. Don't send us anything because we don't need it.
>
> Nothing changes here except to get dryer and colder. Still have a few cows and this year's calf crop. I get out to feed them in the morning and sit by the fire the rest of the day.
>
> Dad is feeling pretty fair for an old man. He gets the blind staggers now and then and sometimes thinks he is going to fall down.
>
> Merry Christmas

Harley and grandchildren Kathy and Doug Johnston with Kent

In 1956 when the nation was in the Cold War with Russia, and uranium was needed for atomic bombs, Kent and J. L. (Wally) Holyoak, owner of the Lund Store, began prospecting with Geiger counters in the hills west of Milford. They filed three mining claims with the Beaver County clerk and recorder. After two deals involving quitclaim deeds, they ended up with an arrangement for William K. Atkinson of Oklahoma City to mine uranium ore on the Desert View claim 27 miles west of the Kalunite siding on the Union Pacific railroad. Atkinson sold only a few shipments of ore in 1959–1960 to the Vitro Uranium Company in Salt Lake City. He sent royalty checks of $4 and $17 each to Dick and Millie as heirs of Kent's estate and checks of $8 and $34 to Wally who hoped for many years that the mine would someday produce more money.

Kent and Harley were informal partners in the farm and ranch operations. Harley's 1956 federal and state income tax reports listed $3,585 in income, $2,391 in expenses and depreciation, and net profit of $1,194. In the spring of 1957, the bottom of the irrigation well at the homestead farm caved in, and sand choked the pump. A well company repaired the damage at a cost of half of the partners' net income for one year.

However, living costs for Harley and Kent were minimal. The two very seldom bought any clothes, railroad water was free, firewood that Kent got from the hills for heating and cooking was free, meat from slaughtered steers was stored in a frozen food locker in Cedar City and was free. Property taxes were only a few dollars per year. The pickup truck and passenger car were approaching ten years of age, but were driven only a thousand miles per year. The creaking old house was adequate for two bachelors.

June 1957 on the range was pleasant with azure skies and gentle breezes. There were tiny pink flowers on the greasewood bushes, large white flowers above prickly leaves on widely scattered desert poppies, patches of green among the sand dunes, and a green tint in the usually tawny bunch grass on the bench land.

Kent had worked several days on the second cycle of irrigation at the farm, and, in the morning cool of June 12, he drove to Homer Green's place, saddled up the old horse, hooked a battered canteen of water on the saddle horn, and rode off to check on the grazing cattle.

The railroad tie fence around corral at Homer Green's place, 2009

It was twelve years since Kent had arrived at the Kempei Tai prison in Tokyo.

Since it was mid-June amid the longest days of the year with sundown at 8 p.m., Harley did not expect Kent to be home before 6 p.m., and he proceeded to fix the usual steak dinner. When Kent was not home at 7 p.m., Harley ate dinner, put Kent's portion in the warming oven, and strolled over to the store to see if Kent was there having a beer.

The store was busy, and Harley stood in the corner near the telephone booth until he had a chance to tell Wally Holyoak that Kent had not come home, saying, "I wonder if something might have happened to him. He's always home well before dark."

Wally said, "Do you know where he went today—to the farm or to look at the cattle?"

"I believe he went out to Homer Green's," Harley replied.

"Okay, I'll send Paul out there to look for him."

Paul, Wally's seventeen-year-old son, drove to Homer Green's place and got a bad feeling when he saw Kent's pickup truck parked beside the corral with the railroad ties fence, a saddle on the fence, and the horse tied to a nearby post. Paul parked his car behind the truck, got out, and called, "Kent, are you okay?"

There was no answer. Paul walked slowly up to the driver's side of the pickup. The door was open, Kent's left arm was hanging out of the door, his right hand was holding a partly opened sack of Bull Durham tobacco. Paul felt Kent's left hand. It was cold, and Paul knew Kent was dead.

Back at the store, Harley saw Paul's face as he came through the door alone, and cried out, "Oh, no!"

Wally telephoned the sheriff and told him what Paul had found. An hour later, a deputy sheriff and ambulance arrived at the store to get directions. Harley went with the deputy to confirm Kent's identity, and the ambulance took the body to the Jensen Mortuary in Cedar City. The consensus was that Kent, like his mother, had a heart attack and had been dead for several hours. When the ambulance driver asked what he should tell the mortuary, Harley said everything would have to wait until his two other children could come home.

The county coroner would examine the body at the mortuary, consult with the sheriff's office, and prepare a death certificate.

The deputy sheriff returned Harley to the store, and, when he had a chance to get Wally alone, he asked, "Was there a Mrs. Johnston that had a heart attack out here a few years ago?"

Wally replied, "Yes, that was this guy's mother. The old guy that went with you and identified his son Kent was her husband. He's all alone here now. We don't know what he's going to do. I guess his other kids will take care of him."

After the ambulance and deputy left, Mrs. Holyoak fixed Harley a cup of tea as he slumped in a chair, shaking his head and wringing his hands. "Wally," he whispered, "Can you call Dick and Millie? Their telephone numbers are in a book at home. Maybe Paul can drive me over there and get it."

"Yeah, sure," Wally replied, "but I don't want to tie up the phone line too long in case the sheriff or the mortuary call for more information. I'm afraid it's going to be a long night. Paul, you better go back to Homer Green's and put the horse in the barn with some hay and make sure there is water there and put the saddle in the barn."

Wally called collect to Dick at his home in Rockford, Illinois, and to Millie at her home in Denver. They were numb over the double whammy in two years and found it hard to realize that Harley, who had counted on a young wife and then on a reliable son to take care of him, was now alone—except for them.

Ever since Mary died, Dick and Millie had almost subconsciously been expecting a call any day that their father had died. When that happened, they thought to themselves, Kent would inherit all the property—and properly so—and would be free to decide whether he would stay in Lund with the farm and ranch or give up and go find a job someplace. The brother and sister had not thought about Kent dying, and, although they would never admit it to each other, they had hoped Kent would continue to be the caretaker until their Dad died.

Millie told Wally she and her husband and their three kids would start the ten-hour drive to Cedar City in the morning, would stay in a motel in Cedar, and be in Lund early the next day. Wally said he and his wife would take care of Harley for a day or two, making sure he got to bed at his home and providing him with meals.

Dick considered flying or taking a train from Rockford to Utah, but figured that driving the family's new Chevrolet Nomad station wagon would work well for the family's trip to Cedar City and Lund. At the end of two days of driving, Dick and Joan and their two kids joined the Vittums in Lund.

Harley was virtually catatonic. When he talked, it was about Mary and how he missed her or about why Kent had died when he seemed to be so healthy—maybe not happy but at least healthy. And he kept asking about the crops at the farm, worried that the alfalfa and newly-planted corn would not survive long without irrigation.

The two families agreed they needed to make funeral and burial arrangements as soon as possible since it had already been almost three days since Kent had died. They drove to Cedar in two cars with their five children and Harley, and spent the day at the Presbyterian Church and at the mortuary where they got copies of the death certificate saying Kent had died of a heart attack. The arrangements, with the 10 a.m. funeral to be held in three days, were much the same as had been made for Mary two years earlier. There was no time to get an obituary in Cedar's weekly newspaper but the local radio station mentioned the funeral schedule in most of its newscasts.

After dinner in Cedar, Dick and his family went to a motel while the Vittums returned to Lund where Joe and the children stayed in the Holyoak's hotel rooms at the store, and Millie stayed at the house with Harley.

With Wally's help and advice from Harley the next day, Dick contacted Lyle Applegate in Milford. Lyle was almost speechless to learn than Kent was dead. He agreed to try to salvage the farm crops through the summer in return for whatever sale value they might have, and, for $50, he would check once a week on Homer Green's place and the cattle until the Johnstons could sell them. Lyle said he and Jewel would attend the funeral in Cedar, and everyone could work out further details after that.

The families then spent most of two days sorting through all the household goods, clothes, financial records and other paperwork in the creaking old and very dusty house. Harley and Kent had left all of Mary's clothes, keepsakes, and other belongings where she had kept them. Dick and Millie had no use for the aged furniture or for Kent's and Mary's old and well-worn clothes so it was agreed much of the stuff would be left in the house for disposition by a buyer of the property, whenever and however such a sale might occur. The sagging old mattresses on which two generations had slept were especially worthless.

The brother and sister carefully selected the few items they particularly wanted to save and that could be crammed into their cars for the long drives back to Denver and Rockford. Dick took the small box of Kent's military service ribbons, several boxes filled with family photographs and samples of paper records, a slim wood-framed mirror that had hung in the living room reflecting the Johnston family members for almost 40 years, a cedar chest that older brother Harlan had made at Wasatch Academy, and Mary's small library of books. Millie took some fancy dishes and a set of silverware.

Perhaps the saddest moments were when the brother and sister climbed into the attic of the old storage building and found a large trunk containing Mary's wedding dress, boxes of photographs, some letters, and a few other personal effects from her Santa Barbara days. The items had been perfectly preserved in the dry desert air.

After sorrow in the attic, Dick and Millie walked together around Lund for an hour, remembering places and events from their childhood, lingering longest at the now-deserted depot and at the now-barren site of the old school house. They visited the Lund Store and thanked the Holyoaks repeatedly for all their help and compassion over the past two years. The families then drove out to Homer Green's place for a last look at the place of Kent's lonely death beside the railroad ties fence.

Since Millie was the oldest child, she volunteered to stay in Lund after the funeral and help Harley with the heart-rending chore of selling all the properties and the cattle. After that, she and Dick would decide what to do with their father. Millie and Harley would have the old blue passenger car to use during efforts to sell everything.

The audience at Kent's funeral was smaller than that for his mother. A few of her friends attended along with the dependable contingent from Lund—the Holyoaks and the Frahskes—plus the Applegates from Milford and several men from the livestock business in the area.

Kent, always the loner, had made a few casual acquaintances in classes at the BAC (Branch Agricultural College), but that was nine years ago. In other small towns, a veteran with Kent's Air Force record would be well-known but his low profile in Lund had made little dent in Cedar City.

The funeral service included traditional hymns, prayers and scripture readings. The Presbyterian pastor's sermon, however, was well-tailored to Kent's singular life and his military record. The pastor emphasized that Mary Johnston's Christianity had been ingrained in her children and was strengthened with Presbyterian values in their high school years at Wasatch Academy. One of those values was "honor thy father and mother" and Kent did that with unwavering devotion, taking care of his parents for ten years in their old age and fulfilling his father's dream of having a farm. "Life is not easy in the Escalante desert out around Lund, and life there is not one that many young men would opt for in today's society, particularly young men of Kent's stature and high IQ. However, it is common knowledge that he was a loner, and he chose loneliness on ranch and farm with his parents although he might have gone to college on the G.I. Bill and found a career elsewhere."

The pastor summarized Kent's military record from his enlistment in the Army Air Force in 1943 to his B-29 bomber missions, his survival as a prisoner of war, and his honorable discharge in 1946. "The Air Force seems to have recognized his above-average abilities and chose him for training as a gunner in the elite B-29 bomber squadrons that would bring the Japanese empire to the surrender table," the pastor added.

"Kent Johnston was a veteran of whom we can all be proud. It is tragic that his life was cut short by an apparent heart attack while he was alone on the cattle ranch near Lund. Although he did not participate in the church, his life followed the teachings of Jesus Christ, and now he can join his mother in heaven for a well-deserved rest."

A cortege of half dozen dusty cars stopped in the Cedar City cemetery, and Kent was lowered into a grave beside his mother with brother Harlan on the other side. The older brother's horizontal headstone had a light gray center framed in dark gray.

HARLAN K. JOHNSTON
1916 ~~~~1943

Kent's horizontal headstone was put in place a month later.

WILLIAM K. JOHNSTON
Sgt 504th Bomb GP AAF
World War II AM & OCL
Jan 15 1921   June 12 1957

The vertical JOHNSTON headstone showed there was a place waiting for Harley to be buried next to Mary.

After a lunch put on by Mary's friends at the church, Dick and family tearfully hugged everybody and set out in the station wagon to return to Rockford.

Millie sat down for half an hour with Lyle and Jewel Applegate to talk about Lyle taking care of the farm and the cattle ranch, probably for the rest of the summer. Then she and her family and Harley went to the mortuary to pay the balance on the bill there and to the *Iron County Record* to compose an advertisement for sale of the ranch and cattle. They returned to Lund, and Joe left early the next morning to drive to Denver. The three Vittum children stayed with their mother in the Johnston family's old house.

Chapter 23

Harley

With considerable trepidation the day after Kent's funeral, Millie began the sad task of taking care of her father and her children in the crumbling old house in Lund while starting a crash course in real estate and livestock sales. The assignment was complicated by questions about the legal status of the estates of Kent and Mary.

The first priority, however, was instant adjustment from life in her totally modern house in Denver with a supermarket nearby to living in a house with bare bulb electric lighting, a wood-fired kitchen stove, and a little store nearby that stocked only canned food.

For the first few days Millie plowed through the somewhat haphazard collection of financial records, talked with Harley about what the family properties would be worth and how to sell the cattle. He had occasional lapses of memory, but for the most part had a fair grasp of business details. There were several thousand dollars in Kent's and Harley's bank accounts. With sale of the cattle and the ranch, homestead farm, and Lund properties, it appeared Harley would have enough money to live on for quite a few years.

Millie and Harley scheduled meetings with his longtime attorneys, Durham Morris and Orville Isom in Cedar City to start sorting out the legal status of Kent's estate and the steps necessary for sale of the cattle and the real estate. Kent did not leave a will.

With his feeling of desolation after Mary's death, Harley had done nothing about her estate, figuring that as her husband he would automatically inherit everything if and when questions arose. Now, in the turmoil over Kent's death, the status of Mary's estate continued in limbo for a year although she had left a will.

Harley and Mary had owned all their real estate in joint tenancy and had made Kent the owner of some other parcels. With Mary and Kent gone and with Harley as the only person likely to be appointed administrator and beneficiary of their estates, there seemed to be no question that he had or soon would have the power to sell or otherwise dispose of all the properties. Two weeks after Kent's death, attorney Isom filed a petition in the Probate Division, Fifth Judicial District Court in Parowan, for John H. Johnston to be the administrator and beneficiary of the estate of William Kent Johnston.

However, additional immediate action was needed in order to expedite sales and ultimate inheritances, especially so Millie could return to Denver and also to protect against complications should anything happen to Harley at age eighty-two. He and the attorneys agreed to start transferring Harley's and Kent's various land ownerships in equal shares to Dick and Millie.

Three weeks after Kent's death, Oscar and Alma Frahske stopped by the Johnston home in Lund. They extended condolences and comments about the tragic chain of events of the past two years and then offered to buy the house and the adjacent acreage. They said they were getting too old to remain on their isolated homestead; their car was too old to be reliable for constant trips to Lund and Cedar City, and gasoline was expensive. They made no direct reference to the Johnston family members' heart attacks, but hinted that they wanted to be "in town" meaning Lund with at least a telephone available for medical emergencies.

Alma and Oscar Frahske at the Johnston home after purchasing it.

The Frahskes were the last remaining homesteaders out of the hundreds who came to the Lund area between 1912 and 1918, and they no longer had any neighbors.

Harley happily agreed to a sale, noting to himself that no one else was likely to want to buy a small and sagging old house in a dying town. He and the Frahskes went to Cedar City together the next day, got the complete file of all deeds to all the Johnston properties from Harley's bank box, and took it to attorney Isom. The Frahskes agreed to buy all of the Johnston property in

Lund, and Isom drew up a sales contract allowing the Frahskes to take possession in September. By then, it was assumed, arrangement for sale of the cattle and other properties would be completed, and Harley would move. The Frahskes, who were in the midst of selling their homestead holdings, gave Harley a $3,000 check.

The plat of the Town of Lund was basically all in Section 21, Township 32S, Range 14W, Salt Lake Meridian. The property sold to the Frahskes included most of Blocks 9 and 13 in the townsite where the old house was located plus 110 acres south and east of the house.

By a warranty deed dated July 5, 1957, J. H. Johnston, "widower," conveyed 1,333 acres to Mildred E. Vittum and Richard S. Johnston. Included was the 320-acre homestead plus parcels in the area that Harley had gradually acquired over the years.

In the meantime, Harley had received a letter from Rulon M. Lyman of Parowan expressing interest in buying the cattle and the ranch property. He had cattle on the range north of the Johnston range with the Sulphur Spring being the unofficial border in between. Harley arranged by telephone for him to inspect the cattle and the real estate involved in the ranch, especially Homer Green's place with its windmill, since that watering hole would be critical to Lyman's expansion plan. Lyman liked what he saw and provided a written offer at a meeting at Harley's bank in Cedar. Harley and Millie agreed to accept a price of $24,000 including $6,000 for the cattle which was paid by check a few days later and $18,000 for the range land.

A contract for the land sale was drawn up with payments on principal and 4.5 percent interest to be made over a ten-year period to Dick and Millie as the ultimate inheritors of Harley's and Kent's properties. The contract was signed December 22, 1957 by Rulon and Mary Lyman after the attorneys cleared up titles, some dated back to the 1920s, to all the scattered parcels, and a ninety-page abstract of title was prepared covering 2,355 acres. Lyman was late on several annual payments in the next few years, and finally in July 1961 he offered a deal to complete the ranch land purchase which Dick and Millie accepted. He paid $12,000 plus $900 in back interest in return for immediate release to him of all deeds and abstracts of title that had been held in bank escrow.

The Probate Court on October 14, 1957, approved Harley, as the surviving father, to receive distribution of Kent's estate. It included

$3,803 in First Security Bank of Cedar City, a 1950 Dodge truck, and 1,182 acres valued at $2 per acre.

Attorney Morris finally got around to Mary's estate in June 1958, filing Mary's will and a petition in the Probate Court for Harley to be the administrator. In October the court issued a Decree of Summary Distribution of all the real estate interests of Mary D. Johnston to J. H. Johnston as her surviving husband. Harley paid Morris $467 for all costs and fees.

In her will, Mary left $6,000 in savings bonds to Dick. It was money that she should have spent on herself to ease the hardships of desert life or that she might have used for a life-saving move to Cedar City but she apparently felt Dick as the youngest child needed it to help with his new family.

Millie and her children had spent almost a month in Lund and were glad to return to their home in Denver after the cattle were sold, and sale of the ranch properties was in process. Accompanied by Harley, she drove the old blue Dodge to Denver. He gave her the car and started living with the Vittums. The financial transactions provided funds for his personal expenses for the rest of his life.

Despite his advanced age, Harley traveled to Lund and Cedar City several times in the last half of 1957 to finish up on the property sales. However, Lund was no longer his home, he no longer had a farm, and he began an Odyssey for the rest of his life seeking a home that didn't exist.

Harley knew that Millie hoped he would not continue to stay with her family in their crowded bungalow in southwest Denver, and, besides, after his many years of peace and quiet, he was not sure he wanted to be around a family of three noisy kids. Among Mary's papers, he had found the address of his younger brother, Earl, who had long since retired from the Union Pacific railroad and was living with his second wife, Hazel, in Lawndale, California. Hazel was about twenty years younger than her husband. He, like Harley, said he wanted a young wife to take care of him.

Harley telephoned Earl early in 1958 and told him what had happened. Harley did not outright say he would like to stay with his brother, but Earl sensed that and told Harley to come to Lawndale when it was convenient, adding that they would see what could be worked out. When Harley caught a train to Earl's home, Millie was relieved but suspected that any arrangement there would not be permanent.

From Lawndale, it was fairly easy for Harley to make a few train trips back to Utah, sometimes with Earl, mainly to finalize probate court proceedings about Mary's estate. In a postcard April 22, 1958, from Lawndale to Mr. and Mrs. J. W. Vittum in Denver, he wrote: "Dear Daughter and family, Well, I'm here yet. Am going up to Utah in a few days and will call you from up there . . . Love, your Dad." His handwriting was a bit shaky but clearly legible.

Harley stayed with Earl for almost a year but without Mary, without his farm, and without the way of life he was used to, he was not very happy. Earl was in his late 70s, and although the brothers did not argue openly, Earl sometimes resented the advice his older brother kept offering. They were two grumpy old men, and the angelic Hazel, although she treated Harley as if she were a nurse, was usually caught in the middle. Harley more than paid his own way, giving Earl a "loan" of several thousand dollars.

There was a sense of relief by Earl and Hazel when Earl's oldest son Gordon, a very successful southern California physician, decided to buy a small ranch near Datil in arid western New Mexico where Earl could live out his longtime dream of being a cattleman. The ranch included a house, a windmill, fifty head of cattle, a few thousand acres of private property, and grazing rights

The deal did not include Harley.

When Harley called Millie about what Earl and Hazel were going to do, she had little choice except to invite her father to stay with her. Earl helped Harley catch a train to Denver, and they said goodbye to each other for the last time. Neither had had much contact with their aging sisters, Lu, Jennie and Ruby, in southern California.

For the trip to Denver, Harley had arranged a one-day stop in Lund. There he got Wally Holyoak to drive him out to the now abandoned homestead farm. Harley walked around the fence one last time, waved goodbye to the farm he had spent a lifetime pursuing, and caught the next northbound train.

Harley's first trip on the Union Pacific railroad was in 1913 when he went from Omaha to Los Angeles hoping to find a place to farm. His ride from California to Colorado to find a place to live was the last time he or a member of his family rode a U.P. train.

Joe Vittum had begun expanding his very profitable Denver-based plumbing supply business, and in September 1959, he completed construction on a four-bedroom home with swimming pool in an upscale neighborhood in southeast Denver. With Harley in mind, he and Millie designed the house to have a guest room and bath behind the garage. Millie lived the rest of her life in this house.

Having Harley live in the guest room gave him total privacy away from constant contact with the three Vittum children who kind of liked having Grandpa around now and then to ask what they had done in school or what they were watching on television.

Harley wrote checks to Joe and Millie to help pay for his room and board, and Millie's background as a nurse provided some health care. However, his arteriosclerosis, increasing frailty and dependency created some tension in the Vittum household. By early 1960 Millie placed Harley in a boarding house where a woman served as caretaker for him and several other old men. Harley confessed that he "kind of liked that old gal" but he became ill, and, after a few months, she sent him back to Millie. In a letter to Dick and Joan, Millie wrote, "Dad is back with me again. It just seems to be inevitable. Each time I think I have found a place for him, it seems like just two minutes and here he is back again"

In the meantime, Dick and Joan had built a modest home in northeast Rockford, Illinois, and son Kirk, their third and last child, was born September 27, 1958. After receiving Millie's letter, Dick felt he

Harley with Dick and his children Kathy, Kirk and Doug

had to take his turn caring for his father so Harley went to Rockford in mid-spring 1960. Dick's and Joan's new house had a walkout basement with a bedroom and bath suitable for Harley.

He spent most of his time alone in the sunny garden level, but he was increasingly aware of the burden he created on a young family. He did not have a lot of solitude because the three children were constantly up and down the stairs and in and out of the lower level sliding door that led to the back yard. Meals were served upstairs, and Harley often needed help on the stairs.

Joan was initially sympathetic but she was working part time in advertising art and was hard-pressed to take care of the children and be a meticulous housekeeper. A slow-moving old man added to the burden. So, after about five months, Harley returned again to the Vittums' home and to Millie's care.

In December 1960, Dick finally realized a dream of going to work as a news reporter for the *Denver Post.* Two years later, he and Joan designed and built a nice house in south suburban Greenwood Village with a mountain view and a walkout basement having a bedroom and bath. However, the time had passed for Harley to live with any of his children.

In 1961, Dick and Millie agreed it was time to find a nursing home for Harley. After some searching for an affordable but pleasant place with a cheerful staff, they placed their father in the Foothills Nursing Home on the east side of Boulder. It was fairly new, very clean and sunny. He had a separate room and bath and three meals a day in a dining room.

At this point, Harley was 86 years old and was in comparatively good health with no major medical problems but he was increasingly frail, subject to colds and to severe acid indigestion which he had not helped over the years by eating baking soda. His mind was still clear but thoughts and speech came slowly. Like most elderly persons in such situations, he did not like the idea of being in an institution, but he was ready to accept it as probably inevitable after his experiences living with relatives. Events and reality had replaced his goal of having a wife to take care of him until he died.

Dick arranged for Harley to receive $100 a month from the Colorado Old Age Pension Fund. The pension plus interest and withdrawals from $12,000 in a Denver bank from the ranch sale would probably pay for his nursing home costs of $300 a month until he died. Harley and Mary had paid little attention over the decades to the U.S. Social Security program so he did not qualify for SS payments. Millie served as her father's financial secretary.

Millie's family and Dick's family took turns visiting Grandpa on Sunday afternoons, and in good weather they sometimes took him on picnics in Boulder Creek Canyon.

He did not complain much about being in the nursing home, but it clearly was not the life he had planned with Mary. He remained mentally alert enough to know when the children had to leave Sunday afternoon to catch Disney shows on television. The nursing home had recreation facilities but Harley was not interested. He dressed and bathed himself and spent most of the time lying on his bed. He had several long white hairs in his nose that he constantly fingered as a nervous habit.

One summer afternoon, Millie got a call from the nursing home staff. Harley had slipped out of the building and began hobbling as fast as he could toward the Boulder Turnpike a few hundred yards away. When the staff caught up with him, he said he wanted to get to the highway to jump in front of a truck. Up until then, no one had realized how tired he was of the nursing home life and probably of life in general.

At age 89, Harley had become so frail he could hardly walk to the Foothills Home dining room or take proper care of his personal hygiene. The director of the home suggested he needed a more intensive level of care than was provided at Foothills.

After several consultations, Millie and Dick moved him late in 1964 to the Cherrelyn Nursing Home in south suburban Englewood. He got the level of care there that he needed, and the location was much closer than Boulder to the homes of the son and daughter. However, his physical and mental condition had deteriorated to the point where he could hardly talk with Dick and Millie on their occasional perfunctory visits. The grandchildren preferred not to see him. When he did talk, it was often about dying and getting it over with.

At Cherrelyn, Harley got a card dated January 14, 1965, for his ninetieth birthday on January 19, from his sister Ruby in Pasadena, California. She noted she had turned 74 the previous month, and said, "Well, we have both had another birthday. Five of us eight children have lived past seventy . . . Everything is about as usual here. Hope you are in good condition. Lots of love from all of us."

On July 5, 1965, a doctor called Millie from the nursing home and said he did not expect Harley to live through the night. Dick and Millie met at the home and found Harley with sunken cheeks, vacant-staring eyes, and labored breathing, propped up on a hospital style bed. He did not visibly acknowledge them. After gently hugging him, they sat in the home's reception room, discussing what to do next. At 10:30 p.m. a nurse came in and told them their father was "gone." She said, "I was checking his monitor when the heart beat line began to waver. He mumbled something about plowing, and then he stopped breathing."

Millie and Dick had a feeling their father was back on a bottom land farm in Missouri on a lovely spring day, plowing a straight furrow behind a mule in the kind of rich black soil he did not find in the Escalante Valley.

The next day, Millie and Dick met with the Arapahoe County coroner at the nursing home where he filled out a death certificate saying the cause of death was simply old age, but technically, it was myocardial infarction or a heart attack. The body was taken to an Englewood mortuary with instructions for the body to be shipped to the Bulloch Mortuary in Cedar City to await funeral and burial. Dick recovered Harley's old black suit and a white shirt from his nursing home closet and had the clothes accompany the body.

Millie and Dick and their families set out in two cars early the next day for the ten-hour drive to Cedar. Making the funeral and burial arrangements was by now almost automatic. There was no time to get an obituary in the weekly newspaper. The group of Mary's friends who had honored her and Kent with post-funeral luncheons had dissipated, and there was no reception for Harley.

After the day-long drive from Denver and a day making the funeral and burial arrangements, the families drove out to Lund to tell the few people still there what was happening. They visited the homestead where the farm had been abandoned; the pump and the engine were gone; the shed was leaning to the northeast under pressure from the usual southwest wind; and brush was inexorably taking over the fields. They visited Homer Green's place which was basically unchanged although the big barn was caving in and the fences were sagging. The windmill still creaked and groaned, and a few of Rulon Lyman's cattle, offspring of Kent's cows, stared at the newcomers.

Mr. and Mrs. Frahske were still living in the old Johnston house. They had deeded the property to their daughter Fay, who made sure her parents were as comfortable as possible with their wish to remain in the desert.

As expected, attendance was scant at the 10 a.m. funeral in the little tan brick Presbyterian Church as Harley Johnston, despite 40 years of ranching and store business in the Escalante Valley, was largely forgotten in Cedar City. The Frahskes came from Lund, and three women members of the church, who mainly remembered Mary, paid their respects. Also present was Don Cartwright of Cedar whose parents had operated a hotel in Lund in the 1930s.

The pastor, Grayson H. Gowen, was new and had little previous knowledge of the Johnston family. He summarized Harley's long and hard-working life in the unforgiving desert, his love of Mary, and his devotion to his four children that included three veterans of World War II. Regardless of the reality that Harley had ignored religion most of his life, a parallel was drawn between the shepherds of the Bible and Harley the sheep rancher. Hymns included *The Old Rugged Cross.*

A few cars followed the hearse to the dry grass cemetery where Harley was buried next to Mary and between the graves of their two older sons. Dick had told the mortuary to issue a work order for $15 to the Nu-Art Memorial Company to engrave the date of Harley's death on the parents' headstone.

Millie and Dick and their families got into their cars and headed back to Denver.

On April 2, 2012, Millie and Dick and several members of their families met in the Cedar City Cemetery to bury the cremation ashes of Doug King Johnston, Dick's oldest son. Millie died June 14, 2012, at her home in Denver and was interred at a Denver cemetery.

On trips to and through Cedar City, Dick visits the Johnston graves where the view to the west remains over low lavender-brown foothills to the eternal desert.

EPILOGUE

By the time the last Johnston left Lund in 1957, the Escalante Valley desert was steadily reverting to solitude, and the heroics of B-29 bomber crews in World War II were a fading memory. But three decades later, Kent's *Sitting Pretty* plane crew began attending reunions around the nation, and major economic developments began materializing in the valley. By 2013 the long-awaited and tortuous process of reviving historic iron mines was a reality. Highly optimistic real estate agents had created residential subdivisions on and around Harley Johnston's homestead south of the ghost town of Lund.

After he came home from the prisoner of war camps in Japan and from the hospitals, Kent turned his back on his bomber days and his crew in the 421st Squadron, 504th Bombardment Group, Twentieth Air Force. However, Bruce A. Yungclas of Webster City, Iowa, became deeply involved in a 504th Bomb Group Association and was determined to learn what had happened to Kent.

In a letter dated March 14, 1990, to the "Postmaster, Lund, Utah," Bruce introduced himself as the radar operator on the B-29 bomber on which William (Bill) Kent Johnston of Lund, Utah, was the tail gunner. Bruce briefly described how they were shot down over Yokohama and were at different prisoner of war camps.

He then wrote,

> I never saw Bill again after I helped him fasten his inflatable dinghy to his parachute harness before he bailed out . . . I remembered that Bill never wrote home much from Tinian so when I sent him a Christmas card in 1945, I didn't have too high hopes for an answer. I kept this up until sometime in the 1950s when the Postmaster at Lund returned the card unopened, saying that Bill was deceased. I made no attempt then to follow up to see what happened to Bill or if there were some of his family still living.
>
> The 504th Bomb Group had its first reunion in 1986, the second in 1988, and will have its third in Portsmouth, New Hampshire, September 5–9, 1990. The crew of the *Sitting Pretty* are the hosts.

> We have lost only one other crew member, radio operator Alan G. Kenniston.
>
> I would like this letter directed to someone who could let us know what caused Bill's death and when. Please use the enclosed addressed stamped envelope for a reply.

The post office in Lund had been closed for many years, but the letter ended up with the postmaster in Cedar City who knew Fay Frahske Burns, and he gave it to her. She wrote Bruce on April 9, saying that she was one of the very few "old timer" residents of Lund and that she knew the Johnston family very well. She enclosed a copy of Kent's newspaper obituary and told Bruce she would send his letter to Kent's sister, Millie, in Denver and brother, Dick, in Westminster, Colorado.

In a lengthy letter April 21, 1990, Millie wrote to Bruce,

> How exciting to hear from you, and I am impressed with your perseverance in tracking down my brother Bill Johnston (We called him Kent) . . . I am very touched that out of Bill's past comes this friend, knowing he is gone but wanting to know about him and his family . . . I would welcome an account of how you met my brother, what you did together . . . He never gave us any details (about being shot down or about prison camp).
>
> . . . He was a faithful loyal son, saddled with the responsibility of living with and looking after our elderly parents and their ranch properties . . .

Millie proposed that a toast, on behalf of her and Dick, be made at the next reunion: "To the crew of the *Sitting Pretty* and all of Bill's comrades in arms in the 504th Bomb Group. We salute you and may God bless you all. Thank you for remembering him and allowing us to remember too . . ."

Bruce responded to Millie on May 11, 1990, with a four-page typed letter that was typical of his extensive writings over forty years about the experiences of the *Sitting Pretty* crew. He sent Millie a copy of his article, *My P.O.W. Experience*, that was included in a collection of memoirs by members of the crew.

In 1991, Bruce joined other 504th Bomb Group members on a visit to Tinian to dedicate an historical site plaque there. In 1996, he visited Japan's Chiba peninsula where he and his crew had bailed out. He was cordially greeted by residents there and in Tokyo in meetings arranged by a former Webster City, Iowa, resident living in Japan.

Bruce relished the reversal of most American and Japanese attitudes that had occurred fifty years after the Pearl Harbor attack. However, some other crew members such as John Ryan continued to hate the Japanese. And some, like Kent, simply preferred to forget.

In a 1994 letter reply to Millie, Wally Moritz, a lieutenant on the *Sitting Pretty* crew and Kent's prisoner of war cellmate, wrote,

> You have asked me about someone I knew a long time ago but has lived with me through these many years. Bill Johnston is with me now and will always be with me . . . I talked with Bill many times (in the prison camp). Could not do it too often . . . Mostly, Bill talked. Yes, Bill did talk, maybe he understood that it helped me . . . Bill Johnston, to put it mildly, helped me endure."

Moritz, who grew up in Brooklyn, New York, recalled that Kent rambled on for many hours in detail about the Utah desert, about raising sheep, about cooking "lamb."

After the war, the Brooklyn kid got married, had two children, went to college, got a master's degree in engineering, and worked in engineering for many years. His letter to Millie concluded,

> "All this would not have occurred if WILLIAM KENT JOHNSTON had not helped me through a very difficult time. Do I remember Bill Johnston? Yes, I sure do!"

The exchange of letters with Bruce Yungclas in 1990 started Millie's long and active involvement in the reunions of Kent's crew and of the 504th Bomb Group Association. In a letter February 5, 1991, Marcus Worde, Kent's B-29 crew captain, welcomed Millie and her family "as representatives of William Kent Johnston" into membership in the "*Sitting Pretty* family" and invited her to a reunion in September 1992 in San Antonio, Texas. She and Dick attended the event where the main speaker was Air Force General Glenn Martin, formerly a colonel in command of the 421st Squadron. Millie participated in most of the 504th reunions thereafter for fifteen years, ending in Albuquerque, New Mexico, in 2007 when the less than 100 who attended were in their 80s or early 90s in age.

On the occasion of the 1990 death of General Curtis LeMay, who had ordered low level B-29 bombings of Japan, Le Triplett, of Greeley, Colorado, longtime president of the 504th association, wrote, "Those of us who flew the first low level night time incendiary raid over Tokyo March 10, 1945, did not hold his name in high esteem that night. Nowhere, no time have I experienced the fear and witnessed the fires of hell as I did that night. I expressed those feelings in a letter to him in 1986." The general sent Triplett a copy of *Iron Eagle*, a massively detailed biography of LeMay by Thomas Coffey.

Beginning on December 7, 1991, in San Antonio, Texas, a large photo of the original *Sitting Pretty* plane and its crew members including Kent was part of a U.S. National Archives exhibit titled "Personal Accounts—Pearl Harbor to V-J Day" that traveled to eleven museums around the nation for four years before ending up in Washington, D.C. Millions of people saw the exhibition. No other B-29 and crew was so honored.

In 1991, *Sitting Pretty* pilot Arthur P. O'Hara of Teaneck, New Jersey, helped write and publish a limited edition, 308-page, illustrated, hard-cover book about the 504th Bomb Group in World War II. Millie got a copy.

The 1957 departure of widower Harley Johnston from Lund somewhat symbolized the end of a half century in the Escalante Valley. The flood of homesteaders had dried up faster than it began. Many of the little towns where Union Pacific railroad steam engines once stopped for water became ghost towns or simply disappeared. Lund's heyday as the gateway to the region's national parks and iron mines ended in the 1970s. The town's population peaked at 190 at the end of the 1920s, then declined to 52 in 1950 and to two in 2013.

Lund's role in the history of western Iron County was acknowledged with a star on a map of the region on a two-foot-by-four-foot metal plaque placed at the "highway" entrance to the ghost town by the county's Statehood Centennial Committee. It was part of the celebration marking Utah's 100 years of statehood in 1996. The plaque gives a history of Lund in seven short paragraphs.

Residents of the region remained concerned for decades that cases of cancer were caused by low-level radioactive fallout from nuclear bomb test sites in southern Nevada from 1951 to 1975. The Escalante Valley was directly in the path of windblown clouds of detectable radioactivity. The worst was a dust cloud May 19, 1953, from a bomb called "Dirty Harry." The U.S. Atomic Energy Commission, despite charges of cover-up, repeatedly won lawsuits or had lawsuits dismissed brought by residents seeking compensation. A study in 1990 by the U.S. Department of Energy and National Cancer Institute concluded that about 180,000 people in the region had been exposed to 0.46 rems of radiation, more than double the average annual background level. Thereafter, Congress created a $100 million fund to compensate possible victims of radiation.

The most bizarre proposal for use of the Escalante Valley desert and most of the entire Great Basin popped up in 1979 during the administration of President Jimmy Carter while the Cold War with Soviet Russia was still hot. It was called the "mulitple protective structures/shelters" version of dispersal of nuclear bomb-tipped MX intercontinental ballistic missiles. Patrick O'Driscoll, a reporter for Reno, Nevada newspapers, summarized the "race track/shell game" proposal in the *Nevada Magazine* February 1982.

The "game," estimated to cost $33.8 billion in 1980 dollars, would have included 200 missiles, 4,600 garage-like "shelters," and 9,000 miles of roads spread over at least thirty rural valleys in central Nevada and 15 in western Utah. Each missile—71 feet long, weighing 96 tons, carrying 10 nuclear warheads—would be shuttled around on giant truck-like transporters using 200 closed-loop roads. Each loop would have 23 garage-like shelters where the trucks would stop at random on their rounds. U.S. Air Force officials contended that Russia could not know where all the U.S. missiles were at any point in time and could not afford to build enough attack missiles to hit the 4,600 shelters.

Economic development organizations in the Las Vegas metropolitan area liked the proposal but rural populations were terrified. Grassroots opposition mushroomed, aided by the Mormon church and Nevada's U.S. senator, Paul Laxalt. Congress worried about the cost, and the scheme slipped over from the Carter administration to President Ronald Reagan (a friend of Laxalt) who vetoed it in October 1982. A plan to re-fit Minuteman missile silos scattered around Midwest and Rocky Mountain states was adopted in 1984.

The valley was explored several times by oil companies to no avail. The Hunt Oil Company drilled a dry hole in 1983 south of Lund. At the end of each project or proposed project, workers left, and the desert snoozed.

However, by the start of the new century, developments beyond the wildest dreams of one-time "desert rats" had occurred in the Escalante Valley.

The stretch of almost flat land hundreds of miles long in the deserts of western Utah has made it a logical corridor not only for the

Escalante and Dominquez trek in 1776 and the Union Pacific railroad in 1900–1905, but also for a variety of public utility lines starting mainly in 1985.

The sparse population and millions of acres under the U.S. Bureau of Land Management have helped make the desert corridor especially desirable for companies needing rights-of-way and easements for pipelines and especially for high-tension electric power lines. Such companies have increasingly run into "not in my back yard" opposition from communities in rural as well as urban areas plus objections by assorted environmental protection organizations

According to Fay Frahske Burns, Lund's longest-term resident, a fiber optics line was placed underground in 1967 along the railroad right-of-way and was paralleled in 1990 by a natural gas line from Wyoming to California.

The most visible utility line in the corridor is the Intermountain Power Project's high voltage 3,000-megawatt transmission line strung on tall steel towers bisecting the Escalante Valley. As described below, the IPP right-of-way is used by a petroleum pipeline and may be used in the future by other electricity power lines. Lund was a staging area for work on the IPP line in 1985 by the Kirby Construction Company that included a temporary plant to make concrete for the bases of the towers. The Los Angeles Department of Water and Power and a consortium of thirty-seven Utah and California utilities formed an Intermountain Power Agency including Rocky Mountain Power which

Intermountain Power Project high-voltage transmission line
bisecting the Escalante Valley

serves the Cedar City region, but does not take power from the IPP. The multi-company agency spent more than $5 billion to build a huge Utah-coal-fired generating plant near Delta and the transmission line to southern California in the 1980s.

Thereafter, economic development projects began popping up around the valley. In the north end, large scale cattle ranching was joined by a massive ultra-modern hog farm and two electricity generation projects. In the desert's southeast corner, a huge greenhouse complex materialized; and at the eastern edge, a rocket fuel plant and an iron ore processing plant were built. The region had finally benefited, at least economically, from its isolation, thin population, wind, and boiling hot groundwater. Southern California is a major beneficiary of the projects. In the process, the population of Iron County increased nearly every year, approaching 50,000 in 2012.

The largest development was, and is, the hog farm started in 1993 by Circle Four Farms which is part of the Murphy Brown/Smithfield Foods conglomerate based in Virginia. A ten-mile-long string of air-conditioned barns stretching along the base of foothills southwest of Milford produces 1.2 million hogs per year for the West Coast market, mainly California. Tall silos and automated factory buildings for storage, production and processing of more than 30,000 tons of feed monthly for the hogs dot an industrial park on Milford's south side. A major menu item for the hogs, shipped in on the Union Pacific railroad, is the residue of grain used in large distilleries.

The total complex, one of the largest of its kind in the world, has an asset value of around $150 million, employs 500 people with an annual payroll of about $17 million, purchases $34 million in supplies from Utah vendors each year, and pays more than $700,0000 annually in local property taxes.

Circle Four Farms barns, 2010

Circle Four Farms hog feed plant, 2010

In 1992, officials of Iron and Beaver Counties and the city of Milford extended an invitation to the company to undertake a hog farm complex and helped the company win a series of local government and state government disputes with environmentalist opponents concerned about odor and water pollution. Industrialized farms of this size for hogs, cattle, and chickens, called Concentrated Animal Feeding Operations (CAFOs), began cropping up in the 1990s around the nation, particularly in poverty-stricken rural areas. Job creation of any kind was welcomed in some places but, in other places, local residents fought off the corporations because of concerns about environmental degradation. Also, animal rights activists decry the treatment of livestock in CAFOs.

Water for Circle Four Farms comes from deep wells and is extensively recycled. A continuing problem has been the 25-foot deep lagoons for continuous treatment of one billion gallons of wastewater. Manure produces useable methane gas and is converted to fertilizer. Shipping of hogs is done by trucks, not by the Union Pacific Railroad.

Despite the economic boost, Milford's population of 1,500 has had split opinions about Circle Four Farms, particularly about the pervasive odor and influx of "outsiders." The operation is highly automated, and a majority of the employees commute from the towns of Beaver and Cedar City. The Cedar commuters drive west through Lund and turn north on a longtime gravel road (often used by Johnston brothers Kent and Dick) along the foothills to a major part of the hog farm operations.

Stories in the *Denver Post,* and in the *Economist*, a weekly magazine based in Britain, said a major Chinese meat production company has offered $4.7 billion for purchase of Smithfield Foods, the world's largest pork producer and maker of famous Smithfield Hams. The deal, which could be the largest takeover of an American company by a Chinese firm, faced a tough review by the U.S. government, but Smithfield shareholders liked the thirty-one percent increase in price over earlier offers. Pork consumption has declined in the U.S., but soared in China.

Although much smaller than the hog farm in terms of economic impact, CML Metals Company's revival of iron mines activity west of Cedar City evokes nostalgic memories in old-timers of the days when the iron ore fed huge steel mills in central Utah and helped win World War II. Vast piles of pink and gray tailings mark previous mining in the district which is three miles wide and twenty miles long.

In 2005, Palladon Ventures LTD out of Vancouver, Canada, began difficult and convoluted efforts to resume mining at several of the iron ore deposits that had been, and still are, served by rail spurs linked to the Union Pacific track between Lund and Cedar City. Ore shipments then went on the UP main line to West Coast ports and on to China. Palladon bought two ore deposits for $10 million, planned to build a plant to concentrate the iron content in ore before shipping it to steel-making customers, and began trading shares of company stock for investment money from Luxor Capital Ventures of New York City. Palladon ran into a series of problems including the world-wide economic downturn in 2008–2009. In 2010 Luxor gained 78 percent of Palladon stock in return for $40 million to keep the project afloat along with an agreement for sale of 600,000 metric tons of ore concentrate to China Kingdom International Minerals and Metals Company, a major Chinese steelmaker.

By 2012, the iron ore project was under the name of CML Metals Company, based in Cedar City, construction of the plant to boost the iron content of shipped ore was completed, and CML had a goal of selling two million tons to China at prices of up to $100 per ton.

A fourteen-page review of iron ore activity near Cedar City from 1850 to March 2013 by Utah Rails.net plus company press releases were the basis of this report.

The perpetual winds that help keep the Escalante Valley dry and that haunted homesteaders have assumed a major new beneficial use in addition to turning isolated windmills for vital water for livestock.

North of Milford, bracketing the border between Beaver and Millard counties, is a forest of towers bearing wind-driven electricity generators. It is called a "wind farm" that was built by First Wind Company of Boston, Massachusetts, starting in 2009. The 165 huge turbines with blades more than a hundred feet long generate 306 megawatts. A company spokesman said the total project cost was almost $600 million including a transmission line north to Delta where it hooks into the super-sized Intermountain Power Project. The power then goes to southern California on the Project's high tension line that bisects the Escalante Valley.

First Wind Company's wind farm near Milford

Under a power purchase agreement with the Southern California Public Power Authority, the Milford-produced electricity sufficient for 64,000 homes is supplied to the cities of Los Angeles and Glendale. They are examples of cities that want to reduce the climate-warming emissions of coal-fired power plants. The second phase of First Wind's Milford project was completed in May 2011, and further expansion is expected. The wind farm, with twenty full-time employees, sprawls across hundreds of acres of U.S. Bureau of Land Management and Utah state government land.

Surprisingly, another power-generating project has popped up in the Escalante Valley about 10 miles south of Milford on the once-muddy banks of what was called Thermo Springs. It is a shiny new plant that creates electricity from underground hot water.

Built in 2007–2008 by Raser Technologies of Salt Lake City at a cost of about $100 million, the plant feeds electricity into a power company substation at Milford. From there, the power is "wheeled" to Raser's customer, the city of Anaheim, California, on the Intermountain Power

Project line. The plant operates on what is called a binary system. In over-simplification, heat from the underground water turns turbines that generate electricity sufficient for 9,000 homes. The company which has eight geothermal plants in western states filed Chapter 11 bankruptcy proceedings in May 2011 in Delaware, listing $108 million in debts and $42 million in assets. The Milford plant was expected to remain in operation.

The hot springs were mentioned the journal of Colonial Spanish explorers Escalante and Dominguez who wandered through the valley in 1776.

Dean Carter of Minersville, near Milford, and his wife Donna Applegate Carter, daughter of Lyle Applegate, the Johnstons' two-times sheep herder, operated the largest cattle ranch in the valley for many years with 1,500 cows on a range stretching twenty miles from near Milford to Lund. It included two feed lots for fattening up to 300 cattle at a time. By 2013, Dean and Donna had retired and turned the ranch operations over to their children.

The livestock and power businesses provide an economic base for Milford, but in some respects, the heart of the town continues to be the Union Pacific railroad whose predecessor railway arrived there in 1880. The UP made Milford a major activity center until cutbacks began in the middle of the 1900s. In an interview in 2009, Larry Whittaker,

Raser Technologies geothermal power plant

a UP employee for thirty-five years, said some mainline trains still change crews at Milford, and a few crews provide short train delivery services in the region. Whittaker's father and grandfather preceded him in railroad work. In their heyday, trains had crews of four on freight trains of fifty cars instead of the two crewmen currently on trains 100 cars long.

In the southeast corner of the Escalante Valley are 26 acres of greenhouses built by Milgro Newcastle, Inc. Milgro wholesales nursery stock such as flowers, bulbs, bare root trees and shrubs around the nation. The project, with a value of more than $3.5 million, started in 1993 with 527,000 square feet of greenhouse space for production of cut flowers. A decade later, it was the nation's largest producer of chrysanthemums. The project has been steadily expanded to 1.1 million square feet under sheet plastic roofs supported by arches and fiberglass walls. The operation utilizes underground hot water at around 200 degrees Fahrenheit to allow year-around production. An elaborate network of plastic pipes and pumps serves the plants from wells 600 to 1,000 feet deep. The water is recycled back into the ground.

The greenhouse complex has 80 to 130 employees, some of them seasonal. Plants are shipped by trucks out of a large trucking facility near St. George, Utah. California-based Milgro Newcastle, with four plants in the United States, was sold recently to Royal Van Zanten, a Dutch company.

Unlike the visible thermal springs for the Raser power plant, the underground hot water near Newcastle was accidentally discovered

Milgro Newcastle, Inc. greenhouses

in 1975 by well drillers seeking farm irrigation water. The water underground in the desert is fed by mountain snow melt.

An industrial plant that makes an oxidizer agent for rocket fuel plus propellant for automobile safety air bags is located about ten miles west of Cedar City on the Union Pacific railroad line from Lund. Known locally simply as AMPAC, it is American Pacific Corporation's Utah Operation. It was built by the Las Vegas, Nevada-based company at a cost of $92 million in 1988, replacing a plant that exploded at Henderson, Nevada. The Cedar City project has 155 employees. Because of the volatile nature of the products, the plant takes extensive security precautions.

Also located west of Cedar a few miles beyond what was once the little town of Iron Springs is a new 30-acre petroleum storage project with capacity for 200,000 barrels. It is owned and operated by the ENEV Pipeline Company which is part of a conglomerate of petroleum companies under the umbrella of HollyFrontier Corporation based in Dallas, Texas. HollyFrontier subsidiaries operate five refineries including one at Woods Cross near Salt Lake City, Utah. The 400-mile ENEV line runs from Woods Cross to the Las Vegas, Nevada, area, mostly in the Intermountain Power Project line's right-of-way.

The IPP route might also be used by both the Zephyr Power Transmission Project for which several years of planning and research began in 2012 and by a relatively new Chokecherry and Sierra Madre wind farm project.

The Zephyr project, scheduled to be completed by 2020, is to be constructed, owned and operated by the Duke-American Transmission Company, a joint venture of Duke Energy Company and American Transmission Company, based in Las Vegas, Nevada. More than 100,000 acres of ranch land in Wyoming are to be the site of a wind energy farm to produce 3,000 megawatts of electricity to be conveyed on a power line southwest through Utah to the Las Vegas, Nevada, area. A project map shows the "proposed" route of the 850-mile line would go through Beaver County past Milford and join the IPP line in Iron County past Newcastle. An "alternative" route would be the Union Pacific railroad right-of-way through Lund and Modena.

A story in the *Denver Post* on July 4, 2013, quoted Denver billionaire Philip Anschutz's Power Company of Wyoming, and said the U.S.

Bureau of Land Management ruled there would be no major adverse human or environmental impacts from the proposed Chokecherry and Sierra Madre project with 1,000 turbines. A 725-mile power line would carry electricity from a Wyoming wind farm southwest through western Utah and southern Nevada to join the southern California power grid.

Then there is perhaps the least known attraction in the Escalante Valley region—a series of wild horse herd areas managed by the U.S. Bureau of Land Management, Cedar City office, under a 1971 federal law, the Wild Free-Roaming Horse and Burro Act. The law says the wild animals "shall be protected from capture, branding, harassment or death . . . as living symbols of the historic and pioneer spirit of the West!" Most of the areas in Iron and Beaver Counties, containing an estimated 1,000 horses, are in the very desolate and arid Wah Wah Mountains northwest of the valley accessible only by obscure roads and trails. Two areas are in hills and mountains south of the valley. A BLM pamphlet gives guidelines for any hardy souls who want to try to see the wild horses. One main access road goes through Lund.

Lund, once the commercial distribution center for southern Utah, became a ghost town in the 1970s. Thereafter, for twenty-five years, the only residents were Judy and Gary Campbell and her brother, J. O. Campbell. They lived in modular houses that the Union Pacific continued to supply with water from an increasingly undependable well and pipeline. Gary first came to Lund to work on the Hunt Oil Company test well, and he and Judy stayed on. They finally moved to Colorado leaving one other couple as Lund's only residents.

Fay Frahske Burns was the last member of a homestead family to live in Lund. She graduated from Cedar City High School in 1942 and then graduated from the Holy Cross Hospital School of Nursing in Salt Lake City a year after Millie Johnston graduated there. Her parents lived in the old Johnston house from the fall of 1957 until her father, Oscar, died in

Dick Johnston and Fay Frahske Burns, 2009

1969. She and her mother, Alma, moved to Salt Lake City where Fay worked as a registered nurse until they returned to Lund to a spacious new house Fay arranged to have constructed late in 1972 on the site of the Johnston home, which was razed.

Fay loved the desert, but there were no jobs there so she wrote to the Utah Board of Regents, the governing body for higher education, saying southern Utah needed a program to produce nurses. She began commuting to Southern Utah University in Cedar City in 1973 when she became the university's first coordinator of the Nursing Cooperative Program affiliated with several other colleges in Utah. Thereafter Fay became the first director of the nursing program as it expanded through the 1970s, producing practical nurses and registered nurses. As an assistant professor, she also taught classes until she retired after her mother's death in 1978. By then there were only a few families living in Lund.

Fay was the unofficial historian of Lund for many years, writing stories about her life there and getting long letter memoirs from former "desert rats." She was visited in 1992 by sisters Amy and Ola of the Norris family that starved out of Lund in 1936. In the summer of 1993, Alice Fourman, reared in Lund in the 1920s, and members of her family had Fay help them look for old homestead sites.

On October 24, 1979, Fay married Merle Burns who had worked on railroad section gangs for 27 years while also maintaining a small cattle ranch near Beryl. They lived in Lund until he died in 1993, and Fay moved to Kanarraville near Cedar City. She visited Lund often until 2005 when she sold the house. "It was awfully hard for me to leave my desert," she recalled in an interview with the author in 2009, but age and health problems required the move. At age 84, her memory was absolutely amazing. She died July 20, 2010, in Cedar City.

In 2009 the venerable Lund store and one-time post office was boarded up, and the roof sagged precariously. Except for two forlorn shells, all of the Union Pacific employee houses were gone but the 80-year-old Couch family house was still recognizable. The one-room school house was moved to Minersville after the school closed in 1947. Fay was instrumental in having the brass bell saved and placed in the Frontier Homestead State Park in Cedar City.

The small but exquisite Colonial Spanish-style depot, the railroad's roundhouse, the landmark tower for railroad well drilling and the big black water tank had all been demolished by the early 1970s. On a rail

Lund Union Pacific train depot, circa 1950s.

The Union Pacific's domestic water well pump housed in Lund, 2009.

siding, several rusting flatbed railroad cars with warped wood decks appeared to have been forgotten by the Union Pacific. With 34,000 miles of track, Union Pacific became the biggest railroad in North America. Lund is not even a fly speck on the railroad's maps.

A 1971 federal law set up Amtrak to assume passenger service from existing railroads, and one Amtrak train passed through Lund at night for a decade.

South of Lund the railroad section town of Zane totally disappeared and only a few vacant buildings remain at Beryl. Modena, near the Nevada border, has had a few residents living in the midst of a dozen tumble-down buildings. A small water tower is the only remnant of Union Pacific facilities.

Chuck Reeve at the J. H. Johnston Ranch near Lund.

However, the century-old Johnston homestead, three miles south of Lund, is in the center of speculation in desert real estate in the area in the 21st Century. It and about 1,000 acres around it are owned by Charles (Chuck) Reeve of Hurricane, Utah, a retired electronics engineer. One of his real estate advertisements in 2013 referred to the "Historic J. H. Johnston Ranch . . ." Reeve grew up near Newcastle, and on quiet days there he could hear the whistles of Union Pacific trains passing through Beryl.

According to Reeve, the Cleo Wood family of Cedar City acquired what once were the Johnston livestock range properties west of the railroad tracks into the foothills, and land speculators out of Las Vegas, Nevada, became the owners of the Johnston properties east of the tracks. A would-be developer named Bill Young acquired the original Johnston homestead of 320 acres and subdivided most of it into the Sun Valley Estates in the 1990s. He used the Johnston well to start an irrigated tree farm which survived long after he lost all his holdings in settlement of a lawsuit.

Reeve noticed the property while flying his own plane over the valley one day and began acquiring parcels in the area at prices of $100 and up per acre including eighty acres of the Johnston homestead and most of the one-acre and five-acre lots in Sun Valley Estates. He built a comfortable cabin out of used railroad ties and experimental adobe bricks on the homestead. The original well had "sanded in" and a new 200-foot deep well was drilled nearby which Reeve maintains, using the Utah State government permit obtained by Harley Johnston in the late 1940s. Reeve uses the well to irrigate the tree farm and to provide water to some of the subdivision lots where a few owners come and go in trailer homes. Two small power companies out of Cedar City provide electric power to the area. Reeve sometimes cultivates test crops on some of the land Harley Johnston first plowed in 1915.

The 2009 Web page for another real estate agent operating in the Lund area offered twenty acres of flat land for $22,000. (In Kent Johnston's estate in probate court in 1957, the land he owned was valued at $2 per acre.) The usually-vacant house in Lund that Fay Frahske Burns built in 1972 plus 120 adjacent acreage has been priced at $200,000, according to Reeve.

The highly-energetic, white haired Reeve has more and bigger dreams than the homesteaders, but so far without much success. With some participation by his son, he set up 200-acre sites for research on use of desert land and on wind and solar power, the Lund Development Group, and a Sun Valley Estates Property Owners Association where Reeve has sold six lots.

Branching off to the east from the railroad tracks south of Lund, a quarter-mile road to the homestead is paralleled by a gravel landing strip, designated UT28, for small planes. At the end of it is a small hangar. Occasionally, a few of Reeve's friends gather in their planes where Harley and Mary Johnston once drove mules and a wagon to Lund.

As part of a two-day automobile tour to see what was happening in the Escalante Valley, Dick Johnston took a graded gravel road west out of Lund across the railroad tracks where locomotive engineers no longer sounded warnings, and there was only silence between the rumbles of a few freight trains. The road cut through the center of what was the Johnston family sheep and cattle ranch. A windmill, a small house, and fences loomed out of the gray-green brush. It was Homer Green's place reincarnated as McRay Wood's place.

Tan tumble weeds were stacked against the railroad tie fence where war veteran Kent Johnston had put his saddle on the fence, sat down in his pickup truck with the door open, and died with a sack of Bull Durham tobacco in his hand, ending the half-century Johnston family saga in the Escalante desert.

In the maze of corrals, greatly expanded from the 1950s, were several horses and huge Black Angus bulls. The windmill appeared to be the same as the one Kent and Harley Johnston kept in repair, but the base was concrete instead of planks. In place of the Johnstons' eight-foot-high galvanized metal tank, a large, circular, three-foot-deep concrete tank received water from the windmill with overflow to the dirt-bank reservoir that Kent and Dick scraped out in 1947. Cattle from the range had access to a section of the concrete water tank and the reservoir.

The only building was a small, fairly new, house with solar energy panels, a propane tank, and frisky dogs in the yard. Slim gray-haired McRay Wood, dressed in Levis, long-sleeved plaid shirt, and white cowboy hat, greeted Dick at the door and invited him into the bachelor-styled living/dining room and kitchen.

McRay grew up as a member of a ranching family in southern Utah. In 1959, his father, Cleo, began assembling a cattle ranch stretching west from the railroad tracks near Lund that eventually included the range that Rulon Lyman had purchased from Harley Johnston. Cleo died in 1986, and his sons inherited the cattle business. His father, McRay's grandfather, once had a herd of sheep and was the last rancher to ship

Aerial view of McRay Wood's ranch (Homer Green's place).

livestock by rail out of Lund. Trucks have totally replaced trains for transporting cattle.

McRay served in the Vietnam War in the 1960s and later survived cancer that he was sure was caused by exposure to Agent Orange which was used to defoliate jungle areas. After several years competing in rodeos, he returned to the cattle business, took over the Lund ranch, and began living there.

As his health declined from emphysema and he became increasingly dependent on oxygen tanks for breathing, McRay began alternating a few days at the ranch with days in Cedar City. He began leasing the desert range land of almost 8,000 acres to his cousin, Worth Brown of Kanab, Utah, who has had an average of 200 cattle per year there. Brown has a permit from the U.S. Bureau of Land Management to graze cattle on BLM land around the range's checkerboard pattern of private land.

McRay died October 1, 2013, in Cedar City, and his ex-wife was in line to succeed him as owner of the Lund ranch and forty acres McRay had acquired adjacent to Harley Johnston's homestead land south of Lund and east of the railroad tracks. Brown hired a replacement for McRay to take care of the herd of cattle. The caretaker sometimes parks his truck near the railroad tie fence covered with tan tumbleweeds.

The "highway" into Lund, 2009.

Bibliography

"The American West." Active Minds lecture. Westminster, CO. March 20, 2013.

Athearn, Robert G. *Union Pacific Country*. University of Nebraska Press, 1976.

"Beautiful Santa Barbara, California." *The Arrowhead*. March 1915.

Bowden, Charles. "The Emptied Prairie." *National Geographic Magazine*. January 2008.

Bradley, James, with Ron Powers. *Flags of Our Fathers*. Bantam Books, 2000.

Brokaw, Tom. *The Greatest Generation*. Random House, 1998.

Burns, Fay Frahske Collection. MS 32. Special Collections, Southern Utah University.

"California." *Encyclopedia Americana*. Americana Corp., 1950.

Campbell, Hardy W. *Campbell's Soil Culture Manual*. University of Nebraska Press, 1902.

Coffey, Thomas M. *Iron Eagle*. Random House, 1987.

Culmsee, Carlton. "Last Free Land Rush." *Utah Historical Quarterly*. 49, no.1 Winter 1981.

Denton, J.R. "Bike Trip Across Nevada." *Denver Post*. November 1, 2001.

The Dominguez-Escalante Journal. edited by Ted J. Warner, translated by Fray Angelico Chavez. University of Utah Press, 1995.

Durham, Michael S. *Desert Between the Mountains*. Henry Holt & Co. 1997.

Glidewell, Donna J. *It Endures Like the Wasatch Mountains*. 1st Books/AuthorHouse, 2003.

Hankins, Esther W. "Beloved Escalante Doctor in Exile." *The Nevadan*. April 22, 1984.

Hanley, Fiske. *History of the 504th Bomb Group in World War II*. 504th Bomb Group Association, 1992.

"Haywire." *High Country News* (Paonia, CO). May 27, 2013.

Hemphill, Mark W. *Union Pacific Salt Lake Route*. Mills Press, 1995.

Hillenbrand, Laura. *Unbroken*. Random House, 2010.

Hinton, Wayne K., and Green, Elizabeth. *With Pick, Shovel, and Hope*. Green Mountain Press, 2008.

Iron County Record (Cedar City, UT).

Laub, Norman. "The Escalante Valley." Janet Seegmiller Collection. Special Collections. Sherratt Library. Southern Utah University.

McGarry, Wendell H. as told to Gwen J. McGarry. *I Am Coming Home*. Southern Utah University Press, 2013.

Merrill, Karen R. *Public Lands and Political Meaning*. University of California Press, 2002.

"Montana's Hi-Line." *National Geographic Magazine*. January 2012.

Nugent, Walter. *Into the West: The Story of Its People*. Vantage, 2001.

O'Driscoll, Patrick. "The Story Behind the Great Dis-Missile." *Nevada/the Magazine of the Real West*. February 1982.

Raban, Jonathan. *Bad Land: An American Romance*. Thorndike Press, 1996.

Seegmiller, Janet Burton. *A History of Iron County–Community Above Self*. Utah State Historical Society and Iron County Commission, 1998.

"How the Homestead Act Transformed America." *Smithsonian Magazine*. May 2012.

Star-News (Pasadena, CA), May 20, 1916.

Stegner, Wallace. *Angle of Repose*. Doubleday. 1971.

Stegner, Wallace. *Wolf Creek: A History, A Story, and A Memory of the Last Plains Frontier*. Penguin Books, 1967.

Thomas, Oliver C., editor. *The Saga of a B-29 Airplane Called "Sitting Pretty" During World War II*. Lubbock, TX, 1988.

Trimble, Stephen. *The Sagebrush Ocean, A History of the Great Basin*. Torrey House Press, 1989.

Vossler, Bill. "Presidential Automobile Firsts." *The Elks Magazine*. July-August 2009.

Walls, Jeannette. *Half-Broke Horses*. Scribner, 2009.

Weidel, Nancy. *Sheepwagon, Home on the Range*. High Plains Press, 2001.

Index

www.ingramcontent.com/pod-product-compliance
Lightning Source LLC
Chambersburg PA
CBHW072134090426
42739CB00013B/3189

* 9 7 8 0 9 3 5 6 1 5 4 5 6 *